T0393250

'From schools of fish to swarms of bees, the biological principle of Swarm Intelligence empowers natural groups to combine their perspectives and make optimized decisions. Richard Kelly's latest thought-provoking book explores how similar principles can be applied to organizations, empowering business teams to optimize their collaborative process'.

Louis Rosenberg, *CEO, Author, Entrepreneur, and Inventor*

'This is truly an uplifting book addressing system leadership and giving us a pathway to achieve systemic change. Combining theory, applications, and supported by examples and research, this book fosters a new generation of collective leaders and systems. This is a moment in time where this book makes a compelling contribution to our thinking on leadership and systems in the decades ahead'.

Mario Chiasson, *President of the Atlantic Education Institute and Director of Research, Innovation and Change Management*

THE NATURE OF BUSINESS TRANSFORMATION

This book is a practical guide for business professionals to develop and improve business intelligence and collective decision-making within their organisation. It proposes a progressive reconfiguration of the traditional business operating system using a nature-inspired framework called swarm facilitation that enables and facilitates collective decision-making.

Organisations have followed the same rigid formula of problem-solving and decision-making for over 100 years. It is dominated by centralised governance and pyramid decision-making. Such an approach is no longer fit for purpose in an environment of employee disengagement, artificial intelligence (AI)/superintelligence, and Covid-19 fallout. By the end of this book, readers will be able to:

- solve organisational problems and challenges collectively using swarm intelligence;
- upgrade and future-proof business operating systems to reflect a more collective decision-making approach fit for the new connected economy and Industry 4.0;
- embrace mindset quotients that support people working in a more networked, self-organising, and collective environment.

The book is important reading for leaders and managers who are focused on building organisational capital and engagement and gaining value from the emerging technology by evolving their business operating system into a digital ecosystem as part of an ongoing digital transformation strategy. It will also appeal to experts working in the field of organisational change and development, both within the organisation and as consultants.

Richard Kelly is a London-based author, keynote speaker, columnist, and leadership and organisational development specialist. He has enjoyed an international career that has spanned 25 years working in the private and public sectors in various senior leadership roles. For the last 15 years, Richard has worked as an independent consultant and entrepreneur based in Europe and South America. Currently, he is the director of a niche UK-based leadership and organisational development consulting company, Swarm Business Solutions, that works with inspirational leaders to support the digital, structural, and behavioural transformation of organisations using the swarm transformation approach outlined in *The Nature of Business Transformation*.

THE NATURE OF BUSINESS TRANSFORMATION

A Swarm Intelligent Approach to Reinventing Organisations

Richard Kelly

Routledge
Taylor & Francis Group

LONDON AND NEW YORK

Cover image: © Getty Images

First published 2022
by Routledge
4 Park Square, Milton Park, Abingdon, Oxon OX14 4RN

and by Routledge
605 Third Avenue, New York, NY 10158

Routledge is an imprint of the Taylor & Francis Group, an informa business

British Library Cataloguing-in-Publication Data
A catalogue record for this book is available from the British Library

Library of Congress Cataloging-in-Publication Data
Names: Kelly, Richard (Business consultant), author.
Title: The nature of business transformation : a swarm intelligent approach to reinventing organisations / Richard Kelly.
Description: Milton Park, Abingdon, Oxon ; New York, NY : Routledge, 2022. | Includes bibliographical references and index.
Identifiers: LCCN 2021040378 | ISBN 9781032104980 (paperback) | ISBN 9781032104966 (hardback) | ISBN 9781003215561 (ebook)
Subjects: LCSH: Organizational change. | Leadership. | Swarm intelligence–Social aspects. | Strategic planning.
Classification: LCC HD58.8.K4579 2022 | DDC 658.4/06–dc23
LC record available at https://lccn.loc.gov/2021040378

ISBN: 978-1-032-10496-6 (hbk)
ISBN: 978-1-032-10498-0 (pbk)
ISBN: 978-1-003-21556-1 (ebk)

DOI: 10.4324/9781003215561

Typeset in Times New Roman
by Newgen Publishing UK

To my family.

CONTENTS

ILLUSTRATIONS

Figures

Tables

ABBREVIATIONS AND ACRONYMS

AAR	After Action Review
ABC	Artificial Bee Colony
ACO	Ant Colony Optimisation
ADS	Autonomous Decision Systems
AGI	Artificial General Intelligence
AI	Artificial Intelligence
AIVA	Artificial Intelligence Virtual Artist
ANI	Artificial Narrow Intelligence
AQ	Adaptive Quotient
AR	Augmented Reality
AS	Ant System Algorithm
ASI	Artificial Swarm Intelligence
BBC	British Broadcasting Corporation
BCO	Bee Colony Optimisation
BIN	Business Intelligence Network
BOS	Business Operating System
Bot	Robot
CA	California
CAS	Complex Adaptive System
CBS	Columbia Broadcasting System
CCWC	Computing and Communication Workshop and Conference

CDO	Chief Data Officer
CDSS	Clinical Decision Support Systems
CEO	Collective Enterprise Optimiser
CEO	Chief Executive Officer
C-factor	Collective Intelligence
CI	Collective Intelligence
CIO	Chief information officer
CIPD	Chartered Institute of Personal Development
Cisco	San Francisco
CNBC	Consumer News and Business Channel
COVID-19	Corona virus disease 2019
CQ	Collaborative Intelligence
CSI	Change style indicator
C-Suite	C Level Executive
CT	Connecticut
CT	Computerised Tomography
D8	Organisation for Economic Cooperation
Daimler AG	Aktiengesellschaft
DARPA	Defense Advanced Research Projects Agency
DNA	Deoxyribonucleic acid
DQ	Digital Quotient
EDT	Eastern Daylight Time
EU	European Union
Fed ex	Federal Express
FT	Financial Times
FW	Future workshops
GCC	General Company Circle
GDSS	Group Decision Support System
G-factor	General Individual Intelligence
GPS	General Problem Solver
GPS	Global Positioning System
GRPI	Goals, Roles, Processes and Interpersonal Relationships
HBR	Harvard Business Review
HCI	Human Computer Interaction
HR	Human Resources
IA	Intelligence Amplification
IBM	International Business Machines Corporation

ICIS	International Conference on Information Systems
ICSI	International Conference on Swarm Intelligence
IJCSIT	International Journal of Computer Science and Information Technologies
IL	Illinois
IMEC	Interuniversity Microelectronics Centre
IN	Indianapolis
Industry 4.0	Fourth Industrial Revolution
Intel	Integrated Electronics
IOT	Internet of Things
IQ	Intelligence Quotient
IT	Information Technology
JLL	Jones Lang LaSalle
KPMG	Klynveld Peat Marwick Goerdeler
L&D	Learning and Development
LD	Leadership development
LOA	Lion Optimisation Algorithm
MA	Massachusetts
MIMO	Multiple-Input Multiple-Output
MIT	Massachusetts Institute of Technology
MR	Magnetic Resonance
MRI	Magnetic Resonance Imaging
NASA	National Aeronautics and Space Administration
NBC	National Broadcasting Company
NJ	New Jersey
NY	New York
OD	Organisational Development
OECD	Organisation for Economic Co-operation and Development
OED	Oxford English Dictionary
OH	Ohio
OR	Oregon
OST	Open Space Technology
PC	Personal Computer
PSO	Particle Swarm Optimisation
PWC	Price Waterhouse Coopers
R&D	Research and Development

Sci-fi	Science fiction
SDL	Self-Directed Learning
SFI	Santa Fe Institute
SML	Swarm Mentor Leaders
SOA	Swarm Optimisation Algorithm
Swarm 1.0	Emergent Swarm Organisation
Swarm 2.0	Planned Swarm Organisation
Swarm 3.0	Business Superorganism
Swarm reps	Swarm Representatives
SWOT	Strengths, Weaknesses, Opportunities and Threats analysis
TSP	Travelling Salesman Problem
TX	Texas
Uk	Unitied Kingdom
US	United States
USD	United States Dollar
VP	Vice President
VR	Virtual reality
VUCA	Volatility, Uncertainty, Complexity, and Ambiguity
Web 1.0	Read-only web
Web 2.0	Read-write web
Web 3.0	Read-write-execute web
WEF	World Economic Forum

PREFACE

I was watching *Bee Movie* by DreamWorks Animation the other day and came to the scene where decorated general, Lou Duca was clutching his clipboard briefing the Pollen Jocks. I have read and researched enough about honeybees (*Apis mellifera*) to know that this kind of leadership doesn't exist in honeybee colonies. And then my thoughts turned to my previous book, *Constructing Leadership 4.0: Swarm Leadership and the Fourth Industrial Revolution*. It was also inspired by honeybees and described a type of leadership that encourages a more enabling and swarm intelligent work environment. Having spent over 25 years developing systems and leaders, it seems I was still hanging on to the belief that a more engaged and connected Industry 4.0 workplace could be achieved solely through leadership. *The Nature of Business Transformation* is less about leadership and more about the business operating systems that cause toxic organisations. I started with the assumption in *The Nature of Business Transformation* that we do not need to create yet another leadership label – such as 'swarm leadership' – but evolve the business operating system. The book's ultimate ambition concerns building a superlative collective environment, a complex adaptive system with no clipboards, and no Lou Lo Duca types.

My academic background is in organisational and behavioural science where I gained a PhD. I have spent my professional life working for different organisations developing leadership and organisational culture. Applying swarm intelligence to the workplace is a niche field. It has a small but impactful body of authors with a diverse range of organisational, academic, and technical and scientific backgrounds. I hope my research and practical experience make me a credible contributor to this field. The book covers everything from biology to artificial intelligence (AI) and I hope I have been able to represent these complex fields in a way that connects with a professional business mind who wants to create a more engaged and collaborative workplace.

I wish to acknowledge all my students and colleagues past and present who have been so supportive. A special mention goes to Dr. Michael Poerner, a senior executive at Mercedes Benz AG, for help with a case study on Daimler AG. Given the polymathic quality of this study, I have had many interesting conversations with natural scientists, computer scientists, AI specialists, and apiarists. I thank you all. My experience talking to apiarists was mixed. It seems that the only area of controversy that my research into honeybees sparked concerned the spelling of honeybee. The community is torn between spelling it as a single word or as two words. H.D. Dade, a titan in the honeybee world who wrote *Anatomy and Dissection of the Honeybee*, spelt it as one word. Another heavyweight, R.E. Snodgrass in *The Anatomy of the Honey Bee*, spells it with two words. I took my inspiration in the end from Microsoft spell check.

Richard Kelly
Kent, United Kingdom

INTRODUCTION

SMALL STEPS AND GIANT LEAPS

'Houston, Tranquillity Base here. The Eagle has landed'. These were the fabled words of Commander Neil Armstrong that crackled through to the Apollo Mission Control Centre in Houston at 4:18 pm EDT on Sunday 20 July 1969 affirming that the Apollo 11 Lunar Module, 'Eagle', had landed on the moon's surface. The moon landing was watched live on television by over 600 million viewers, a broadcasting record at the time, and even more tuned into the radio. But the lunar landing nearly never happened because approximately 8 minutes earlier, the mission was close to being aborted. An obscure error code, called the 1202 alarm, suddenly flashed up, causing the normally sangfroid Armstrong to voice concern – 'Give us a reading on the 1202 programme alarm', he urged.[1]

There was a lot riding on this decision. President Kennedy had set the challenge of putting a man on the moon by the end of the decade in the early 1960s and the entire nation got behind the project. The country's image, technological reputation, and cold war rivalry were at stake.[2] What happened next is a striking example of collective decision-making. Gene Kranz was the experienced NASA flight director who was responsible overall for the success and safety of the mission, but Kranz deferred the decision to a 26-year-old Mission Guidance Officer, Steve Bales, who in turn deferred it to a 25-year-old NASA engineer, John 'Jack' Garman.

DOI: 10.4324/9781003215561-1

During a landing simulation two weeks before the mission, an unknown alarm code flashed on the screen prompting Bales to abort the simulated mission. In the simulation debrief, Kranz tasked Bales to match every alarm code with a required action. Bales delegated the task to Garman. When code 1202 flashed up, there was one person in Apollo Mission Control Centre who knew what it meant and what to do. Garman consulted his handwritten notes and saw that it was just a warning signal that the computer was temporarily overloading and that the landing could continue. Garman responded, 'If it doesn't occur too often, we're fine'. Bales relayed to Kranz, 'We're go on that, Flight', and Armstrong and Aldrin were given the 'go' to ignite the Eagle's decent engine. And the rest, as they say, is history.

The code 1202 situation is not just an interesting backstory to the lunar landing, it is central to NASA's success. The decision-making leading up to touchdown which rescued the mission did not happen by chance. Collective decision-making (a 'hivemind of expertise' as it is described by Kevin Fong) was built into the organisational culture. Steve Bales was later to remark for a BBC radio documentary presented by Fong:

> We didn't make decisions at the highest level possible. We shoved them down to the lowest level. Now, the flight director, for instance, had to understand the inputs he was getting. But everybody had their piece of the pie, and we didn't try to share it too much because we didn't have time. Make the decisions at the lowest level, where people know what they're doing and what they're talking about, rather than elevating everything to the top. Let's build this thing from the ground up; not from the top down.[3]

The reason why NASA successfully landed a man on the moon (and I pointedly ignore all the conspiracy theories surrounding studio shoots) was not solely due to its technical abilities, but also because NASA's organisational structures and mindsets were linked to its technical mission. Simply put, NASA's business operating system (BOS) was about shared responsibility and decision-making and every aspect of its transformative journey that landed astronauts on the moon contributed to this.

The Apollo 11 lunar landing highlights the core themes of this book. It has been over half a century since Neil Armstrong first walked on the moon, but the lessons learned in getting him there are still relevant today. So, what are these lessons and themes?

Walk the talk

The first step on the lunar surface is really the story of a passionate and engaged organisation where different generations worked together; where diversity of thought and ideas was respected; where adaptiveness, agility, collaboration, and curiosity were not buzzwords posted on walls or featured in organisational handouts but were played out every day in conversations and meetings across the organisation. As we have seen, it was also a collective/hivemind culture. It is a sad truth that in the 60 years since NASA was founded, modern organisations still struggle to achieve anything comparable in terms of organisational culture. This book has 'transformation' and 'reinventing' in its title. One of the book's central ideas is that organisations run off a BOS which is the modus operandi and engine of the organisation. Many modern organisations' BOSs still reflect out-of-date organisational values, mindsets, and structures. They need an urgent upgrade. This book shares a nature-inspired process to upgrade the BOS.

Focus on the system not personalities

At the press conference on the astronaut's return, Buzz Aldrin acknowledged that the lunar landing was a collective endeavour and not three men in a module. The astronauts enjoyed hero status when they returned to earth, but they publicly acknowledged the role every NASA employee played and the collective nature of the enterprise. An organisational personality cult pervades, but it needs to be abandoned and the system needs to be deformalised. This book goes into great detail about how to transform structures, systems, and mindsets and, inspired by superorganisms, develop complex adaptive systems as an enabling environment for collective intelligence and decision-making. It makes some bold recommendations about phasing down and phasing out management and leadership and deformalising the system.

Make sure everything is wired together

'Houston, we have a problem', is a phrase that was never actually said in a NASA context. When a problem is identified, collective organisations turn to problem-solving. This is achieved through connection and connectivity. The three-system transformation outlined in the book (organisational, digital, and behavioural) all contribute to building this connection and connectivity. The book explores an organic honeycomb structure which glues the complex adaptive cells and systems together. Communication and knowledge sharing run through its grid. This honeycomb structure is both emergent and planned and extends across three swarm phases known as the swarm transformation. The entire enterprise, supported by the honeycomb structure, is working towards being a complex adaptive system and business superorganism. Technology in the form of advanced data analytics and decision augmentation will support this connectivity, but technology alone is not the fix; structures and mindsets also need to be part of the mix.

Be led by intelligence

NASA spent a decade putting astronauts on the moon. It was a learning organisation. Its triumphs and fatalities, technological breakthroughs, and technological breakdowns all contributed to the story of astronauts walking on the moon. Being intelligence-led and not knowledge-led is key to superorganisms. This relates to the 'natural' in the title. This book is about swarm intelligence. When honeybees (*Apis mellifera*) forage or relocate to new nesting sites or hives, they act on sensemaking intelligence which they share with the colony for a collective decision to be made. What has foraging honeybees got to do with the Apollo 11 lunar landing? Think of the lunar module as a worker bee who flies from the colony and transmits intelligence for the group to decide collectively on the way forward. This is the essence of swarm intelligence and a hivemind. This book uses swarm intelligence from the natural world to help build self-organising complex adaptive swarm systems that give collective perspective on business intelligence; what is more, it is not facilitated or led by alpha leaders.

To go from the Apollo mission to the mission of the book, *The Nature of Business Transformation* concerns changing the traditional BOS from a personality and knowledge-led hierarchy to a complex adaptive system that solves problems, creates ideas, and makes decisions through swarm intelligence. It does this in small steps and giant leaps. The small step is the swarm transformation change process; the giant leap is technology. It uses an algorithm modelled on house-hunting honeybees, as an inspiration to build a swarm-based organisation. Transforming the business is seen as a system-wide endeavour that is executed through three incremental phases known as swarm transformation. The book explores in a highly practical way the organisational, digital, and behavioural systems that need to be evolved to accommodate swarm; the organisational change and development initiative; and the swarm facilitation process that helps transform the organisation. One of the key enablers to push the organisation to a fully connected and swarm intelligent superorganism is technology. This book explores how intelligent systems will help organisations to augment swarm and take a giant step forward for the collective workplace of the future.

The book is divided into two parts: theory and application. Here is a brief flavour of each chapter.

Chapter 1 is a theory chapter about business transformation. It explores how out-of-date BOSs create dissonant and monocratic organisational cultures lacking in engagement and agility. Such dinosauric cultures are a turn-off for young talent and will leave organisations ill-prepared to survive in the new economy and Industry 4.0. The chapter proposes an upgraded BOS, BOS 2.0, which is modelled on complex adaptive systems.

Chapter 2 is a theory chapter on swarm intelligence and honeybees. It explores how superorganism activity is being modelled into algorithms that drive artificial intelligence (AI) applications. The chapter examines how honeybees (*Apis mellifera*) use a collective approach when relocating nests. This approach (which includes the famous 'waggle dance') is modelled into a flow diagram, known as the swarm flow model, and used as an algorithm for collective decision-making/swarm facilitation in organisations.

Chapter 3, the final part of the theory section, explores the limitations, individually and in groups, of human mental processing. It looks to technology and intelligent systems as an enhancement of collect intelligence, idea generation, and decision making. This will prove to be a major game changer for building swarm-based organisations.

Chapter 4 begins Part 2 of the book which is about applying ideas. This chapter outlines the swarm transformation that will be a blueprint for the rest of the book. The three swarm phases are local human swarms (Swarm 1.0), augmented swarms (Swarm 2.0), and business superorganisms

(Swarm 3.0). The chapter highlights three levers that will expedite the swarm transformation. Lever 1 relates to the system transformation which applies to structures, technology, and behaviours. Lever 2 is the organisational change and development model which will be a phased approach and a hybrid between planned and emergent change. Lever 3, drawing inspiration from the swarm flow model based on the study of relocating honeybees, represents swarm facilitation.

Chapter 5 applies the swarm transformation blueprint to human swarms working on local meetings or events. Swarm 1.0 is a local complex adaptive cell bivouacked within a traditional structure. It is a local swarm community consisting of a business process owner, trusted advisors, a business intelligence network, and a swarm cluster. The swarm community is formed by the business process owner to approach local meetings and events in a more collective way. A business challenge emerges from the business intelligence network. A self-organising swarm cluster and swarm teams work on the challenge and come up with ideas and recommendations for the business process owner to take forward. It follows the swarm facilitation process and collaborates using human participatory technologies.

Chapter 6 applies the swarm transformation blueprint to organised swarms. Swarm 2.0 is an organisational-led initiative that creates strategic swarm communities across the enterprise to work on global business challenges that emerge from automated business analytics and intelligence. Swarm clusters, augmented by intelligent systems, come up with best-fit solutions to organisational challenges. The chapter explores the system, technology, and behavioural transformations needed for this swarm-based model and details the change and development initiative that will support it. Swarm 2.0 is a human and machine collaboration that self-organises through swarm facilitation rather than human facilitation.

Chapter 7 applies the swarm transformation blueprint to the creation of business superorganisms. Swarm 3.0 is about scaling-up swarm communities. It is also about organisational choice and decision. Business superorganisms are self-organising, interconnected, and integrated entities without formal governance or leadership. The organisation needs to come together and collectively assess whether it wants to become such a business superorganism. This will require greater augmented intelligence and a reconfiguration of organisational governance and power towards becoming a more collective decision-making, intelligence-led, and hivemind enterprise.

The conclusion presents a timeline that details the swarm transformation in five clear stages – ranging from setting up human swarms to becoming a business superorganism. The purpose of this timeline is to provide a clear step-by-step guide to adopting swarm and includes transitions and milestones to form a swarm-based organisation. The chapter ends by directly appealing to business leaders to prepare for Industry 4.0 by appraising their BOS and future-proofing their organisations to embrace the new post-Covid/AI business reality that is facing them.

Notes

1 Source: Royal Museums Greenwich, 'Apollo 11 Moon Landing: Minute by Minute', www.rmg.co.uk/discover/explore/space-stargazing/space-exploration/apollo-11-moon-landing-minute-minute, accessed 29 May 2021.

2 Mark R. Whittington, 'How the Flight of Apollo 11 Won the Cold War', *The Hill*, 21 July 2018, https://thehill.com/opinion/international/398164-how-the-flight-of-apollo-11-won-the-cold-war, accessed 29 May 2021.

3 Steve Bales, interviewed by Kevin Fong, '13 Minutes to the Moon', *BBC Sounds*, Season 1, Ep. 02, 'Kids in Control', realeased on 22 May 2019, www.bbc.co.uk/sounds/play/w3csz4dk, accessed 29 May 2021, 33.15–34.02.

Part 1

THEORY

1

BUSINESS TRANSFORMATION

FROM THE OLD BOSS TO THE NEW BOS

Have you ever stopped to wonder why so many leadership development programmes are full of modules about influencing, motivating, effective decision-making, managing conflict, and the like? It's because leaders are seen as influencers, motivators, decision-makers, and problem solvers. We are repeatedly told that modern businesses are putting diversity, agility, and collaboration at the heart of their business operation; and yet, here we are in the 2020s and ideas and decisions in large organisations typically follow a classic pyramid approach where key initiatives, ideas, and decisions are formulated by a handful of senior C-suite decision makers who force their ideas down the organisational scalar chain. No wonder Matthew and Gilbert Fairholm opine that 'the corporation and other large employers may be among the last bastions of a stifling bureaucratic dictatorship defined by chains of dominance and submission'.[1] It reminds me of the story of Walt Disney who sought input from employees through surveys and then sacked them if they didn't implement the idea in the way he wanted.[2] This behaviour is beautifully exemplified in a Work Chronicles comic strip (Figure 1.1) reproduced here with permission.

Unfortunately, this is a common behaviour in most modern workplaces. Despite all the interpersonal awareness programmes leaders have attended, they still seem to manage to create forbidding environments that deter

DOI: 10.4324/9781003215561-3

Figure 1.1 Brainstorming session.

Source: Work Chronicles.

engagement. The problem is, for over 60 years, we have seen leadership development as a fix – that we can somehow reprogramme managers and leaders into being servant leaders. It's like trying to change the behaviour of a goldfish who is swimming around in circles in a round goldfish bowl; the energy should go into changing the bowl, not changing the fish.[3] As someone who has worked for over 25 years in leadership development, I have come to conclude that individuals are not to blame; culture and systems produce this toxic behaviour. Patrick Hoverstadt is right when he says that we are 'much more puppets of the systems we create than we [are] their masters'.[4]

We don't need yet another transformational leadership initiative; we need a radical business transformation. We need to fundamentally change and rewire the organisational culture from a business operating system (BOS) that rewards and glorifies monocracy to one that embraces swarmocracy, a swarm-like decision-making culture. We need to connect with the energy and spirit of the Apollo 11 lunar landing and – in a post-Covid world – reinvent our organisations by upgrading the very BOSs that drive them.

Ted Gee defines a BOS as 'the common structure, principles and practices necessary to drive the entire organization'.[5] It's lamentable that over 60 years since NASA was established, many modern organisations still have untenable BOSs. Traditional organisations fool themselves that they foster democratic problem-solving and decision-making and that everyone's views are considered. The reality is quite different; the modern workplace is a hotbed of cognitive elitism and transactional leadership, masquerading as collective intelligence (CI).

The theme above of individual executives making all the decisions and presuming they know all the answers denotes an alpha leader mentality. Arun Kumar and Nagarajan Meenakshi depict alpha executives as 'not happy unless they are the ones calling the shots… [and] get stressed when they are not entrusted with important decisions'.[6] The authors go on to claim that 70% of all senior executives are alpha types. Despite years of transformational leadership journeys, this pervasive culture of alpha decision-making and partisanship is, unfortunately, rife in traditional companies.

Business Operating System 1.0

In most traditional organisations, the BOS follows a sequential and centrally directed formula which promotes rational decision-making. This was modelled by Charles Citreon in 2011 (Figure 1.2). As he explains, the arrows signify the sequence; the rounded boxes are the decision process; and the square boxes are additional parameters.

BOS version 1.0 is a traditional approach for arriving at rational decisions within organisations. It can be characterised as rational based[7]; focused on individualistic choice behaviour[8]; information-led rather than intelligence-led where information is sought to reduce uncertainty and justify the decision-making process[9]; and, as Charles Citreon explains in his commentary, it is typically executed by a high-status decision

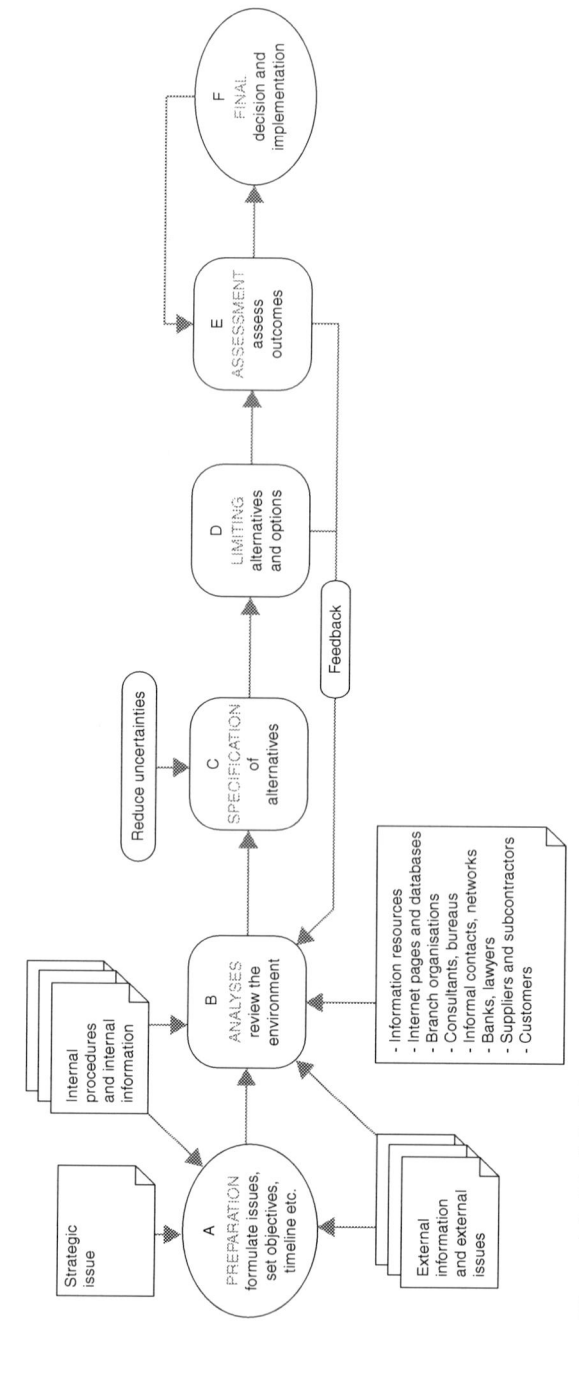

Figure 1.2 Model of the phases of a rational decision-making process.

maker who is perceived to have greater cognitive abilities than everyone else. Such alpha decision makers seek data and information to test their preconfigured ideas and assumptions with the broader community. They do this in the form of a needs analysis/assessment based on shepherded information rather than independent business intelligence.

This classic BOS, or series of decision-making algorithms, has remained unchanged since the last century, despite valiant attempts from the 1970s onwards to move away from transactional to transformational leadership – away from leading through coercion and conditioning to cultivating followership. Companies have poured billions[10] into trying to deradicalise alpha leadership and to promote more open and engaging workplaces and a culture of shared responsibility and decision-making. We have to fess up, as behavioural developmentalists, that this approach has had its problems.

Four factors that reinforce the classic business operating system

1. Culture and conditioning structures

'That's the way we've always done things round here' is an oft-heard sentiment in workplaces across the globe.[11] We see from the work of Weber through to Skinner and Foucault that the organisational culture and structure can shape and reinforce BOSs and related dissonant behaviours.[12] As I said in my previous book, 'It simply isn't enough or effective to mentally reconfigure individual leaders in isolation from the broader ecosystem in which leaders lead'.[13]

2. Alpha leaders are venerated in most organisations

Arun Kumar and Nagarajan Meenakshi, you recall, reported that 70% of all senior executives are alpha types, a statistic researched by Kate Ludeman and Eddie Erlandson.[14] Alpha leaders, mostly recruited from top universities, are still seen as natural leaders and are highly rewarded and esteemed in organisations. The perception of natural strong (heroic) leadership has persisted through the centuries. Two of the nineteenth-century greatest proponents of the superior entitled self were Thomas Carlyle and Friedrich Nietzsche. Thomas Carlyle wrote his 'Great Man' theory in 1841 and Friedrich Nietzsche outlined his Übermensch theory in 1883, an independent being who is master unto himself and not influenced by 'herd morality'. The heroic self and natural leader even found its way into popular culture and the cult of American superherodom that still exists today in blockbuster releases.

3. The industry is still influenced by classical management legacies

The dominant organisational mindset at the start of the twentieth century was classical management theory. These included Frederick Taylor's 1911 scientific management theory in his *The Principles of Scientific Management* which formed the genesis of transactional leadership, and Max Weber's 1944 theories on bureaucracy in *Rationalism and Modern Society*. The core of classical management theory is centralised decision-making. 'Centralisation' is the eighth principle of Henri Fayol's 14 management principles which Fayol, a French industrialist and contemporary of Max Weber, published in his celebrated 1916 work, *Industrial and General Administration*. Fayol was of the view that decision-making should be carried out by a concentrated few. This is followed by his ninth principle, the scalar chain, which indicates 'the chain of superiors ranging from the ultimate authority to the lowest ranks'.[15] Fayol's apostles include Luther Gulick (1937), Bernard Chester (1939), and Lyndall Urwick (1943). The idea of the concentrated few continued in later studies where the individual decision maker is deemed to be more efficient,[16] spontaneous,[17] creative,[18] and intuitive. We will be exploring some of these issues further in Chapter 3 when we look at individual versus central decision-making in relation to group paralysis, social loafing, polarisation, and groupthink.

4. It is reinforced through leadership development programmes

The way leadership development programmes condition leaders was characterised at the start of this chapter. Such programmes endorse and reinforce the idea of alpha leadership as a single source of influence and power (even though in recent times it has been softened by theories of

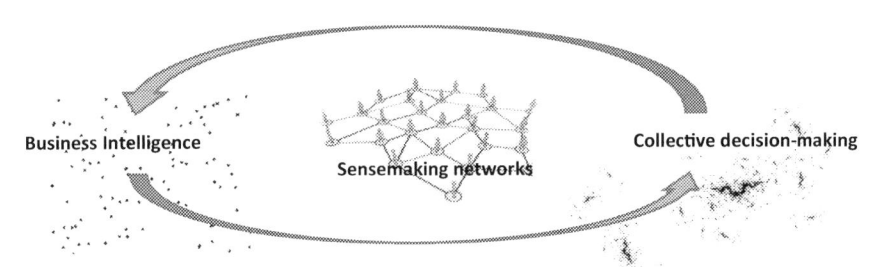

Figure 1.3 Business Operating System Version 2.0.

transformational leadership). Leadership is part of a tenacious succession rite where leaders are identified, nurtured, and promoted by a strong oligarch. They are preselected, assessed for potential, and trialled/tested in the management arena for their leadership qualities which are largely defined by cognitive elitism.

Towards a new Business Operating System (BOS 2.0)

This book calls for a new BOS that departs from linearity and is fit for purpose for Industry 4.0 and the new economy. Figure 1.3 sketches a model that embraces heterogeneity and collective decision-making.

BOS 2.0 is a complex adaptive system (CAS) that makes collective sense of organisational intelligence using agreed criteria and simple algorithms that are processed through interconnected, self-organising, sensemaking networks. Here, collective decisions emerge through collaboration, optimisation, feedback loops, and group consensus or swarm. This dense sentence will be carefully unpacked in this chapter, but a simple headline would proclaim: *In BOS 2.0., decision-making as the function of the executive is rigorously challenged.*

Contained in this sentence are six principles or properties that encapsulate the new BOS.

Six core properties of BOS 2.0

1. Complex adaptive system (CAS)

BOS 2.0 is a CAS. The field of CAS was defined at the Santa Fe Institute (SFI) in New Mexico in the mid-1980s under the leadership of George

Cowan. It embraced a broad group of disciplines, building on the work carried out in fields such as complexity science, chaos theory, biology, computer science, systems theory, artificial intelligence, and game theory.[19] It lacked a precise definition for a period because of the interdisciplinary and evolutionary nature of the field, but this was addressed in the 1990s.[20] One of the most comprehensive definitions emerged in 2008 by Zimmerman, Lindberg, and Plsek, who break the term down:

> Each word is significant. 'Complex' implies diversity – a great number of connections between a wide variety of elements. 'Adaptive' suggests the capacity to alter or change – the ability to learn from experience. A 'system' is a set of connected or interdependent things... A CAS has a densely connected web of interacting agents each operating from their own schema or local knowledge.[21]

John Holland also offered a concise definition of CAS as 'systems that involve many components that adapt or learn as they interact'.[22] CASs are all around us in nature as well as in human systems, including economies and organisations. The choice we have is to either embrace the complexity or manage it. For example, in organisations, you either seek to control complexity through constructing hierarchies or you embrace it via open ecosystems. Herbert Simon opined that complexity depends on the attitudes and mindsets we have. He reflected, 'How complex or simple a structure is depends critically upon the way in which we describe it'.[23] Simon believes we have an inherent hierarchical perspective and illustrates this with an example of drawing a human face where we typically outline the shape of the head first. Hierarchy has been the mainstay of organisations for centuries. It is understandable why hierarchy has persisted – it is structured, predicable and achieves economies of scale (Taylor 1911); it creates a clear chain of command and quick decision-making (Weber 1922); and it can be a motivating force (Jaques 1990). This study starts with the premise that organisational hierarchy impedes open networks, CI, and decision-making and that progressive organisations need to create more open ecostructures and digital ecosystems to flourish in Industry 4.0.[24] BOS 2.0 is a CAS because there are no hierarchies, no exact sequences or procedures, but a whole-system complex intelligence where self-organising agents sensemake and form a collective point of view which will be increasingly supported by smart technology.

2. Emergence

Jeffrey Goldstein considers emergence as, 'the arising of novel and coherent structures, patterns and properties during the process of self-organization in complex systems'.[25] An everyday example of emergence can be found in bootleg trails or desire paths which are well-trodden convenient shortcuts leading away from a planned pathway. Within complexity theory, emergence is associated with self-organisation and complex systems. Emergence also strongly correlates to the natural world of swarm and optimisation where the strength and power of superorganisms evolve 'from low-level rules to higher-level sophistication'.[26] The term is widely accredited to the psychologist George Henry Lewes who talked about 'Life being an emergent' in *Problems of Life and Mind* in 1874.[27] The general principle of emergence is also central to John Stuart Mill and Charles Darwin's philosophies. Emergence spans many disciplines. It fell out of usage and into a 'submergence'[28] as a concept during the first part of the twentieth century to be reincarnated in the complexity theory era. This has resulted in it being a rather ambiguous and disputed term. It has also led to two distinct schools of emergentism – strong and weak emergence.[29] BOS 2.0 is emergent in nature. Ideas and decisions do not come from the executive, and they are not designed or scripted but emerge from the CAS through self-organising agents. This is a 'strategy by discovery' and not a strategy by design.[30]

3. Self-organising

At the Wyss Institute for Biologically Inspired Engineering at Harvard University, a remarkable breakthrough in science took place on a makeshift tabletop. The Self-Organising Systems Research Group has successfully developed a low-cost self-organising robot called a Kilobot that is 33 mm in diameter, communicates with neighbours up to 7 cm with distance sensing, and moves around using vibrating motors and infrared light. Kilobots are programmed to work in large swarms and can form any collective shape without human intervention. Just a few seed Kilobots can set in motion a 1024-Kilobot swarm activity that creates complex shapes such as the letter K or a starfish. Its commercial implications are already emerging, and it is gaining scientific recognition.[31] The Kilobots are following the basic principles of self-organising systems. Eugene Pleasants Odum and Gary W. Bennet provide a useful definition of the concept, linking self-organisation with complex systems and emergence:

> Self-organization can be defined as the process whereby complex systems consisting of many parts tend to organize to achieve some sort of stable, pulsing state in the absence of external interference.[32]

The idea of self-organising systems has a messy etymology. Like other categories in this section, the term evolved over time and has been hacked by multiple disciplines, including computer science,[33] chemistry,[34] physics,[35] and biology and evolutionism.[36] The concept featured in Kant's 1790 *Critique of Judgement* in relation to living organisms and has been referenced throughout history from Democritus to Descartes. It resurfaced in the twentieth century as a major constituent of cybernetics and complexity science. Cybernetician William Ross Ashby explored self-organising systems in relation to humans and machines in his classic 1947 paper. He wrote, 'a machine can be at the same time (a) strictly determinate in its actions, and (b) yet demonstrate a self-induced change of organisation'.[37] Controversy exists around self-organising systems. Geoff Mulgan argues in *Big Mind: How Collective Intelligence Can Change our World* (2018) that even self-organisation needs some degree of structure. Self-organising systems can lead to collective stupidity as much as CI.[38] It is relatively easy to mislead a crowd of disembarking passengers at an airport if you walk stridently in a certain direction – the crowd will tend to follow you. Central to BOS 2.0 are self-organising sensemaking networks that initiate business intelligence and create decisions without executive direction or steer.

4. Collective intelligence (CI)

Many view Aristotle as a champion for collectivism when he wrote in *The Politics* that good men 'may be better, not individually but collectively'.[39] There have been a steady stream of early thinkers following Aristotle who have conceptualised some form of CI, including Condorcet, Diderot, Hegel, and Moritz Lazarus and Heymann Steinthal's Völkerpsychologie. *In Big Mind: How Collective Intelligence Can Change Our World*, Geoff Mulgan provides a great example of early CI. He tells the story of Richard Chenevix Trench who convinced sponsors of the Oxford English Dictionary (OED) to compile the dictionary using an army of unpaid volunteers to help map the language.[40] Twentieth-century authors who have written about CI include Galton, Habermas, Wells, Lévy, and Bloom. Pierre Lévy dedicated much time to the subject and provides a classic definition of CI as 'a form of *universally distributed intelligence*, constantly enhanced, coordinated in real time, and resulting in the effective mobilization of skills'.[41] For Lévy, CI is about mutual recognition and enrichment where 'no one knows everything, everyone knows something, all knowledge resides in humanity'.[42] Related concepts include open innovation,[43] collective impact,[44] crowdsourcing,[45] and open source.[46] H.G. Wells' vision of a world encyclopaedia (a 'world intelligence') has become a reality.[47] Wikipedia went live with its first edit on 15 January 2001 with a domain registered by Jimmy Wales and Larry Sanger.[48] The principle of Wikipedia is one where global users edit and evolve the content and it is widely held to be a supreme example of CI. CI has undoubtedly come of age in the computer and Internet/ Wikipedia era. In recent times, it has acquired scientific status where, similar to the g-factor (general individual intelligence), the group c-factor (CI) is measured.[49] BOS 2.0 embraces CI. Whereas BOS 1.0 is more information-led with individual decision makers seeking out information to justify preconfigured decisions, BOS 2.0 is intelligence-led where the whole system contributes to the decision-making process.

5. Interconnectivity

Interconnectivity is the way in which agents relate and connect to one another in a CAS. The idea of an immersive space where self-organising (interconnecting) agents can coordinate behaviour, collaborate, and work out direction based on whole system/CI that feeds back into the CAS is absolutely critical to BOS 2.0. There are three core elements that contribute to this interconnectedness.

- Collaboration
  To collaborate is to push your own mental boundaries and partner with others. It has become a popular concept in modern business studies as we have moved towards teamworking and decentralised operations. Many studies, including my book *Constructing Leadership 4.0: Swarm Leadership and the Fourth Industrial Revolution*, focus on building collaborative intelligence (CQ), a term coined by William

Isaacs in *Dialogue: The Art of Thinking Together* (1999), which Dawna Markova and Angie McArthur describe as a 'measure of your ability to think with others on behalf of what matters to us all... to dignify the differences in how we think and use them to face complex challenges'.[50]

- Diversity and competition of ideas
  Interconnected systems function best in diverse environments where there exists a rich competition of ideas. A system's approach to encouraging diverse ideas comes when organisations promote cross-functional collaborations in which participants are invited to engage in problem-solving and decision-making outside of their defined discipline. This has become known as the 'Medici Effect' where participants create 'intersectional ideas'[51] in a cross-functional environment made up of different fields, disciplines, and cultures that provoke non-conditioned diverse thinking and results.

- Coordination
  Sivave Mashingaidze defines coordination as the 'appropriate organization in space and time of the tasks required to solve a specific problem'.[52] In the digital and information age, an increasing use of technology such as advanced data analytics and intelligent systems has improved information filtering and strengthened the way we crunch data so that consensus decision-making avoids some of the pitfalls of traditional human decision-making. This subject will be explored in the coming chapters.

BOS 2.0 is an interconnected system of diverse collaborative networks which come together to coordinate ideas and perspectives to reach collective group decisions.

6. Simple rules

In *The Perfect Swarm*, Len Fisher looks at how simple rules define superorganisms, 'The modern science of complexity has shown that collective behavior in animal groups (especially those of insects such as locusts, bees and ants) emerges from a set of very simple rules for interaction between neighbors'.[53] Eric Bonabeau and Christopher Meyer link this to human behaviour arguing that 'complex collective behavior can emerge from individuals following simple rules'.[54] Donald Sull and Katherine Eisenhardt believe that simple rules lead to better decisions and 'are shortcut strategies that save time and effort by focusing our attention and simplifying the way we process information'.[55] They researched early tech companies such as Intel and Cisco during the Internet boom and discovered that the organisational success factor was based on specified simple rules. Such an approach 'helped companies to bridge the gap between strategy and execution – to make on-the-spot decisions and adapt to rapidly changing circumstances, while keeping the big picture in mind'.[56] In a Harvard Business Review (HBR) article reporting their findings, they provide a good case study of the Brazilian Rail Authority and give some generic guidelines on setting simple rules, including identifying bottlenecks, focusing on data, encouraging users to craft the rules, making concrete/specific rules, and keeping them up to date.[57] BOS 2.0 follows specific rules and frameworks. BOS 1.0, with all its strict hierarchies and linearity is, in fact, fairly complex and involved. Individual leaders need to conduce, influence, motivate, and manage conflict to promote their ideas. Any real resistance and they fall back on status, power, control, and conditioning. Despite being a CAS, BOS 2.0 uses a clear business process, swarm facilitation, and starts with the principle that the solution or decision lies in the group – it just needs an agreed set of rules and mechanisms to help surface the ideas. We will see in Chapter 2 that swarm facilitation is a simple process with clear properties and gateways for identifying issues, collaborating, filtering data, and establishing group consensus.

Why now?

The central theme of this chapter which will thread throughout the book is that the old BOS is no longer relevant or fit-for-purpose; it hasn't served the business well for several decades. It has led to a dysfunctional workplace which even transformational leadership could not fix. Despite many transformations, established organisations, factories, and offices still have legacies going back to previous centuries. There is a building sense of urgency to upgrade organisations once and for all and I believe now is the time. Why? There are at least four reasons driving the need for business transformation.

1. The rise of Industry 4.0 and the smart economy

Artificial and augmented intelligence is proving to be a game changer. Sundar Pichai, CEO of Google, recently remarked that AI will be more profound a change than electricity or fire.[58] Smart apps and platforms are driving the connected economy and transforming the economic model.[59] The new technology is creating an unprecedented organisational, cultural, and digital transformation that outdated BOSs can't handle. The traditional or classic BOS depicted in Figure 1.1 doesn't make sense in a modern volatile/uncertain/complex/ambiguous (VUCA)[60] business context. We are living in a more complex and connected world which requires a more agile, adaptive, interconnected, self-organising BOS.

2. A new generation of workers who want to work in a more engaging workplace

A hesitancy by many established businesses to flatten their decision-making pyramids and adopt a more collective approach has created employee engagement issues, particularly with the millennial generation who are digital natives and have core values around collaboration and meaningful work. Put simply, millennials and digital natives who make up the largest working group do not thrive in a stifling BOS.[61] Attracting and retaining young talent in the workplace is going to require a more adaptive, agile, flexible, and collective business environment. Lack of collective decision-making is one of the key factors behind disengagement in the workplace, particularly among a younger generation who want to contribute.[62]

3. The growth of social media that exposes this problem

Executives with dysfunctional alpha leadership behaviours are under the spotlight. There have been some recent high-profile cases where organisational leaders have been removed from their posts because of adverse social media publicity that has caused major reputational damage. Recent examples include Uber's Travis Kalanick[63] and KPMG's Bill Michael[64] – both these senior executives were alpha leaders who called the shots and made some disastrous gaffes that compromised the company they led. It is easy to blame individual followers for allowing it to happen (for lacking the courage to voice and challenge this alpha behaviour), but the reality is that it has been part of a tenacious conditioning culture within modern organisations for decades – social media has brought it more to light and has highlighted the need for a genuine change of attitudes, behaviours, and working practices.

4. Coronavirus pandemic

The coronavirus pandemic outbreak has done more to advance the case for rethinking BOSs than any other single factor. Covid-19 has raised some rather intriguing debates and discussions about human presence and how we work together. Prior to Covid-19, there existed a culture of presentism (which is very much part of the BOS 1.0 paradigm). In 2013, Marissa Mayer, ex CEO of Yahoo, hit the headlines when an internal Yahoo memo was leaked where she was forcing presenteeism:

> To become the absolute best place to work, communication and collaboration will be important, so we need to be working side-by-side. That is why it is critical that we are all present in our offices. Some of the best decisions and insights come from hallway and cafeteria discussions, meeting new people, and impromptu team meetings. Speed and quality are often sacrificed when we work from home. We need to be one Yahoo!, and that starts with physically being together.[65]

For decades, it has been perceived that human presence and presentism are critical for productivity (an issue we will explore in Chapter 3). Even tech entrepreneur, Steve Jobs, who developed so much of the digital technology we rely on today, was a firm advocate of human presence.[66] The debate on human presence in online environments has trended during the coronavirus pandemic, where many people have been connecting online. The pandemic has entirely debunked the myths and false assumptions around homeworking and productivity. A recent Chartered Institute of Personal Development (CIPD) report, for example, has shown a significant rise in productivity during the Covid-19 crisis where many have worked from home.[67] This is already leading to discussions of shaking up the workplace and having hybrid working models. Henry Mance comments in an article published in the *Financial Times*:

> In a few short months, the office era – that period when working in an office was the default setting for the professional class – has died. The key space where white-collar workers interact will no longer be the four walls of an office; it will be the four sides of a screen.[68]

This is enhancing the network economy and digital transformation and may prove to be, as Henry Mance asserts in his *Financial Times* article, a defining moment in the shift away from old structures and practices. Attitudes seem to be changing, but the debate is still divided with some still calling for face-to-face interaction. We will see in later chapters how nascent technology is creating better human-computer interaction (HCI) which has the potential to shift attitudes further.

The backdrop to this opening chapter is business transformation. David Cruise, Director of Business Transformation at Change Associates, characterises business transformation as a 'process of fundamentally changing the systems, processes, people and technology across a whole business or business unit, to achieve measurable improvements in efficiency, effectiveness and stakeholder satisfaction'.[69] The verb 'transform' is from the Latin *transformare* meaning to change in shape or metamorphose and describes a shift from current reality to future state. In the context of BOSs, the business transformation represents a fundamental change in business operations and involves rewiring the enterprise from centralised decision-making through bosses and hierarchies (BOS 1.0) to a more collective approach through collaborative networks via swarm communities increasingly supported by intelligent systems (BOS 2.0). This is a shift from monocracy to swarmocracy. The catalyst for this business transformation – it's beating heart – is based on a swarm algorithm inspired by house-hunting honeybees. Let's explore this now.

Notes

1   Matthew R. Fairholm and Gilbert W. Fairholm, *Understanding Leadership Perspectives: Theoretical and Practical Approaches* (New York, NY: Springer, 2009), 54.

2 Story cited in Rajeev Peshawaria, *Open Source Leadership: Reinventing When There's No More Business As Usual* (New York, NY: McGraw-Hill, 2017), 53.

3 Inspired by Andrea Derler, 'Better Pond, Bigger Fish', Deloitte United States, 23 January 2017, www2.deloitte.com/us/en/insights/deloitte-review/issue-20/developing-leaders-networks-of-opportunities.html, accessed 29 May 2021. I used a similar example in Richard Kelly, *Constructing Leadership 4.0: Swarm Leadership and the Fourth Industrial Revolution* (Basingstoke: Palgrave Macmillan, 2018).

4 Patrick Hoverstadt, *The Fractal Organization: Creating Sustainable Organizations with the Viable System Model* (Chichester: Wiley, 2008), 20.

5 Ted Gee, *Hope is Not a Strategy: Simple Solutions for Doing Business in the 21st Century* (Indianapolis, IN: Dog Ear Publishing, 2008), 85.

6 Arun Kumar and Nagarajan Meenakshi, *Organizational Behavior, A Modern Approach* (New Delhi: Vikas, 2009), 375.

7 Chun Wei Choo argues, 'Organizational decision making is rational in spirit (and appearance) if not in execution: the organization is intendedly rational even if its members are only boundedly so'. Chun Wei Choo, *The Knowing Organization: How Organizations Use Information to Construct Meaning, Create Knowledge and Make Decisions* (New York, NY: Oxford University Press, 2006), 13.

8 Source: Samuel A. Kirkpatrick, 'Psychological Views of Decision-Making', in Cornelius P. Cotter (ed.), *Political Science Annual: An International Review*, Vol. 6 (Indianapolis, IN: Bobbs-Merrill, 1975), 36.

9 Charles Citroen succinctly equates rational decision-making with information when he writes, 'Information on the internal and external environment of the organisation is a crucial factor in the process of decision-making by executives in industry'. Charles L. Citroen, 'The Role of Information in Strategic Decision-Making', *International Journal of Information Management*, 31, 2011, 493–501, 493.

10 Trainingindustry.com estimated that leadership development spend was approximately $3.5 billion in 2019. 'The Leadership Training Market', *Training Industry*, 28 March 2019 (updated 20 November 2020), https://trainingindustry.com/wiki/leadership/the-leadership-training-market/, accessed 29 May 2021.

11 Source: 'The Gorilla Story' in Walter R. Olsen and William A. Sommers, *A Trainer's Companion: Stories to Stimulate Reflection, Conversation, Action* (Dallas, TX: AHA, 2004), 100–103.

12 Max Weber, *Rationalism and Modern Society: New Translations on Politics, Bureaucracy, and Social Stratification*, trans. by Tony Waters and Dagmar Waters (eds.) (Basingstoke: Palgrave Macmillan, 1944/2014), 114; B.F. Skinner, 'Two Types of Conditioned Reflex: A Reply to Konorski and Miller', *Journal of General Psychology*, 16, 1937, 272–279; Michel Foucault, 'The Subject and Power', *Critical Inquiry*, 8, 4, 1982, 777–795.

13 Richard Kelly, *Constructing Leadership 4.0: Swarm Leadership and the Fourth Industrial Revolution* (Basingstoke, Palgrave Macmillan, 2018).

14 Kate Ludeman and Eddie Erlandson, 'Coaching the Alpha Male', *Harvard Business Review*, May 2004, https://hbr.org/2004/05/coaching-the-alpha-male, accessed 20 October 2021.

15 Henri Fayol, *General and Industrial Management*, trans. by Constance Storrs (London: Pitman, 1916/1949), 34.

16 Collective decision-making is perceived as slowing down the decision-making process. For example, see Michael A. Hitt and Dennis R. Middlemist, *Organizational Behavior: Applied Concepts* (Chicago, IL: Science Research Associates, 1981) and Jerald Greenberg and Robert Baron, *Behaviour in Organizations: Understanding and Managing the Human Side of Work* (Eaglewood Cliffs, New Jersey: Prentice Hall International, 1983/1995). This is a contested view. Some studies have considered that smaller teams are more likely to succeed in their goals. For example, Marjorie E. Shaw, 'A Comparison of Individuals and Small Groups in the Rational Solution of Complex Problems', *The American Journal of Psychology*, 44, 3, 1932, 491–504, Joseph Wolfe, Thomas Chacko, 'Team-Size Effects on Business Game Performance and Decision-Making Behaviors', *Decision Sciences*, 14, 2007, 121–133.

17 Some argue that large groups are more cautious in making decisions than individuals. This is the view of Neil Malamuth and Seymour Feshbach, 'Risky Shift in a Naturalistic Setting', *Journal of Personality*, 40, 1972, 38–49. This is against the general view from such commentators as James A.F Stoner, 'Risky and Cautious Shifts in Group Decisions: The Influence of Widely Held Values', *Journal of Experimental Social Psychology*, 4, 4, 1968, 442–459, who argue that groups take more risks than individuals in decision-making.

18 There is a view that large groups produce less creativity and innovation. See, for example, Thomas J. Bouchard et al., 'Brainstorming Procedure, Group Size, and Sex as Determinants of the Problem-Solving Effectiveness of

Groups and Individuals', *Journal of Applied Psychology*, 59, 2, 1974, 135–138; Solomon E. Asch, 'Studies of Independence and Conformity: 1. A Minority of One Against A Unanimous Majority', *Psychological Monographs: General and Applied*, 70, 9, 1956, 1–70.

19 Jason Brownlee provides some good background and literature review on complex adaptive systems. Jason Brownlee, 'Complex Adaptive Systems', *Technical Report 070302A, Complex Intelligent Systems Laboratory, Centre for Information Technology Research*, April 2007, www.semanticscholar.org/paper/Complex-adaptive-systems-Brownlee/44de012ccf9ff522ab6ed6dfb6 6c75e39e986be1#paper-header, accessed 29 May 2021.

20 Arthur et al. (1997) describe complexity in an economic context by providing six 'features' of complex adaptive systems went on to define CAS as three properties. Murray Gell-Mann (1994) usefully goes on to provide four characteristics of a CAS. Brian Arthur, et al., 'Introduction: Process and Emergence in the Economy', in W. Brian Arthur, Steven Durlauf, and David A. Lane (eds.), *The Economy as an Evolving Complex System II* (Reading, MA: Addison-Wesley Pub. Co, 1997), 1–4; Murray Gell-Mann, 'Complex Adaptive Systems', in George A. Cowan, David Pines, and David Meltzer (eds.), *Complexity: Metaphors, Models, and Reality* (Boston, MA: Addison-Wesley, 1994), 17–45.

21 Brenda Zimmerman et al., *Edgeware: Lessons from Complexity Science for Healthcare Leaders* (Irving, TX: VHA Inc., 2008), 8. Serena Chan, paraphrasing Murray Gell-Mann, argues:

> *Plexus* means braided or entwined, from which is derived *complexus* meaning braided together, and the English word 'complex' is derived from the Latin. Complexity is therefore associated with the intricate inter-twining or inter-connectivity of elements within a system and between a system and its environment.
>
> Serena Chan, 'Complex Adaptive Systems', *Research Seminar in Engineering Systems*, 31 October 2001, https://www.studocu.com/en-gb/document/university-of-south-wales/strategic-systems-thinking/complex-adaptive-systems/5721382, accessed 29 May 2021

22 John H. Holland, 'Studying Complex Adaptive Systems', *Journal of Systems Science and Complexity*, 19, 2006, 1–8, https://link.springer.com/article/10.1007/s11424-006-0001-z, accessed 29 May 2021.

23 Henry Simon, 'The Architecture of Complexity', *Proceedings of the American Philosophical Society*, 106, 6, 1962, 467–482, www.scirp.org/(S(lz5mqp453 edsnp55rrgjct55))/reference/ReferencesPapers.aspx?ReferenceID= 1227703, accessed 29 May 2021, 481.

24 Steve Jobs said in an interview at the D8 conference, 'You have to be run by ideas, not hierarchy'. Steve Jobs, 'Steve Jobs in 2010 at D8 Conference (Full Video)', interviewed by Walt Mossberg and Kara Swisher, Filmed 1 June 2010 in Southern California, 1:35.53, www.youtube.com/watch?v= i5f8bqYYwps, accessed 29 May 2020.

25 Jeffrey Goldstein, 'Emergence as a Construct: History and Issues', Emergence: Complexity & Organization, 1, 1, 1999, 49–72, www. researchgate.net/publication/243786253_Emergence_as_a_Construct_ History_and_Issues, accessed 16 June 2020, 40.

26 Steven Johnson, *Emergence: The Connected Lives of Ants, Brains, Cities, and Software* (New York: Scriber, 2001), 18.

27 George Henry Lewes, *Problems of Life and Mind*, Volume 1 (Boston and New York: Houghton, Miffin and Company, 1874), 174.

28 Peter A. Corning, 'The Re-Emergence of "Emergence": A Venerable Concept in Search of a Theory', *Complexity*, 7, 6, 2002, 18–30, www. researchgate.net/publication/279236945_The_re-emergence_of_emer- gence_A_venerable_concept_in_search_of_a_theory, accessed 29 May 2021, 18.

29 See David J. Chalmers, 'Strong and Weak Emergence', in Philip Davies and Paul Clayton (eds.), *The Re-Emergence of Emergence: The Emergentist Hypothesis From Science to Religion* (Oxford: Oxford University Press, 2006).

30 David Gray and Tomas Vander Wal, *The Connected Company* (San Mateo, CA: O'Reilly Media, 2012), 227.

31 Source: 'Kilobots: A Thousand-Robot System', *Wyss Institute*, https://wyss. harvard.edu/media-post/kilobots-a-thousand-robot-swarm/, accessed 29 May 2021.

32 Eugene Pleasants Odum and Gary W. Bennet, *Fundamentals of Ecology*, (1953, Pacific Grove,CA: Thomson Brook/Cole, 2005) 355.

33 Such as John Holland, *Adaption in Natural and Artificial Systems* (1992, Cambridge, MA: MIT Press, 1975) and Yang Xin-She et al. 'A Framework for Self-Tuning Optimization Algorithm', *Neural Computing and Applications*,

23, 7–8, 2013, 2051–2057, www.researchgate.net/publication/258160428_A_framework_for_self-tuning_optimization_algorithm, accessed 29 May 2021.

34 For example, Gregoire Nicolis and Ilya Prigogine, *Self-Organization in Nonequilibrium Systems: From Dissipative Structures to Order through Fluctuations* (CA: Wiley-Interscience, 1977).

35 For example, Hermann Haken, *The Science of Structure: Synergetics* (New York, NY: Van Nostrand Reinhold, 1984).

36 Such as the following authors: Humberto R. Maturana and Francisco J. Varela, *The Tree of Knowledge: The Biological Roots of Human Understanding* (Boston, MA: New Science Library/Shambhala, 1987); Erich Jantsch, *The Self-Organizing Universe: Scientific and Human Implications of the Emerging Paradigm of Evolution* (Oxford: Pergamon Press, 1980); Stuart A. Kauffman, *Origins of Order: Self Organization and Selection in Evolution* (New York: Oxford University Press, 1993); Brian C. Goodwin, *How the Leopard Changed its Spots: The Evolution of Complexity* (Princeton, NJ: Princeton University Press, 2001).

37 W.R. Ashby, 'Principles of the Self-Organizing Dynamic System', *The Journal of General Psychology*, 37, 2, 1947, 125–128, www.tandfonline.com/doi/abs/10.1080/00221309.1947.9918144, accessed 29 May 2021, 125.

38 A good explanation of this can be found in this recorded lecture, 'Designing Collective Intelligence: Mobilising Humans and Machines to Address Social Needs', Nesta/Sage event, 17 September 2018, *You Tube*, posted as 'Collective Intelligence—The What Why and How', 24 January 2019, https://youtu.be/h4EClp7o28Q?t=410, accessed 29 May 2021.

39 Aristotle, *The Politics*, trans. by H. Rackham (Cambridge, MA: Harvard University Press, 1944), Book 3, 1281b.

40 Geoff Mulgan, *Big Mind: How Collective Intelligence Can Change our World* (Princeton, NJ: Princeton University Press, 2018), 48. This was subject of the 2019 movie, *The Professor and the Madman*.

41 Pierre Lévy, *Collective Intelligence: Mankind's Emerging World in Cyberspace*, trans. by Robert Bononno (Cambridge, MA: Perseus books, 1997), 13.

42 Pierre Lévy, *Collective Intelligence*, 20.

43 A term coined by Henry Chesbrough – 'Open Innovation means that valuable ideas can come from inside or outside the company and can go to market from inside or outside the company as well'. Henry Chesbrough, *Open Innovation: The New Imperative for Creating and Profiting from Technology* (Boston, MA: Harvard Business School Press, 2003), 43.

44 Collective impact is where leaders and organisations collaborate with external stakeholders. The term was coined by John Kania and Mark Kramer in 2011.

45 This is a portmanteau term coined by Wired Magazine editors Jeff Howe and Mark Robinson in 2005 to mean outsourcing work to the crowd (typically via the Internet).

46 Good Source: Eric S. Raymond, *The Cathedral and the Bazaar: Musings on Linux and Open Source by an Accidental Revolutionary* (Sebastopol, CA: O'Reilly & Associates, 1999).

47 H.G. Wells, *World Brain* (New York, NY: Doubleday, 1938), 17.

48 'History of Wikipedia', open source contribution, https://en.wikipedia.org/wiki/History_of_Wikipedia, accessed 29 May 2021.

49 Good Source: Anita Williams Woolley et al., 'Evidence for a Collective Intelligence Factor in the Performance of Human Groups', *Science*, 330, 6004, 2010, 686–688, www.researchgate.net/publication/47369848_Evidence_of_a_Collective_Intelligence_Factor_in_the_Performance_of_Human_Groups, accessed 29 May 2021. See also 'Collective Intelligence Factor C', *Wikipedia*, open source contribution, https://en.wikipedia.org/wiki/Collective_intelligence, accessed 29 May 2021.

50 Dawna Markova and Angie McArthur, *Collaborative Intelligence: Thinking with People Who Think Differently* (New York, NY: Spiegel & Grau, 2015), Introduction.

51 Frans Johansson, *The Medici Effect: Breakthrough Insights at the Intersection of Ideas* (Boston, MA: Harvard Business School Press, 2006), 17.

52 Sivave Mashingaidze, 'Benefits of Collective Intelligence: Swarm Intelligent Foraging', *Journal of Governance and Regulation*, 3, 4, 2014, 193–201, www.researchgate.net/publication/311565345_Benefits_of_collective_intelligence_Swarm_intelligent_foraging_an_ethnographic_research, accessed 29 May 2021, 198.

53 Len Fisher, *The Perfect Swarm: The Science of Complexity in Everyday Life* (New York, NY: Basic Books, 2009), 2

54 Eric Bonabeau and Christopher Meyer, 'Swarm Intelligence: A Whole New Way to Think about Business', *Harvard Business Review*, 2001, https://hbr.org/2001/05/swarm-intelligence-a-whole-new-way-to-think-about-business, accessed 29 May 2021. See also Chapter 3 ('The World of Simple

Programs') of Stephen Wolfram (2002) where he explores how simple rules can generate complicated behavior. Stephen Wolfram, *A New Kind of Science* (Champaign, IL: Wolfram Media, Inc., 2002).

55 Donald Sull and Kathleen M. Eisenhardt, *Simple Rules: How to Thrive in a Complex World* (London: John Murray, 2015), 5.

56 Donald Sull and Kathleen M. Eisenhardt, 'Simple Rules for a Complex World', *Harvard Business Review*, September 2012, https://hbr.org/2012/09/simple-rules-for-a-complex-world, accessed 29 May 2021.

57 Donald Sull and Kathleen M. Eisenhardt 'Simple Rules for a Complex World'.

58 Source: Catherine Clifford, Google CEO: A.I. is More Important than Fire or Electricity, CNBC, 1 February, 2018, www.cnbc.com/2018/02/01/google-ceo-sundar-pichai-ai-is-more-important-than-fire-electricity.html, accessed 29 May 2021.

59 See, for example, Paul Krugman, *The Self-Organizing Economy* (Oxford: Blackwell, 1996); Tony Killick (ed.), *The Flexible Economy: Causes and Consequences of the Adaptability of National Economies* (London: Routledge, 1994); W. Brian Arthur et al., 'The Economy as an Evolving Complex System 2', *Santa Fe Institute Studies in the Science of Complexity, Proceedings Volume XXVII* (Reading, MA: Addison-Wesley, 1997), www.researchgate.net/publication/237357182_The_Economy_as_an_Evolving_Complex_System_II, accessed 29 May 2021.

60 The VUCA axiom stands for Volatile, Uncertain, Complex and Ambiguous and was a term used at the US Army War College in their strategic leadership programme. Herbert Barber talks of the etymology of the term in a 1992 *Journal of Management Development* paper where he credits Warren Bennis and Burton Nanus (1986) for inspiring the axiom. H.F. Barber, 'Developing Strategic Leadership: The US Army War College Experience', *Journal of Management Development*, 11, 6, 1992, 4–12.

61 See, for example, Brigid Schulte, 'Millennials Want an End to Hierarchies in the Workplace', *Chicago Tribune*, 21 June 2015, www.chicagotribune.com/dp-millennials-want-an-end-to-hierarchies-in-the-workplace-20150622-story.html, accessed 29 May 2021. Don Tapscott argues that the millennial generation are 'exceptionally curious, self-reliant, contrarian, smart, focused, able to adapt, high in self-esteem, and possessed of a global orientation'.

Don Tapscott, *Growing up Digital: The Rise of the Net Generation* (New York, NY: McGraw Hill, 1998), 209.

62 See: Jennifer Robison, 'What Millennials Want is Good for Your Business', *GALLUP Workplace*, 22 March 2019, www.gallup.com/workplace/248009/millennials-good-business.aspx#:~:text=Millennials%20don't%20want%20a,they%20do%20best%20every%20day, accessed 29 May 2021. A recent GALLUP publication stated 85% of global employees are disengaged in the workplace. Source: 'What is Employee Engagement and How Do You Improve It?' *GALLUP*, www.gallup.com/workplace/285674/improve-employee-engagement-workplace.aspx, accessed 29 May 2021.

63 Former CEO and founder of Uber resigned as CEO in 2017 in the face of pressure from investors after six months of scandals culminating in an incident with an Uber driver that went viral on social media. In 2019, he relinquished all ties with Uber. He was brash and fostered a 'toxic work culture that encouraged sexual harassment and bullying'. Source: 'Uber Co-Founder Travis Kalanick to Resign from Board of Directors', *Guardian*, 24 December 2019, www.theguardian.com/technology/2019/dec/24/uber-co-founder-travis-kalanick-to-resign-from-board-of-directors, accessed 29 May 2021.

64 Australian born Bill Michael was KPMG's UK chair until he stepped down in February 2021. Well known in the organisation as a strong personality, he went into a tirade during an online call with staff telling them to stop moaning and 'playing the victim card' over the Coronavirus pandemic. His comments were leaked online by insiders and he was forced to resign. Source: Mark Sweney and Joanna Partridge, 'KPMG's Bill Michael Resigns after Telling Staff to Stop Moaning', *The Guardian*, 12 February 2021, www.theguardian.com/business/2021/feb/12/kpmg-bill-michael-resigns-after-telling-staff-to-stop-moaning, accessed 29 May 2021.

65 Source: Kara Swisher, ' "Physically Together": Here's the Internal Yahoo No-Work-from-Home Memo for Remote Workers and Maybe More', *All Things D*, 22 February 2013, http://allthingsd.com/20130222/physically-together-heres-the-internal-yahoo-no-work-from-home-memo-which-extends-beyond-remote-workers/, accessed 29 May 2021.

66 Walter Issacson, Steve Job's biographer, recorded an interview with Steve Jobs when he said,

> There's a temptation in our networked age to think that ideas can be developed by email and iChat... That's crazy. Creativity comes from spontaneous meetings, from random discussions. You run into someone, you ask what they're doing, you say 'Wow', and soon you're cooking up all sorts of ideas.
>
> Walter Issacson, *Steve Jobs, 2011* (London: Little, Brown, 2013), 397

67 'More Employers Reporting Increased Productivity Benefits from Homeworking Compared to Last Summer, New CIPD Research Finds', CIPD, 1 April 2021, www.cipd.co.uk/about/media/press/010421home working-increased-productivity#gref, accessed 29 May 2021. Homeworking is not for everyone. A 2017 *Eurofound* report indicated that 41% of remote homeworkers showed higher levels of stress compared with their office counterparts. Source: Jon Messenger et al., 'Working Anytime, Anywhere: The Effects on the World of Work', *Eurofound and the International Labour Office, Publications Office of the European Union, Luxembourg, and the International Labour Office, Geneva*, 2017, www.ilo. org/wcmsp5/groups/public/---dgreports/---dcomm/---publ/documents/ publication/wcms_544138.pdf, accessed 29 May 2021.

68 Henry Mance, 'The Rise and Fall of the Office', *Financial Times*, 15 May 2020, www.ft.com/content/f43b8212-950a-11ea-af4b-499244625ac4, accessed 29 May 2021.

69 David Cruise, 'What is Business Transformation?' *Change Associates*, 10 July 2017, www.changeassociates.com/blog/post/what-is-business-transformation#:~:text=Business%20Transformation%20is%20the%20 process,efficiency%2C%20effectiveness%20and%20stakeholder%20sat-isfaction, accessed 29 May 2021.

Bibliography

Allport, Flloyd H., 'The Influence of the Group upon Association and Thought', *Journal of Experimental Psychology*, 1920, 3:159–182.

Aristotle, *The Politics*, trans. by Harris Rackham (Cambridge, MA: Harvard University Press, 1944).

Arthur, Brian W., Durlauf, Steven, and Lane, David A., 'Introduction: Process and Emergence in the Economy', in *The Economy as an Evolving Complex*

System II, eds. Arthur, Brian W, Steven Durlauf, and David A. Lane (Reading, MA: Addison-Wesley Pub. Co, 1997) 1–4.

Asch, Solomon, Eliot, 'Studies of Independence and Conformity: 1. A Minority of One against a Unanimous Majority', *Psychological Monographs: General and Applied*, 1956, 70 (9):1–70.

Ashby, William Ross, 'Principles of the Self-Organizing Dynamic System', *The Journal of General Psychology*, 1947, 37 (2):125–128.

Barber, Herbert F., 'Developing Strategic Leadership: The US Army War College Experience', *Journal of Management Development*, 1992, 11 (6):4–12.

Bechara, Antoine, Damasio, Hanna, Tranel, Daniel, and Damasio, Antonio R., 'Deciding Advantageously before Knowing the Advantageous Strategy', *Science*, 1997, 275 (5304):1293–1295.

Belovicz, Meyer W. and Finch, Frederic E., 'A Critical Analysis of the "Risky Shift" Phenomenon', *Organisational Behavior and Human Performance*, 1971, 6 (2):150–168.

Bennis, Warren and Nanus, Burton, *Leaders: The Strategy for Taking Charge* (New York: Harper & Row, 1986).

Bernard, Chester, *The Functions of the Executive* (Cambridge, MA: Harvard Business Press, 1939/1950).

Bonabeau, Eric and Meyer, Christopher, 'Swarm Intelligence: A Whole New Way to Think about Business', *Harvard Business Review*, May 2001, https://hbsp.harvard.edu/product/R0105G-PDF-ENG, accessed 19 October 2021.

Bouchard, Thomas J., Barsaloux, Jean, and Drauden, Gail, 'Brainstorming Procedure, Group Size, and Sex as Determinants of the Problem-Solving Effectiveness of Groups and Individuals', *Journal of Applied Psychology*, 1974, 59 (2):135–138.

Brownlee, Jason, 'Complex Adaptive Systems', *Technical Report 070302A, Complex Intelligent Systems Laboratory, Centre for Information Technology Research*, April 2007, www.semanticscholar.org/paper/Complex-adaptive-systems-Brownlee/44de012ccf9ff522ab6ed6dfb66c75e39e986be1#paper-header, accessed 16 June 2020.

Carlyle, Thomas, *On Heroes, Hero-Worship and the Heroic in History* (New Haven, CT and London: Yale University Press, 1841/2013).

Chalmers, David J., 'Strong and Weak Emergence', in *The Re-Emergence of Emergence: The Emergentist Hypothesis from Science to Religion*, eds. Philip Davies and Paul Clayton (Oxford: Oxford University Press, 2006).

Chan, Serena, 'Complex Adaptive Systems', *Research Seminar in Engineering Systems*, 31 October 2001, https://www.studocu.com/en-gb/document/university-of-south-wales/strategic-systems-thinking/complex-adaptive-systems/5721382, accessed 29 May 2021.

Chesbrough, Henry, *Open Innovation: The New Imperative for Creating and Profiting from Technology* (Boston, MA: Harvard Business School Press, 2003).

Choo, Chun Wei, *The Knowing Organization: How Organizations Use Information to Construct Meaning, Create Knowledge and Make Decisions* (New York, NY: Oxford University Press, 2006).

Citroen, Charles L., 'The Role of Information in Strategic Decision-Making', *International Journal of Information Management*, 2011, 31:493–501.

Corning, Peter A., 'The Re-Emergence of "Emergence": A Venerable Concept in Search of a Theory', *Complexity*, 2002, 7 (6):18–30, www.researchgate.net/publication/279236945_The_re-emergence_of_emergence_A_venerable_concept_in_search_of_a_theory, accessed 29 May 2021.

David Cruise, 'What is Business Transformation?', *Change Associates*, 10 July 2017, www.changeassociates.com/blog/post/what-is-business-transformation#:~:text=Business%20Transformation%20is%20the%20process,efficiency%2C%20effectiveness%20and%20stakeholder%20satisfaction, accessed 29 May 2021.

Derler, Andrea, 'Better Pond, Bigger Fish', *Deloitte United States*, 23 January 2017, www2.deloitte.com/us/en/insights/deloitte-review/issue-20/developing-leaders-networks-of-opportunities.html, accessed 29 May 2021.

Fairholm, Matthew R. and Fairholm, Gilbert W., *Understanding Leadership Perspectives: Theoretical and Practical Approaches* (New York, NY: Springer, 2008).

Fayol, Henri, *General and Industrial Management*, trans. by Constance Storrs (1916, London: Pitman, 1949).

Fisher, Len, *The Perfect Swarm: The Science of Complexity in Everyday Life* (New York, NY: Basic Books, 2009).

Foucault, Michel, 'The Subject and Power', *Critical Inquiry*, 1982, 8 (4):777–795.

Gee, Ted, *Hope is Not a Strategy: Simple Solutions for Doing Business in the 21st Century* (Indianapolis, IN: Dog Ear Publishing, 2008).

Gell-Mann, Murray, 'Complex Adaptive Systems', in *Complexity: Metaphors, Models, and Reality*, George A. Cowan, David Pines, and David Meltzer, eds. (Boston, MA: Addison-Wesley, 1994a) 17–45.

Gell-Mann, Murray, *The Quark and the Jaguar: Adventures in the Simple and the Complex* (New York, NY: Freeman/Holt Paperbacks, 1994b).

Gladwell, Malcolm, *Blink: The Power of Thinking without Thinking* (New York, NY: Back Bay Books, 2007).

Goldstein, Jeffrey, 'Emergence as a Construct: History and Issues', *Emergence: Complexity & Organization*, 1999, 1 (1):49–72, www.researchgate.net/publication/243786253_Emergence_as_a_Construct_History_and_Issues, accessed 16 June 2020.

Goodwin, Brian C., *How the Leopard Changed its Spots: The Evolution of Complexity* (Princeton, NJ: Princeton University Press, 2001).

Goodwin, Brian C., 'Beyond the Darwinian Paradigm: Understanding Biological Forms', in *Evolution: The First Four Billion Years*, Michael Ruse and Joseph Travis, eds. (Cambridge, MA: Harvard University Press, 2011).

Gray, David and Vander W., Tomas, *The Connected Company* (San Mateo, CA: O'Reilly Media, 2012).

Greenberg, Jerald and Baron, Robert A., *Behaviour in Organizations: Understanding and Managing the Human Side of Work* (Eaglewood Cliffs, New Jersey: Prentice Hall International, 1983/1995).

Gulick, Luther, 'Notes on the Theory of Organization', in *Papers on the Science of Administration*, Luther Gulick and Lyndall Urwick, eds. (New York, NY: Institute of Public Administration, 1937).

Haken, Hermann, *The Science of Structure: Synergetics* (New York, NY: Van Nostrand Reinhold, 1984).

Hecht, Ben, 'Collaboration is the New Competition', *Harvard Business Review*, 2013, https://hbr.org/2013/01/collaboration-is-the-new-compe.

Hitt, Michael A. and Middlemist, Dennis R., *Organizational Behavior: Applied Concepts* (Chicago, IL: Science Research Associates, 1981).

Holland, John, *Adaption in Natural and Artificial Systems* (1992, Cambridge, MA: MIT Press, 1975).

Holland, John H., 'Studying Complex Adaptive Systems', *Journal of Systems Science and Complexity*, 2006, 19:1–8, https://link.springer.com/article/10.1007/s11424-006-0001-z, accessed 29 May 2021.

Hoverstadt, Patrick, *The Fractal Organisation: Creating Sustainable Organizations with the Viable System Model* (Chichester: Wiley, 2008).

Howe, Jeff, 'The Rise of Crowdsourcing', *Wired*, 1 June 2006, www.wired.com/2006/06/crowds/, accessed 29 May 2021.

Isaacs, William, *Dialogue: The Art of Thinking Together: A Pioneering Approach to Communicating in Business and in Life* (New York, NY: Doubleday, a Division of Random House, 1999).

Issacson, Walter, *Steve Jobs: The Exclusive Biography* (2011, London: Little Brown, 2013).

Janis, Irving, *Victims of Groupthink, a Psychological Study of Foreign-Policy Decisions and Fiascoes* (Boston, MA and Houghton, MI, Mifflin, 1972).

Jantsch, Erich, *The Self-Organizing Universe: Scientific and Human Implications of the Emerging Paradigm of Evolution* (Oxford: Pergamon Press, 1980).

Jaques, Elliot, 'In Praise of Hierarchy', *Harvard Business Review*, 1990, https://hbr.org/1990/01/in-praise-of-hierarchy, accessed 29 May 2021.

Johansson, Frans, *The Medici Effect: Breakthrough Insights at the Intersection of Ideas* (Boston, MA: Harvard Business School Press, 2006).

Johnson, Steven, *Emergence: The Connected Lives of Ants, Brains, Cities, and Software* (New York, Scriber, 2001).

Kahneman, Daniel, *Thinking, Fast and Slow* (2011, London: Penguin, 2013).

Kania, John and Kramer, Mark, 'Collective Impact', *Stanford Social Innovation Review*, 2011, https://ssir.org/articles/entry/collective_impact, accessed 29 May 2021.

Kauffman, Stuart A., *Origins of Order: Self Organization and Selection in Evolution* (New York: Oxford University Press, 1993).

Kelly, Richard, *Constructing Leadership 4.0: Swarm Leadership and the Fourth Industrial Revolution* (Basingstoke: Palgrave Macmillan, 2018).

Killick, Tony (ed.), *The Flexible Economy: Causes and Consequences of the Adaptability of National Economies* (London: Routledge, 1994).

Kirkpatrick, Samuel A., 'Psychological Views of Decision-Making', in *Political Science Annual: An International Review*, Vol. 6, Cornelius P. Cotter, ed. (Indianapolis, IN: Bobbs-Merrill, 1975).

Klein, Gary, *The Power of Intuition: How to Use Your Gut Feelings to Make Better Decisions* (New York, NY: Crown Publishing, 2007).

Krugman, Paul, *The Self-Organizing Economy* (Oxford: Blackwell, 1996).

Kumar, Arun and Meenakshi, Nagarajan, *Organizational Behavior: A Modern Approach* (New Delhi: Vikas, 2009).

Latané, Bibb, Williams, Kipling and Harkins, Stephen, 'Many Hands Make Light the Work: The Causes and Consequences of Social Loafing', *Journal of Personality and Social Psychology*, 1979, 37 (6):822–832.

Lévy, Pierre, *Collective Intelligence: Mankind's Emerging World in Cyberspace*, trans. by Robert Bononno (Cambridge, MA: Perseus books, 1997).

Lewes, George Henry, *Problems of Life and Mind*, Volume 1 (Boston and New York: Houghton, Miffin and Company, 1874).

Ludeman, Kate and Erlandson, Eddie, 'Coaching the Alpha Male', *Harvard Business Review*, May 2004, https://hbr.org/2004/05/coaching-the-alpha-male, accessed 20 October 2021.

Malamuth, Neil and Feshbach, Seymour, 'Risky Shift in a Naturalistic Setting', *Journal of Personality*, 1972, 40:38–49.

Mance, Henry, 'The Rise and Fall of the Office', *Financial Times*, 15 May 2020, www.ft.com/content/f43b8212-950a-11ea-af4b-499244625ac4, accessed 29 May 2021.

Markova, Dawna and McArthur, Angie, *Collaborative Intelligence: Thinking with People Who Think Differently* (New York, NY: Spiegel & Grau, 2015).

Mashingaidze, Sivave, 'Benefits of Collective Intelligence: Swarm Intelligent Foraging', *Journal of Governance and Regulation*, 2014, 3 (4):193–201, www.researchgate.net/publication/311565345_Benefits_of_collective_intelligence_Swarm_intelligent_foraging_an_ethnographic_research, accessed 29 May 2021.

Maturana, Humberto R. and Varela, Francisco J., *The Tree of Knowledge: The Biological Roots of Human Understanding* (Boston, MA: New Science Library/Shambhala, 1987).

Mayo, Elton, *The Human Problems of an Industrial Civilization* (New York, NY: The Macmillan Co., 1933).

Messenger, Jon, Vargas Llave, Oscar, Gschwind, Lutz, Boehmer, Simon, Vermeylen, Greet, and Wilkens, Mathijn, 'Working Anytime, Anywhere: The Effects on the World of Work', *Eurofound and the International Labour Office, Publications Office of the European Union, Luxembourg, and the International Labour Office, Geneva*, 2017, www.ilo.org/wcmsp5/groups/public/---dgreports/---dcomm/---publ/documents/publication/wcms_544138.pdf, accessed 29 May 2021.

Mulgan, Geoff, *Big Mind: How Collective Intelligence Can Change Our World* (Princeton, NJ: Princeton University Press, 2018).

Nicolis, Gregoire and Prigogine, Ilya, *Self-Organization in Nonequilibrium Systems: From Dissipative Structures to Order through Fluctuations* (New York: Wiley-Interscience, 1977).

Nietzsche, Friedrich, *Thus Spoke Zarathustra*, trans. by Reginald John Hollingdale (Harmondsworth: Penguin, 1883/1969).

Olsen, Walter R. and Sommers,, William A., 'The Gorilla Story', in *A Trainer's Companion: Stories to Stimulate Reflection, Conversation, Action* (Dallas, TX: AHA, 2004).

Peshawaria, Rajeev, *Open Source Leadership: Reinventing When There's No More Business As Usual* (New York, NY: McGraw-Hill, 2017).

Raymond, Eric S., *The Cathedral and the Bazaar: Musings on Linux and Open Source by an Accidental Revolutionary* (Sebastopol, CA: O'Reilly & Associates, 1999).

Ringelmann, Max, 'Recherches sur les moteurs animés: Travail de l'homme' [Research on Animate Sources of Power: The Work of Man]', *Annales de l'Institut National Agronomique*, 1913, 2nd series, 12:1–40.

Robison, Jennifer, 'What Millennials Want Is Good for Your Business', *GALLUP Workplace*, 22 March 2019, www.gallup.com/workplace/248009/millennials-good-business.aspx#:~:text=Millennials%20don't%20want%20a,they%20do%20best%20every%20day, accessed 29 May 2021.

Schulte, Brigid, 'Millennials Want an End to Hierarchies in the Workplace', *Chicago Tribune*, 21 June 2015, www.chicagotribune.com/dp-millennials-want-an-end-to-hierarchies-in-the-workplace-20150622-story.html, accessed 29 May 2021.

Shaw, Marjorie E., 'A Comparison of Individuals and Small Groups in the Rational Solution of Complex Problems', *The American Journal of Psychology*, 1932, 44, 3:491–504.

Skinner, Burrhus Frederic, 'Two Types of Conditioned Reflex: A Reply to Konorski and Miller', *Journal of General Psychology*, 1937, 16:272–279.

Simon, Herbert, 'The Architecture of Complexity', *Proceedings of the American Philosophical Society*, 1962, 106 (6):467–482.

Stoner, James, 'Risky and Cautious Shifts in Group Decisions: The Influence of Widely Held Values', *Journal of Experimental Social Psychology*, 1968, 4 (4):442–459.Sull, Donald and Eisenhardt, Kathleen M., 'Simple Rules for a Complex World', *Harvard Business Review*, September 2012.

Sull, Donald and Eisenhardt, Kathleen M., *Simple Rules: How to Thrive in a Complex World* (London: John Murray, 2015).

Sweney, Mark and Partridge, Joanna, 'KPMG's Bill Michael Resigns after Telling Staff to Stop Moaning', *The Guardian*, 12 February, 2021, www.theguardian.com/business/2021/feb/12/kpmg-bill-michael-resigns-after-telling-staff-to-stop-moaning, accessed 29 May 2021.

Swisher, Kara, '"Physically Together": Here's the Internal Yahoo No-Work-from-Home Memo for Remote Workers and Maybe More', *All Things D*, 22 February 2013, http://allthingsd.com/20130222/physically-together-heres-the-internal-yahoo-no-work-from-home-memo-which-extends-beyond-remote-workers/, accessed 29 May 2021.

Tapscott, Don, *Growing up Digital: The Rise of the Net Generation* (New York, NY: McGraw Hill, 1998) 209.

Taylor, Frederick W., *The Principles of Scientific Management* (New York, NY and London, Harper & Brothers, 1911).

Triplett, Norman, 'The Dynamogenic Factors in Pacemaking and Competition', *The American Journal of Psychology*, 1898, 9 (4):507–533.

Urwick, Lyndall, *The Elements of Administration* (New York, NY: Harper, 1943).

Weber, Max, *Economy and Society: An Outline of Interpretive Sociology*, trans. by Ephraim Fichoff, et al. (Berkeley: University of California Press, 1922/1979).

Weber, Max, *Rationalism and Modern Society: New Translations on Politics, Bureaucracy, and Social Stratification*, trans. by Tony Waters and Dagmar Waters, eds. (Basingstoke: Palgrave Macmillan, 1944/2014) 114.

Wells, Herbert George, *World Brain* (New York, NY: Doubleday, 1938).

Woolley, Anita W., Chabris, Christopher F., Pentland, Alex, Hashmi, Nada, and Malone, Thomas W., 'Evidence for a Collective Intelligence Factor in the Performance of Human Groups', *Science*, 2010, 330 (6004):686–688, www.researchgate.net/publication/47369848_Evidence_of_a_Collective_Intelligence_Factor_in_the_Performance_of_Human_Groups, accessed 29 May 2021.

Wolfe, Joseph and Chacko, Thomas I., 'Team-Size Effects on Business Game Performance and Decision-Making Behaviors', *Decision Sciences*, 2007, 14:121–133.

Wolfram, Stephen, *A New Kind of Science* (Champaign, IL: Wolfram Media, Inc., 2002).

Xin-She, Yang, Suash, Deb, Martin, Loomes, and Mehmet, Karamanoglu, 'A Framework for Self-Tuning Optimization Algorithm', *Neural Computing and Applications*, 2013, 23 (7–8):2051–2057, www.researchgate.net/publication/258160428_A_framework_for_self-tuning_optimization_algorithm, accessed 16 June 2020.

Zimmerman, Brenda, Lindberg, Curt, and Plsek, Paul, *Edgeware: Lessons from Complexity Science for Healthcare Leaders* (Irving, TX: VHA Inc., 2008).

2

HOW HONEYBEES CAN HELP US REINVENT ORGANISATIONS

A few years ago, when I was attending a conference in Texas, I stood on Congress Avenue Bridge in Austin on a warm summer evening waiting with a sizeable crowd to witness an amazing natural spectacle. A busy urban bridge surrounded by concrete office blocks seemed an odd place to nature watch; yet 150,000 people gather here every summer at sunset. As the light faded, people around me were adjusting the settings on their cameras and phones in expectation of what was to come. Suddenly from under the bridge, and to the delight of the amassed spectators, there appeared a great swarm of Mexican free-tail bats. They nest in the safe and warm crevices under the bridge and feed on mosquitoes, bugs, and pests around the riverbank at sunset.[1]

I first became aware of bat watching on Congress Avenue Bridge from watching a 2009 BBC documentary, *One Million Heads, One Beautiful Mind*.[2] I have been fascinated by natural swarms since childhood and simply had to experience it for myself. The documentary's clever title links to swarm intelligence, a term coined by Gerardo Beni and Jing Wang in the context of developing cellular robotics.[3] The documentary provides many examples of how natural swarms, and certain social groups, work as a self-organising collective system that promotes vigilance, migration, and foraging. Bonabeau et al. characterise swarm intelligence succinctly

DOI: 10.4324/9781003215561-4

as 'the emergent collective intelligence of groups of simple agents'.[4] In the natural world, social groups such as birds, bees, ants, locusts, fish, wildebeests, etc. have limited intelligence when they act alone, but a strong collective intelligence when they act as a group. This increases their chance of survival.

In recent times, the principle of natural swarm behaviour has been applied to many systems, including human behaviour, business systems, and artificial intelligence and robotics. In this study, I am interested in how the principles of swarm intelligence can be applied in modern organisations to generate more self-organising and collective decision-making without the need for high-level planning or decisions. For such a change, a business transformation will be needed. Chapter 1 outlined a business transformation that spanned from the classic rational and sequential approach with decision-making steered by alpha leaders down the scalar chain of command (Business Operating System Version 1.0) (BOS 1.0) to a transformational, self-organising complex adaptive system that embraces collective decision-making (BOS 2.0) that is inspired by natural swarm intelligence. This chapter introduces the background and principles of swarm and how it can help transform organisation's BOSs and set them on the path to being business superorganisms.

'Birds do it, bees do it, even educated fleas do it'

You may recognise this lyric from Cole Porter's song, *Let's Do It (Let's Fall in Love)*. But this is not about falling in love; it's about swarming. And it's not just birds, bees and fleas that swarm. Several other social species swarm, including wildebeests, ants, cockroaches, locusts, fish, and termites. These species share one thing in common: they are superorganisms that typically work as collective agents rather than single entities to optimise their chance of survival. The idea of optimising something through collective endeavour is at the heart of swarm intelligence and swarm transformation.

These swarm activities have been modelled by computer scientists and made into practical algorithms. Yovat Noah Haran describes an algorithm as 'a methodical set of steps that can be used to make calculations, resolve problems and reach decisions'.[5] There is a growing family of swarm-based metaheuristic and optimisation algorithms[6] that include cuckoos (cuckoo search algorithm) based on parasitism; bats (bat algorithm) based on echolocation; fireflies (firefly algorithm); and glow-worms (glow-worm algorithm) both based on light emission.[7] Moreover, research is currently being carried out on swarm-based algorithms inspired by pack animals such as lions and wolves.[8] All of these bio-algorithms have practical applications in machine and artificial intelligence and are essential for the practice and evolution of swarm in the business.

The following sections look at a few examples of how bio-inspired swarm activity in nature can be modelled into swarm-based algorithms.

Ants

I have always been captivated by ant superhighways. It's well documented that they achieve this collective behaviour through laying pheromone trails. The term 'pheromone' was first introduced by Peter Karlson and Martin Lüscher in 1959, based on the Greek word *pherein* (meaning to transport) and *hormone* (meaning to stimulate).[9] It is a deposited chemical substance – or scent – that ants use to mark their route and direct the exploring colony to a specific resource, place, or task within a parameter space.[10] This form of indirect communication is known as stigmergy, a term coined by zoologist Pierre-Paul Grassé in 1959 to describe how ants and other social groups communicate through concentrated chemical cues and messaging.

The way ants establish a near-optimal path towards a goal was modelled by an ant system algorithm (AS) in 1991 by Alberto Colorni et al. In this metaheuristic bio-algorithm, artificial ants notate their position and solution for later ant simulations to locate and find better solutions.[11] It was originally modelled to solve the familiar travelling salesman problem (TSP).[12] A flow chart of ant swarm behaviour known as ant colony optimisation (ACO) is represented in Figure 2.1.

The AS led to the variant, ACO which has become a highly popular baseline search algorithm for solving combinatorial optimisation and routing problems with a specific and predefined source and destination (known as path to goal).[13] Popular practical applications for ant-based algorithms such as ACO include data mining,[14] machine learning, vehicle routing,[15] logistics,[16] assembly-line balancing, resource allocation and scheduling,[17] passenger boarding,[18] aerospace control, network and

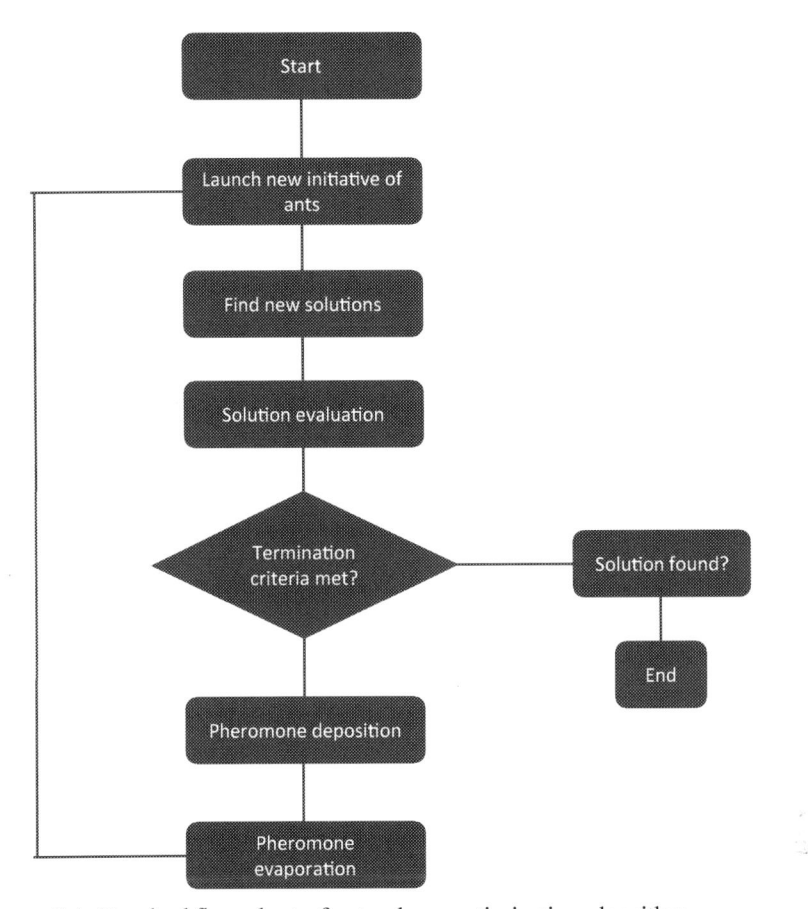

Figure 2.1 Standard flow chart of ant colony optimisation algorithm.

Source: Kiran Khurshid, et al., 'Flow Chart Depicting the Structure of ACO Algorithm', Fig 2, in 'Application of Heuristic (1-Opt Local Search) and Metaheuristic (Ant Colony Optimization) Algorithms for Symbol Detection in MIMO Systems', *Communication and Network*, 3, 2011, 200–209, www.researchgate.net/publication/221007721_Application_of_ant_colony_optimization_based_algorithm_in_MIMO_detection, accessed 29 May 2021.

telecommunications optimisation,[19] data compression in the domain of image processing, blockchains,[20] and factory operations.[21]

Birds and fish

Surrounded by hills and forests at the University of Konstanz in Germany, Iain Couzin, Director of the Max Planck Institute for Animal Behaviour, and a group of researchers spend their days staring at a large water tank housed in what looks like an industrial warehouse with white sheeting, lighting, and camera equipment. The group are studying the collective intelligence of swarming sticklebacks. Under these controlled conditions, areas of moving light and shade are reproduced in the tank to simulate a natural environment. In the wild, sticklebacks have a silver lustre and are prone to predators if they wonder out of shaded areas. The school navigates collectively through the tank and cluster in the alternating areas of shade. Iain Couzin and his team have attached sensors to the fish's dorsal fin so that their movements can be monitored and tracked on a computer screen. They discovered that solitary sticklebacks in the tank do not behave in the same manner as the school and swim incautiously in the unshaded parts of the tank – in the wild, they would make tasty snacks for any passing heron or kingfisher. Collective superorganisms, on the other hand, have more reach, intelligence and chance of survival than the lone stickleback. The school swarms to keep the group safe from predators without any centralised authority or control. Starlings do pretty much the same thing. Benedict Hogan, who has worked on computer simulations of murmurating starlings, observes how a flock of starlings become denser when predators are nearby. Hogan says, 'we have evidence that suggests that starlings could indeed be safer from predation in larger and denser flocks, through the confusion of predators'.[22]

Swarming bird flocks such as starling murmuration and schools of fish that include sardine runs and tuna tornados are among the most spec-tacular sights in nature. The way they synchronise together is breathtaking, particularly when computer image analysis highlights that they have no knowledge about the global environment and only communicate through the movement they feel with their direct neighbours (technically known as allelomimesis or non-verbal behaviour between near neighbours) where individual particles mimic their nearest neighbours to achieve cohesion).[23] This is a rule-based phenomenon. In 1986, Craig Reynolds developed a model of flocking using three simple rules: (i) move away from very nearby neighbours (avoid); (ii) adopt the same direction as those that are close by (align); and (iii) avoid becoming isolated (approach).[24]

The principle of exploring particles with adjusting values searching in a multidimensional space for an optimal position that accommodates their

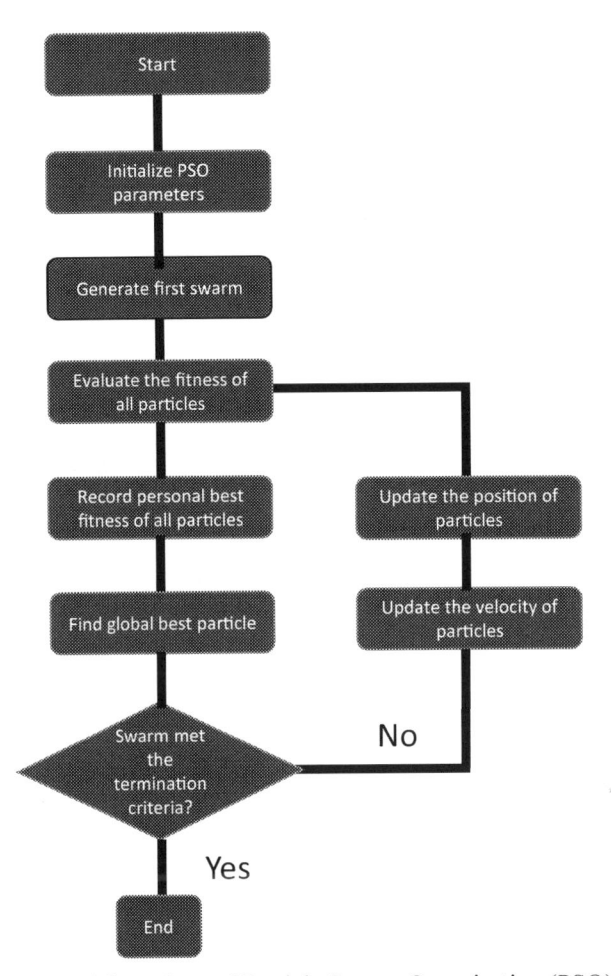

Figure 2.2 Standard flow chart of Particle Swarm Organisation (PSO).

Source: Roohollah Kalatehjari, ASA Rashid, N. Ali, and Mohsen Hajihassani, 'The Contribution of Particle Swarm Optimization in Three-Dimensional Slope Stability Analysis', *The Scientific World Journal*, June 2014, www.hindawi.com/journals/tswj/2014/973093/, accessed 29 May 2021. Open access and permission granted direct from author, Roohollah Kalatehjari.

own volition (personal best) in relation to the optima efficiency of their immediate environment (global best),[25] is modelled in a global optimisation algorithm known as particle swarm optimisation (PSO). A flow chart of basic PSO is represented in Figure 2.2.

Inspired by computer software simulations from schools of fish and flocks of birds, PSO is a population-based optimisation technique developed in 1995 by James Kennedy and Russell Eberhart.[26] They originally developed computer software simulations of birds flocking around food sources before realising that their algorithm served general optimisation problems where the goal of the algorithm is to have optimising particles swarm in a defined search space using four PSO programmed rules of separation, alignment, cohesion, and desire factor.[27]

PSO and its many variants have practical application in environments where single particles function within a broader group, optimising both personal and group best through allelomimesis. This swarm model has been used to predict the 'social forces' of crowd behaviour such as the Mexican Wave seen in stadiums where crowd members replicate their neighbour's behaviour without knowledge of global behaviour or environment.[28] PSO is a widely used algorithm especially in computer intelligence and image analysis where particle positions are allelomimetic and clearly defined. Everyday examples of modern algorithmic PSO application include path planning for driverless cars,[29] path planning in swarm robotics,[30] image classification, facial and iris recognition, traffic incident detection, digital photography, and fruit quality grading.[31]

Honeybees

We have already seen how the activities of ants, fish, and birds have been modelled by data scientists to produce swarm intelligent algorithms that have practical applications in the modern world. Honeybees have likewise inspired optimisation algorithms based on their foraging activities. Honeybees (*Apis mellifera*) have an incredible range – they can travel up to 10 km from their nests in the pursuit of pollen and nectar food source.[32] Nearly a quarter of the bee population are foragers.[33] Forager bees do random searches until they discover a promising food patch and then they localise and refine their search by targeting food sources (an optimum food source is known as best fitness). Back at the colony, follower bees are recruited by scout bees who do a 'miniaturized reenactment'[34] of their foraging by communicating the quality, distance, and direction of the food source to the rest of the colony using their wingbeats and bodies in a communication ritual known as waggle dancing, a term coined by Nobel laureate, Karl von Frisch.[35] On the 'dance floor', the foraging bee moves in a straight line (a waggle run) to indicate the direction of the patch. The speed and duration of the dance signifies the distance and the frequencies of waggles and buzzing signifies the quality.[36]

An algorithm, known as the Bees Algorithm, which models the natural foraging patterns and habits of honeybees and their quest to find best fitness and optima solutions, was created by D.T. Pham et al. in 2005. It is a population-based search algorithm that is combinational, metaheuristic and in the swarm-based optimisation family of algorithms (SOA). A flow chart of this bee behaviour is represented in Figure 2.3.

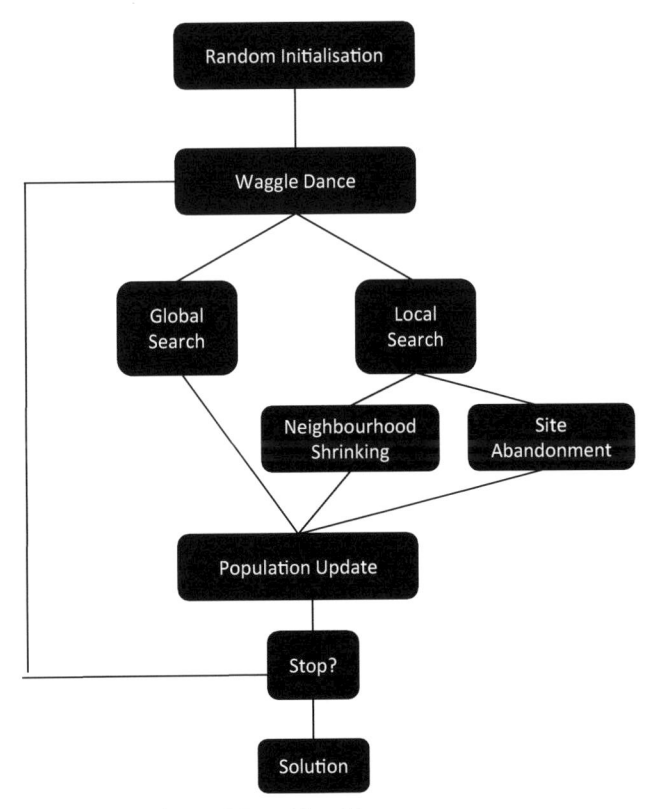

Figure 2.3 Basic flow chart of Bee Algorithm.

Source: Adapted from D.T. Pham and Marco Castellani, 'The Bees Algorithm: Modelling Foraging Behaviour to Solve Continuous Optimization Problems', *Sage Journals*, 223, 12, 2009, 2919–2938, https://journals.sagepub.com/doi/abs/10.1243/09544062JMES1 494, accessed 29 May 2021.

Several bee-inspired algorithm variants and hybrids exist, including the well-known Artificial Bee Colony (ABC) and Bee Colony Optimisation (BCO).[37] Practical applications for Bees Algorithm can be found in solving continuous optimisation problems[38] and decision-making[39] spread across a variety of fields, including magnetic resonance (MR) imaging, pattern recognition,[40] machine vision,[41] robot control,[42] and rostering and scheduling.[43]

The business transformation journey outlined in this book is inspired by honeybees. The behaviour and patterns of the honeybee when searching for a new home provide a perfect formula for modelling a transformational business process that optimises business intelligence and promotes collective decision-making. Let's investigate this now.

Thomas Seeley, professor in biology at Cornell University, has been studying the honeybee (*Apis mellifera*) for most of his life. The following description of the life cycle of honeybees and their annual relocation is taken from Seeley's publication, *Honeybee Democracy*. The sequencing and even whole phrases from the book are reproduced here. In *Honeybee Democracy*, Seeley reflects, 'the single best demonstration of the superorganismic nature of a honeybee colony is the ability of a honeybee swarm to function as an intelligent decision-making unit when choosing its new home'.[44] Each year 10,000 honeybees (two-thirds of the colony) prepare to leave the nest and set up home with the old queen to propagate the species. The preparation for this mass departure starts with the rearing of approximately ten new queens and preparations are made for the mother queen's imminent departure by slimming her down. Forager bees double hat as scout bees and they keep an eye on the weather conditions (which needs to be sunny and warm for the journey) and the state of the developing queens (swarming occurs when the new queens reach pupal stage and have their cell sealed). When conditions are ready, the scout bees buzz around the nest signalling to the resting bees to get flight ready. The hive sounds like 'the engine of a Formula One race car making an all-out acceleration'.[45] The prime swarm leave the nest with the mother queen and form a bivouac. They settle on a tree branch or something resembling it and form a beard-shaped cluster for hours and even days whilst smaller clusters of scout bees search the neighbourhood for suitable accommodation. Sometimes bees can cluster in rather unusual places such as on the wing of a plane causing delay to flights.[46] The nest-site scouts return to the bivouac and, using the waggle dance, help the swarm make sense of their environment, and arrive at a group decision. Here they undergo a recruitment dance where they all try to convince the cluster of the merits of their discoveries. Honeybees seek to arrive at a position, or quorum, through noises and gestures just like city traders.[47]

Thomas Seeley has carried out some practical field experiments on Appledore Island, off the coast of Maine, and discovered that honeybees have a very clear set of preferences for a new location in terms of cavity volume, entrance height, and size.[48] In filmed experiments, Seeley labels the bees with coloured dots for individual identification, sets up potential nests, and observes the process.[49] Nest-site scouts quickly discover the strategically placed locations and return to the bivouac and try to re-enactment the mission. They point their heads in the direction of the potential nest and use wingbeats to signal desirability. Sometimes, they will physically head butt rivals to knock them out of the negotiation. The scout bees are trying to promote their discovery as most desirable to recruit follower bees by physically trying to knock out competitor bidding (again just like city traders). Once the swarm community decodes and makes sense of the intelligence and reaches a group decision, they act collectively and swarm to the preferred location. Then a process of regeneration begins. The old queen will start building the new colony and producing for the new nest. Meanwhile back at the original colony, the appointment of a new queen and the replenishment of the mother colony commences.

An algorithm for house-hunting honeybee activity can be represented by a simple flow model (see Figure 2.4).

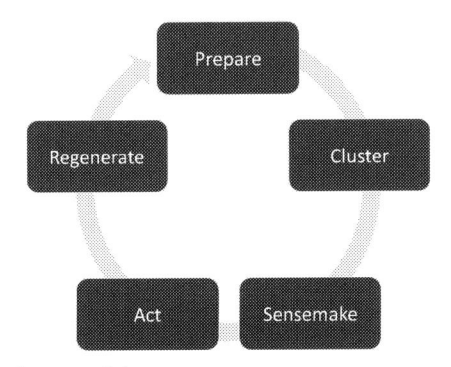

Figure 2.4 Swarm flow model.

This swarm flow model will prove to be an important algorithm for swarm facilitation. It will be frequently referred to in subsequent chapters.

Business transformation and relocating honeybees

Part 2 of the book is a comprehensive deep dive into how to build a swarm-based organisation modelled on the activity of relocating honeybees. There are three primary areas where honeybee house-hunting activities inspire the type of business transformation expounded in this book: swarm transformation, swarm facilitation, and business superorganisms.

Swarm transformation

Swarm transformation refers to the entire end-to-end journey of the organisational change programme. It takes places over three distinct phases. In Swarm 1.0, the business improvement process is local and emergent and is facilitated using human ingenuity and resources. Swarm 2.0 is a more planned and strategic change model that covers a percentage of the organisation and one where intelligent systems augment human ideation and decision-making. Swarm 3.0 is a scaled-up version of Swarm 2.0. It is known as a business superorganism where the entire organisation is swarm based. In Swarm 3.0, creative decision-making across the enterprise is augmented by intelligent systems. Chapter 4 will introduce a change model, known as the accelerate model, that guides and transitions the organisation between these three swarm phases.

Swarm facilitation

Swarm facilitation refers to the ideation and decision-making cycle. It follows the same algorithmic pattern as the house-hunting bees modelled in the swarm flow model (see Figure 2.4). Swarm facilitation is the end-to-end process for intelligence gathering, ideation, and decision-making using swarm. Let's look at the swarm facilitation stages:

1. Prepare

In *Honeybee Democracy*, Thomas Seeley observes that honeybees make lots of preparation when relocating nests. They act with 'persistent intention to gather information'.[50] Such preparation involves the entire colony and is self-organised; there is no one entity directing or coordinating the effort. A common misconception is that the queen bee is a hierarchical leader. As Thomas Seeley says, 'the mother queen is not the workers' boss. Indeed, there is no all-knowing central planner supervising the thousands and thousands of worker bees in a colony. The work of a hive is instead governed collectively by the workers themselves'.[51] The preparation phase of swarm facilitation is also intelligence-led and self-organising. We saw in Chapter 1 that traditional decision-making is information-led (usually conducted through business needs assessments). In swarm facilitation, intelligence is prepared and harvested though enterprise-wide networks and communities rather than being plotted in the C-Suite and forced down the organisational scalar chain. Business intelligence comes from the entire system: from customers, users, stakeholders, partners, social media, competitors, and the like, and it is channelled through sensemaking swarm community networks. All of these require preparation. We will see how this plays out in future chapters.

2. Cluster

During house hunting, honeybees split into self-organising diverse clusters. The most dramatic of these clusters are when the relocating honeybees leave the mother colony and form a beard-like bivouac to figure out their next steps. Swarm facilitation also involves clustering. Acting on intelligence, a swarm cluster forms to make sense of the patterns, formulate challenges and brainswarm solutions. This swarm cluster is an independent diverse group of individuals or agents that actively work on a critical business challenge, problem, or idea in order to create a new process, solve a problem, or reach a collective decision. This group is cross-functional (and can include external stakeholders such as clients/customers and external partners) and it is made up of different expertise and experience. That said, each member should have some practical or theoretical stake in the challenge, problem, or idea. Swarm facilitation thrives on diverse perspective and plural decision-making that promotes what Frans Johansson calls the 'Medici Effect' where different fields, disciplines, and cultures intersect to produce diverse thinking and 'intersectional ideas'.[52] Future chapters will go into minutia detail concerning how these swarm clusters are formed at different swarm transformation levels and how the intelligence is processed and distilled.

3. Sensemake

Honeybees make sense of their adaptive environment; they modify their surroundings to suit their needs, they process the intelligence, they focus on the critical issues that promote and sustain their colony, and they use a mechanism to filter information (waggle dancing). Sensemaking is also a key part of swarm facilitation. The swarm community needs to gather business intelligence and make sense of it. Again, it is not individual leaders or executives that facilitate and work on these problems, it should be done through the business networks and swarm clusters. It has been mentioned that, like relocating honeybees, the swarm cluster breaks down into smaller working groups called swarm teams. These swarm teams brainswarm on the key challenge during swarm meets and feed ideas back to the larger swarm cluster in the manner of human waggle dancing where the group establish a collective view and unify around common purpose. We will explore in later chapters the mechanisms to help achieve such sensemaking, including the use of smart technology to process and filter data and intelligence.

4. Act

Honeybees gather as much intelligence as they can before they act. Once a quorum is reached, the honeybees swarm to their new location. The swarm cluster needs to arrive at a collective sensemaking view (or best fitness) and presents it back to the community in an implementation and execution phase where ideas and suggestions can be accepted, rejected, or refined. More will be said about this in future chapters.

5. Regenerate

In *Teeming: How Superorganisms Work to Build Infinite Wealth in a Finite World*, Tamsin Woolley-Barker opines, 'Superorganism societies are focused entirely on one thing: making each generation more successful than the last'.[53] The verb 'to regenerate' is from the Latin *regeneratus*, meaning 'created again'. A honeybee colony focuses on regeneration and generativity. Two-thirds of a honeybee population relocate to form a new propagating colony. They do this as a survival mechanism, but also because it gives an opportunity for the mother colony and the new colony to replenish. Generativity is also important in the honeybee world. Generativity is a term coined by psychoanalyst Erik Erikson in 1950 to mean 'establishing and guiding the next generation'.[54] Honeybees are a very generative species. This is evident not only in the reproduction of the young and the relocation of the colony, but also in the way honeybees look out for each other. A striking example of this can be found in Jürgen Tautz's *The Buzz About Bees: Biology of a Superorganism*:

> To help the young foragers find their way home, older bees occasionally stand in front of the hive entrance, open the Nasanov glands at the ends of their abdomens, and release a scent called geraniol, a chemical compound that smells like geraniums. The geraniol is spread through the area by scenting bees fanning their wings.[55]

There are other examples from the natural world where superorganisms look out for each other such as Matabele ants who nurse their injured comrades or vampire bats who donate blood to their immediate neighbours.[56] Just as in a honeybee colony, swarm facilitation is about constant regeneration and generativity. Ideas come from the business community and are recycled back into it. This approach is not ego-led but it is about nurturing and encouraging the system to attain a collective view for the good of the enterprise.

The swarm facilitation process that mirrors the honeybee swarm flow model (Figure 2.4) is a self-organising complex adaptive system where intelligence, ideas, and decisions come from the collective group, rather than from individual decision makers. Traditional organisations facilitate knowledge; swarm organisations facilitate intelligence. It has conceptual links to BOS 2.0 that was characterised in Chapter 1 as a collective, interconnected, emergent self-organising complex adaptive system channelled through simple rules. Swarm facilitation is a flow process that facilitates the BOS transformation. Its nature is also a collective, self-organising, interconnected, emergent complex adaptive system that functions on simple rules. As in a honeybee colony, there is no central authority in swarm facilitation (such as a facilitator steering or leading things). Dennis Kinlaw draws a clear distinction between the act of facilitation and the role of the individual facilitator – 'When team-managed facilitation is fully functioning in a team, the requirement for individuals to occupy the role of facilitator becomes less and less frequent'.[57] In the shift to BOS 2.0, this book reconceptualises facilitation. It rejects wholesale the legacy of the traditional facilitator from the old BOS who is an organisationally sponsored human resource who guides groups through prescriptive designs, oftentimes forcing group consensus through timebound rigid processes. Swarm facilitation comes about because it anticipates a paradigm shift in the BOS and group decision-making where we enter the age of collective group intelligence, augmented by smart and collaborative tech. It rejects conventional (centralising) roles and considers that traditional human facilitators have a shelf life.[58] As we shift to a new BOS, away from a linear and centrifugal logic to a decentralised and collective decision-making that is enabled by participatory methods and (increasingly) digital facilitation, executive decision makers, central designers, and coordinating facilitators skilled in human heuristics and social intelligence[59] will be phased out.

Business superorganisms

Bert Hölldobler and E. Wilson described a superorganism as 'a colony of individuals self-organized by division of labor and united by a closed system of communication'.[60] In Chapter 1, we described BOS 1.0 as dinosauric. Tamsin Woolley-Barker comments, 'we want organizations to adapt continuously, nimbly, with no fossilized, rigid, slow and costly layer of management, what we need is a living thing. *What we need is a superorganism*'.[61] A business superorganism is the natural end game of swarm transformation where the capacity of the collective supersedes individual capacity and the complex adaptive system, augmented by intelligent systems, is connected and networked to operate as a swarm community. They will be like a slime mould, an amoebic coalescence of interconnections, networks and resources spread across the enterprise and beyond and focused on instantly solving critical business challenges identified through automated business intelligence and collaborative networks.[62] A business superorganism is not defined by bricks and mortar, personalities or rigid structures and governance, it is organic and networked – a complex adaptive networked ecosystem with clusters or cells of self-organising, self-resourced, cross-functional swarm communities that focus on critical business needs through the gradual support of smart technology. A business superorganism is defined by its brand, with no central headquarters or a traditional CEO. It is a nexus for people and ideas where organisations know at any given moment the full snapshot of the enterprise. There is no need for management, supervisors, and analysts in this world – the swarm shapes and moulds the enterprise.

This chapter veered into the natural world and explored how we can model the behaviour and patterns of certain superorganisms to produce swarm algorithms that have useful applications in the modern world. A major inspiration has been house-hunting honeybees who have a fascinating way of relocating hives and nests through group consensus. Their unique methodology inspired the swarm flow model. This model forms the basis for swarm facilitation which is the end-to-end process for intelligence gathering, ideation and decision-making using swarm in an organisational context. It reinvents the way we work with business intelligence, facilitates collective ideation and decision-making, and contributes to the BOS upgrade. The model, spanning from human swarms to business superorganisms, will be used in the three phases of adopting swarm (swarm transformation) that will be explored in later chapters. A key catalyst for the advancement of the swarm organisation will be technology. Chapter 3 explores how intelligent systems can augment human mind and group processing and evolve the organisation's swarm quotient.

Notes

1   Source: 'A Postcard from the Field: The Bats of Austin', *Dateline NBC, YouTube*, posted 23 September 2016, www.youtube.com/watch?v=oLBoZIO3Seo, accessed 29 May 2021.

2   'One Million Heads, One Beautiful Mind', *Swarm: Nature's Incredible Invasions*, Episode 2 of 2, *BBC1*, 11 January 2009, www.bbc.co.uk/programmes/b00gq43y, accessed 29 May 2021.

3   Gerado Beni and Jing Wang, 'Swarm Intelligence in Cellular Robotic Systems', *Proceed. NATO Advanced Workshop on Robots and Biological Systems, Tuscany, Italy, June 26–30 (1989)* (Berlin, Heidelberg: Springer, 1993), 703–712.

4   Eric Bonabeau, Marco Dorigo, and Guy Theraulaz, *Swarm Intelligence: From Natural to Artificial Systems* (New York: Oxford University Press, 1999), preface xi.

5   Yuval Noah Harari, *Homo Deus: A Brief History of Tomorrow* (2015, New York, NY: Harper Perennial, 2018), 97.

6   Metaheuristic algorithms are a swarm class of search algorithms that optimise problems and cover vast search spaces. Optimisation algorithms are 'search methods where the goal is to find an optimal solution to a problem, in order to satisfy one or more objective functions, possibly subject to a set of constraints'. Baris Yuce, Michael S. Packianather, Ernesto Mastrocinque, and Duc Truong Pham, 'Honey Bees Inspired Optimization Method: The Bees Algorithm', *Insects*, 4, 4, 2013, 646–662, www.researchgate.net/publication/259383112_Honey_Bees_Inspired_Optimization_Method_The_Bees_Algorithm, accessed 5 November 2020. Other excellent general resources here include Jing Yang et al., 'Swarm Intelligence in Data Science: Applications, Opportunities and Challenges', in Ying Tan, Yuhui Shi, and Milan Tuba (eds.) *Advances in Swarm Intelligence. ICSI 2020 Lecture Notes in Computer Science*, Vol. 12145 (Cham: Springer), https://doi.org/10.1007/978-3-030-53956-6_1, accessed 29 May 2021; Javier Del Ser et al., 'Bio-Inspired Computation: Where We Stand and What's Next', *Swarm and Evolutionary Computation*, 48, 2019, 220–250.

7   Source: Yang Xin-She, *Nature-Inspired Optimization Algorithms* (London: Elsevier, 2014).

8   See, for example, Ali Kaveh and Soroush Mahjoubi, 'Lion Pride Optimization Algorithm: A Meta-Heuristic Method for Global Optimization Problems', *Scientia Iranica*, 25, 6, 2018, 3113–3132, www.researchgate.net/publication/327109473_Lion_Pride_Optimization_Algorithm_A_meta-heuristic_method_for_global_optimization_problems, accessed 29 May 2021; Maziar Yazdani and Fariborz Jolai, 'Lion Optimization Algorithm (LOA): A Nature-Inspired Metaheuristic Algorithm', *Journal of Computational Design and Engineering*, 3, 2016, 24–36, www.sciencedirect.com/science/article/pii/S2288430015000524, accessed 29 May 2021; C. Liu, et al., 'The Wolf Colony Algorithm and Its Application', *Chinese Journal of Electronics*, 20, 2, 2011, 212–216, www.researchgate.net/publication/285935995_The_Wolf_Colony_Algorithm_and_Its_Application, 29 May 2021; Husheng Wu, et al., 'New Swarm Intelligence Algorithm – Wolf Pack Algorithm', *Journal of Systems Engineering and Electronics*, 35, 11, 2013, www.researchgate.net/publication/264928582_New_swarm_intelligence_algorithm-wolf_pack_algorithm, accessed 29 May 2021.

9   Peter Karlson and Martin Lüscher, ' "Pheromones": A New Term for a Class of Biologically Active Substances', *Nature*, 183, 1959, 55–56, www.nature.com/articles/183055a0, accessed 29 May 2021. An important contributor to this field was Edward O. Wilson, *The Insect Societies* (Cambridge, MA: The Belknap Press of Harvard University Press, 1971).

10 J.L. Deneubourg, et al. famously demonstrate this effect in the double bridge experiment where a bifurcating trail was set up and exploring ants established an optimal route. Jean-Louis Deneubourg, et al., 'The Self-Organizing Exploratory Pattern of the Argentine Ant', *Journal of Insect Behavior*, 3, 2, 1990, 159–168, www.researchgate.net/publication/301232799_The_Self-Organizing_Exploratory_Pattern_of_the_Argentine_Ant, accessed 29 May 2021.

11 Alberto Colorni, Marco Dorigo, and Vittorio Maniezzo, 'Distributed Optimization by Ant Colonies', in *Conference Proceedings of ECAL91 – European Conference on Artificial Life*, January 1991, www.researchgate.net/publication/216300484_Distributed_Optimization_by_Ant_Colonies, accessed 29 May 2021. In 1994, Erik Lumer and Baldo Faieta also studied the collective reactions of ants and developed sets of Algorithms that replicated the way ant colonies responded to their environment. Erik Lumer and Baldo Faieta, 'Diversity and Adaptation in Populations of Clustering Ants', in *Proceedings of the Third International Conference on Simulation of Adaptive Behavior: From Animals to Animats* (Cambridge, MA: MIT Press, 1994), 501–508.

12 The TSP is a standard AI optimisation problem posing the following conundrum: 'Given a list of cities and the distances between each pair of cities, what is the shortest possible route that visits each city and returns to the origin city?' This standard statement for the TSP has unclear origins. The problem itself dates back over nine decades. Source: Nigel Cummings, 'A Brief History of the Travelling Salesman Problem', *The Operational Research Society* (website), June 2000, www.theorsociety.com/about-or/or-methods/heuristics/a-brief-history-of-the-travelling-salesman-problem/, accessed 29 May 2021.

13 Source: Hazem Ahmed and Janice Glasgow, 'Swarm Intelligence: Concepts, Models and Applications', *Queens University Technical Report 2012-585*, February 2012, https://pdfs.semanticscholar.org/116b/67cf2ad2c948533e6890a9fccc5543dded89.pdf, accessed 29 May 2021.

14 Good resource: David Martens, et al., 'Editorial Survey: Swarm Intelligence for Data Mining', *Machine Learning*, 82, 1, 2011, 1–42, https://link.springer.com/article/10.1007/s10994-010-5216-5, accessed 29 May 2021.

15 Pina Petroli, a fuel oil distribution company based in Switzerland, overcame its vehicle routing problems and achieved fleet utilisation through computing the shortest path per delivery truck based on ACO. Source: Andrea E. Rizzoli, et al., 'Planning and Optimisation of Vehicle Routes for Fuel Oil Distribution', in D.A. Post (ed.), *Proceedings from MODSIM 2003* (Publishing Address Unspecified: Modelling and Simulation Society of Australia and New Zealand, 2003), 2024–2029.

16 An interesting case study concerns how Southwest Airlines solved a cargo optimisation problem using ACO by routing cargo through connecting aircraft rather than storing it in central hubs. This solution saved the company millions of dollars each year. Source: Eric Bonabeau and Christopher Meyer, 'Swarm Intelligence: A Whole New Way to Think about Business', *Harvard Business Review*, May 2001, https://hbr.org/2001/05/swarm-intelligence-a-whole-new-way-to-think-about-business, accessed 29 May 2021.

17 Good resource: Neha D. Yadav and Mohit Mehta, 'An Efficient Algorithmic Approach for Multicast Scheduling Using Ant Colony Optimization', *International Journal of Computing and Corporate Research*, 3, 4, 2013, www.semanticscholar.org/paper/AN-EFFICIENT-ALGORITHMIC-APPROACH-FOR-MULTICAST-ANT-Yadav-Mehta/9f8c9eea8fee239175e1bc5f7f295128c8a12c22, accessed 29 May 2021.

18 Doug Lawson used 'mathematically-modelled ants to determine the most efficient way of boarding a plane, which turns out to be open seating'. Source: 'Small Wonders: What Ants Can Teach Us', *CBS News*, 24 July 2011, www.cbsnews.com/news/small-wonders-what-ants-can-teach-us/, accessed 29 May 2021.

19 Good sources: Selcuk Okdem and Dervis Karaboga, 'Routing in Wireless Sensor Networks Using an Ant Colony Optimization (ACO) Router Chip', *MDPI Sensors*, 9, 2, 2009, 909–921, www.mdpi.com/1424-8220/9/2/909, accessed 29 May 2021; Xin-She Yang, et al., *Bio-Inspired Computation in Telecommunications* (Burlington, MA: Morgan Kaufmann, 2015). Jesal Shethna writes,

> Engineers at Hewlett Packard devised a huge number of "digital ants" that can be sent along uncongested networks. This helped telecom center agents to divert traffic through those routes. If an uncongested

route suddenly became crowded the "digital ants" will slow down or evaporate. This helps agents ignore the routes and look elsewhere. Some of the leading telecom companies such as British Telecom, France Telecom, and MCI WorldCom were the early adopters of such innovations.

> Source: Jesal Shethna, 'Swarm Intelligence Applications', *Ecubar Project Management Blog*, www.educba.com/swarm-intelligence-applications/, accessed 29 May 2021

20 Good source: Eduardo Castelló Ferrer, 'The Blockchain: A New Framework for Robotic Swarm Systems', *MIT Media Lab*, 75, 2017, https://arxiv.org/pdf/1608.00695.pdf, accessed 29 May 2021.

21 'Unilever optimized its plant schedules using swarm intelligence algorithm, managing the complexities of a chemical plant when traditional practices couldn't do it'. Source: Jesal Shethna, 'Swarm Intelligence Applications', *Ecubar Project Management Blog*, www.educba.com/swarm-intelligence-applications/, accessed 5 November 2020.

22 Benedict Hogan, cited in 'Birds of a Feather Flock Together to Confuse Potential Predators', *University of Bristol Press Release*, 18 January 2017, www.bristol.ac.uk/news/2017/january/starlings-confuse-predators-.html, accessed 29 May 2021.

23 Peter Miller in *The Smart Swarm* writes,

> the basic mechanisms of adaptive mimicking – *coordination, communication*, and *copying* – can unleash powerful waves of energy or awareness that race across a population, whether it's made up of starlings or caribou, stimulating the kind of coherent behavior we normally associate with centralized cognition.
>
> Peter Miller, *The Smart Swarm: How Understanding Flocks, Schools, and Colonies, Can Make us Better at Communication, Decision Making and Getting Things Done* (New York, NY: Avery, 2010), 163

24 Craig W. Reynolds, 'Flocks, Herds and Schools: A Distributed Behavioral Model', Computer Graphics, 21, 4, July 1987, 25–34. Commentators such as Sumpter (2006) believe that the dramatic movement and swarm acrobatics of vortices, hourglasses and parabolas are generated by individuals in the group slightly varying these rules. D.J.T. Sumpter, 'The Principles of Collective Animal Behaviour', *Philosophical Transactions of the Royal Society*

B: Biological Sciences, 361, 1465, 2006, 5–22, https://royalsocietypublishing.org/doi/pdf/10.1098/rstb.2005.1733, accessed 29 May 2021.

25 Source: Terry Clark, 'Search Algorithm Series: PSO', *Medium*, 18 December 2017, https://medium.com/@iamterryclark/swarm-intelli-eb5e46eda0c3, accessed 29 May 2021.

26 James Kennedy and Russell C. Eberhart, 'Particle Swarm Optimization', in *Proceedings of IEEE International Conference on Neural Networks, Perth, Australian*, 4, 1995, 1942–1948.

27 Source: 'Swarm Technologies', in *Swarm Intelligence*, TechFerry website, www.techferry.com/articles/swarm-intelligence.html, accessed 29 May 2021.

28 Source: Len Fisher, *The Perfect Swarm: The Science of Complexity in Everyday Life* (New York, NY, Basic Books, 2009). Another key resource on Mexican Waves: Illés Farkas, et al., 'Mexican Waves in an Excitable Medium', *Nature*, 419, 6903, 2002, 131–132, www.researchgate.net/publication/11162381_Mexican_Waves_in_an_Excitable_Medium, accessed 29 May 2021.

29 See Yadhu Prakash, et al., 'Incorporation of Swarm Intelligence in Autonomous Cars', *International Journal of Computer Science and Information Technologies (IJCSIT)*, 5, 5, 2014, https://pdfs.semanticscholar.org/490a/7f5263d43428c309cdad6a980377a1262e4d.pdf, accessed 29 May 2021.

30 See Metin Taylan Das, et al., 'Robotic Applications with Particle Swarm Optimization (PSO)', in *Proceedings 2013 International Conference on Control, Decision and Information Technologies (CoDIT), Hammamet, Tunisia*, 6–8 May 2013, https://ieeexplore.ieee.org/document/6689537, accessed 29 May 2021.

31 'The Fruit Grading System', posted by *Interesting Engineer* (IE), *Facebook*, www.facebook.com/interestingengineering/videos/351215465711952/, accessed 29 May 2021.

32 Source: Tom T.D. Seeley, *The Wisdom of the Hive: The Social Physiology of Honey Bee Colonies* (Cambridge, MA: Harvard University Press, 1995), 46.

33 Source: Baris Yuce, et al., 'Honey Bees Inspired Optimization Method: The Bees Algorithm', *Insects*, 4, 4, 2013, 646–662, www.researchgate.net/publication/259383112_Honey_Bees_Inspired_Optimization_Method_The_Bees_Algorithm, accessed 5 November 2020, 650.

34 Source: Tom T.D. Seeley, *The Wisdom of the Hive*, 36.

35 Karl von Frisch, 'Geruchssinn der Bienen', Film: IWF/C56, 1927 available at Plan Bienen, http://planbienen.net/2014/06/geruchssinn-der-bienen-by-karl-von-frisch-1927/, accessed 29 May 2021. It should be noted that in Chapter 2 of Len Fisher, *The Perfect Swarm: The Science of Complexity in Everyday Life,*, Fisher debunks the idea of waggle dancing as a sole means of communication in favour of a theory of an invisible leader.

36 This description of waggle dancing can be found in El-Ghazali Talbi, *Metaheuristics: From Design to Implementation* (Hoboken, NJ: John Wiley & Sons, 2009), 257.

37 See Davidovic et al. (2015) for an excellent resource of bee-inspired algorithms. Tatjana Davidovic, et al., 'Bee Colony Optimization Part 1: The Algorithmic Overview', *Yugoslav Journal of Operations Research*, 25, 1, 2015, 33–56, www.researchgate.net/publication/276387288_Bee_Colony_Optimization_-_part_I_The_algorithm_overview, accessed 29 May 2021.

38 Good source: Duc Truong Pham and Marco Castellani, 'The Bees Algorithm: Modelling Foraging Behaviour to Solve Continuous Optimization Problems', *Sage Journals*, 2009, Volume 223, issue (12):2919–2938, 1 December 2009, https://journals.sagepub.com/doi/abs/10.1243/09544062JMES1494, accessed 29 May 2021.

39 Good source: Pavol Navrat, et al., 'Bee Hive at Work: A Problem Solving, Optimizing Mechanism', in *Conference Proceedings: Nature & Biologically Inspired Computing*, 2009, www.researchgate.net/publication/224105840_Bee_Hive_At_Work_A_Problem_Solving_Optimizing_Mechanism, accessed 29 May 2021.

40 Good source: Erik Cuevas, et al., 'Image Segmentation Using Artificial Bee Colony Optimization', in I. Zelinka, V. Snášel, and A. Abraham (eds.), *Handbook of Optimization. Intelligent Systems Reference Library*, Vol. 38 (Berlin, Heidelberg: Springer, 2013).

41 Good explanation of machine vision: Tom Merritt, 'Top 5 Things to Know about Machine Vision', *Tech Republic*, 6 June 2017, www.techrepublic.com/article/top-5-things-to-know-about-machine-vision/, accessed 29 May 2021.

42 Good source: Ahmed Haj Darwish et. al., 'Using the Bees Algorithm for Wheeled Mobile Robot Path Planning in an Indoor Dynamic Environment', *Cogent Engineering*, 5, 1, 2018, www.researchgate.net/publication/322442504_Using_the_Bees_Algorithm_for_wheeled_mobile_robot_path_planning_in_an_indoor_dynamic_environment, accessed 29 May 2021.

43 Good source: M. Rajeswari, 'Directed Bee Colony Optimization Algorithm to Solve the Nurse Rostering Problem', *Computational Intelligence and Neuroscience*, 4 April 2017, www.ncbi.nlm.nih.gov/pmc/articles/PMC5394913/, accessed 29 May 2021.

44 Thomas D. Seeley, *Honeybee Democracy* (Princeton, NJ and Oxford: Princeton University Press, 2010), 27.

45 Thomas D. Seeley, *Honeybee Democracy*, 41.

46 Source: James Draper, 'That'll Create a Buzz! Packed Plane is Grounded for 90 Minutes after Huge Swarm of BEES Settles on its Wing', *Daily Mail*, 26 September 2017, www.dailymail.co.uk/travel/travel_news/article-4921404/Packed-plane-grounded-BEES-settle-wing.html, accessed 29 May 2021. See also Helen Coffee, 'Flights Delayed after Planes Surrounded by Swarms of Bees', *Independent*, 3 December 2020, www.independent.co.uk/travel/news-and-advice/flight-bees-swarm-india-vistara-aircraft-b1765876.html, accessed 29 May 2021.

47 Inspired by Peter Miller who likens waggle dancing to brokers working in a stock market. Peter Miller, *The Smart Swarm*, 38.

48 Thomas D. Seeley, *Honeybee Democracy*, 43.

49 Source: 'How Bees Use Swarm Intelligence to Make Decisions', *You Tube*, Video 5:97, 17 February 2014, www.youtube.com/watch?v=j34jgRkOe18, accessed 29 May 2021. Technology has taken over from using colour dots. New research at the University of Washington uses antennae and harmonic radar technology as well as high tech sensors in bee backpacks. Source: Sarah McQuate, 'Researchers Create First Sensor Package that Can Ride Aboard Bees', *University of Washington News*, 11 December 2018, www.washington.edu/news/2018/12/11/sensor-bees/, accessed 29 May 2021.

50 Thomas Seeley, *Honeybee Democracy*, 62.

51 Thomas Seeley, *Honeybee Democracy*, 5.

52 'When you step into the Intersection, you can combine concepts between multiple fields, generating ideas that leap in new directions – what I call intersectional ideas'. Frans Johansson, *The Medici Effect: Breakthrough Insights at the Intersection of Ideas, Concepts, and Cultures* (Boston, MA: Harvard Business School Press, 2004), 17.

53 Tamsin Woolley-Barker, *Teeming: How Superorganisms Work to Build Infinite Wealth in a Finite World* (Ashland, OR: White Cloud Press, 2017), 4.

54 Erik Erikson, *Childhood and Society* (1950, New York, NY: W.W. Norton, 1963), 267.

55 Jürgen Tautz, *The Buzz about Bees: Biology of a Superorganism* (Berlin and London: Springer, 2008), 89.

56 University of Würzburg, 'Medical Care for Wounded Ants', *ScienceDaily*, 13 February 2018, www.sciencedaily.com/releases/2018/02/180213223403.htm, accessed 29 May 2021; see also Michal Greshko, 'Why Female Vampire Bats Donate Blood to Friends', *National Geographic*, 17 November 2005, www.nationalgeographic.com/news/2015/11/151117-vampire-bats-blood-food-science-animals/, accessed 29 May 2021.

57 Dennis Kinlaw, *Team Managed Facilitation: Critical Skills for Developing Self-Sufficient Teams* (San Diego, CA: Pfeiffer, 1993), 13.

58 This is a controversial view. There are commentators that maintain the role of the facilitator is secured well into the future, believing that an increase in work population diversity will always require a skilled facilitator to manage group dynamics. For example, Brandon Klein, 'What "Facilitation" Really Means and Why It's Key to the Future of Work', *Fast Company*, 15 September 2017, www.fastcompany.com/40467377/what-facilitation-really-means-and-why-its-key-to-the-future-of-work, accessed 29 May 2021. AI and future of work studies from Oxford, McKensie, PWC, EU Commission, OECD, World Bank, Bank of England, consistently suggest that occupations that fall in the category of knowledge work who are involved in developing people or decision making are among the least likely occupations to be automated.

59 Source: 'A facilitator demonstrates a heuristic, rather than algorithmic, approach to problem solving'. Lawrence Susskind (ed.), et al., *The Consensus Building Handbook: A Comprehensive Guide to Reaching Agreement* (Thousand Oaks, CA: Sage, 1999), 287–323, 309.

60 Bert Hölldobler and Edward O. Wilson, *The Superorganism: The Beauty, Elegance, and Strangeness of Insect Societies* (New York, NY: W.W. Norton, 2009), *Note to the General Reader*, xvi. It is widely acknowledge that the term superorganism was conceptualised by James Hutton in 1788, but popularised by William Morton Wheeler in 1928.

61 Tamsin Woolley-Barker, Teeming, Prologue.

62 The slime mould is a common study for researchers of superorganisms. It is the subject of Gaia Vince's article, Gaia Vince, 'In Praise of Slime Molds', *The American Scholar*, 24 June 2015, https://theamericanscholar.org/in-praise-of-slime-molds/, accessed 29 May 2021. Tamsin Woolley-Barker mentions it in *Teeming*, and it is the subject of Suzanne Simard's Ted Talk, Suzanne Simard, 'The Networked Beauty of Forests', Ted Ed, https://ed.ted.com/lessons/the-networked-beauty-of-forests-suzanne-simard, accessed 29 May 2021.

Bibliography

Ahmed, Hazem and Glasgow, Janice, 'Swarm Intelligence: Concepts, Models and Applications', *Queens University Technical Report 2012-585*, February 2012, https://pdfs.semanticscholar.org/116b/67cf2ad2c948533e6890a 9fccc5543dded89.pdf, accessed 29 May 2021.

Barnes, Harry Elmer, 'Some Reflections on the Possible Service of Analytical Psychology to History', *Psychological Review*, 1921, 8 (1):22–37.

Beni, Gerardo and Wang, Jing, 'Swarm Intelligence in Cellular Robotic Systems', in *Proceed. NATO Advanced Workshop on Robots and Biological Systems, Tuscany, Italy, June 26–30 (1989)* (Berlin, Heidelberg: Springer, 1993) 703–712.

Bonabeau, Eric, Dorigo, Marco, and Theraulaz, Guy, *Swarm Intelligence: From Natural to Artificial Systems* (New York and Oxford: Oxford University Press, 1999).

Bonabeau, Eric and Meyer, Christopher, 'Swarm Intelligence: A Whole New Way to Think About Business', *Harvard Business Review*, May 2001, https://hbr.org/2001/05/swarm-intelligence-a-whole-new-way-to-think-about-busin ess, accessed 29 May 2021.

Clark, Terry, 'Search Algorithm Series: PSO', *Medium*, 18 December 2017, https://medium.com/@iamterryclark/swarm-intelli-eb5e46eda0c3, accessed 29 May 2021.

Colorni, Alberto, Dorigo, Marco, and Maniezzo, Vittorio, 'Distributed Optimization by Ant Colonies', in *Conference Proceedings of ECAL91 – European Conference on Artificial Life*, January 1991, www.researchgate.net/publication/216300484_Distributed_Optimization_by_Ant_Colonies, accessed 29 May 2021.

Cuevas, Erik, Sención-Echauri, Felipe, Zaldivar, Daniel, and Pérez, Marco, 'Image Segmentation Using Artificial Bee Colony Optimization', in *Handbook of Optimization. Intelligent Systems Reference Library*, Vol. 38, eds. Ivan Zelinka, Václav Snášel, and Ajith Abraham (Berlin, Heidelberg: Springer, 2013).

Cummings, Nigel, 'A Brief History of the Travelling Salesman Problem', *The Operational Research Society* (website), June 2000, www.theorsociety.com/about-or/or-methods/heuristics/a-brief-history-of-the-travelling-salesman-problem/, accessed 29 May 2021.

Das, Metin Taylor, Důlger, Lale Canan, and Das, Gůlesin Sena, 'Robotic Applications with Particle Swarm Optimization (PSO)', in *Proceedings 2013*

International Conference on Control, Decision and Information Technologies (CoDIT), Hammamet, Tunisia, 6–8 May 2013, https://ieeexplore.ieee.org/document/6689537, accessed 29 May 2021.

Darwish, Ahmed Haj, Joukhadar, Abdulkader, and Kashkash, Mariam, 'Using the Bees Algorithm for Wheeled Mobile Robot Path Planning in an Indoor Dynamic Environment', *Cogent Engineering,* 2018, 5 (1), www.researchgate.net/publication/322442504_Using_the_Bees_Algorithm_for_wheeled_mobile_robot_path_planning_in_an_indoor_dynamic_environment, accessed 29 May 2021.

Davidovic, Tatjana, Teodorovic, Dusan, and Selmic, Milica, 'Bee Colony Optimization Part 1: The Algorithmic Overview', *Yugoslav Journal of Operations Research,* 2015, 25 (1):33–56, www.researchgate.net/publica-tion/276387288_Bee_Colony_Optimization_-_part_I_The_algorithm_overview, accessed 29 May 2021.

Del Ser, Javier, Osaba, Eneko, Molina, Daniel, Yang, Xin-She, Salcedo-Sanz, Sancho, Camacho, David, Das, Swagatam, Suganthan, Ponnuthurai N., Coello, Carlos A., and Herrera, Francisco, 'Bio-Inspired Computation: Where We Stand and What's Next', *Swarm and Evolutionary Computation,* 2019, 48:220–250.

Deneubourg, Jean-Louis, Aron, Serge, Goss, Simon, and Pasteels, Jacques M., 'The Self-Organizing Exploratory Pattern of the Argentine Ant', *Journal of Insect Behavior,* 1990, 3 (2):159–168, www.researchgate.net/publication/301232799_The_Self-Organizing_Exploratory_Pattern_of_the_Argentine_Ant, accessed 29 May 2021.

Erikson, Erik, *Childhood and Society* (New York, NY: W.W. Norton, 1950).

Farkas, Illés, Helbing, Dirk, and Vicsek, Tamás, 'Mexican Waves in an Excitable Medium', *Nature,* 2002, 419 (6903):131–132, www.researchgate.net/publi-cation/11162381_Mexican_Waves_in_an_Excitable_Medium, accessed 29 May 2021.

Ferrer, Eduardo Castelló, 'The Blockchain: A New Framework for Robotic Swarm Systems', *MIT Media Lab,* 2017, 75, https://arxiv.org/pdf/1608.00695.pdf, accessed 29 May 2021.

Fisher, Len, *The Perfect Swarm: The Science of Complexity in Everyday Life* (New York, NY, Basic Books, 2009).

Grassé, Pierre-Paul, 'La reconstruction du nid et les coordinations inter-individuelles chez' Bellicositermes natalensis et Cubitermes sp, La theorie de la stigmergie: Essai 'd'interpretation du comportement des termites constructeurs', *Insectes Sociaux*, 1959, 6:41–81.

Greshko, Michael, 'Why Female Vampire Bats Donate Blood to Friends', *National Geographic*, 17 November 2005, www.nationalgeographic. com/news/2015/11/151117-vampire-bats-blood-food-science-animals/, accessed 29 May 2021.

Harari, Yuval Noah, *Homo Deus: A Brief History of Tomorrow* (2015, New York, NY: Harper Perennial, 2018).

Hölldobler, Bert and Wilson, Edward O., *The Superorganism: The Beauty, Elegance, and Strangeness of Insect Societies* (New York, NY, W.W. Norton, 2009).

Hutton, James, 'Theory of the Earth; or an Investigation of the Laws Observable in the Composition, Dissolution, and Restoration of Land upon the Globe', *Transactions of the Royal Society of Edinburgh*, 1788, 1:209–304.

Johansson, Frans, *The Medici Effect: Breakthrough Insights at the Intersection of Ideas, Concepts, and Cultures* (Boston, MA: Harvard Business School Press, 2004).

Kalatehjari, Roohollah, Rashid, Ahmad Safuan A., Ali, Nazri, and Hajihassani, Mohsen, 'The Contribution of Particle Swarm Optimization in Three-Dimensional Slope Stability Analysis', *The Scientific World Journal*, special issue, volume June 2014, www.hindawi.com/journals/tswj/2014/973093/, accessed 20 October 2021.

Karlson, Peter and Lüscher, Martin, '"Pheromones": A New Term for a Class of Biologically Active Substances', *Nature*, 1959, 183:55–56, www.nature. com/articles/183055a0, accessed 29 May 2021.

Kaveh, Ali and Mahjoubi, Soroush, 'Lion Pride Optimization Algorithm: A Meta-Heuristic Method for Global Optimization Problems', *Scientia Iranica*, 2018, 25 (6), 3113–3132, www.researchgate.net/publication/327109473_Lion_Pride_Optimization_Algorithm_A_meta-heuristic_method_for_global_optimization_problems, accessed 29 May 2021.

Kennedy, James, and Eberhart, Russell C., 'Particle Swarm Optimization', in *Proceedings of IEEE International Conference on Neural Networks, Perth, Australian*, Vol. 4, 1995, 1942–1948.

Khurshid, Kiran, Irteza, Safwat, and Khan, Adnan A., 'Flow Chart Depicting the Structure of ACO Algorithm', Fig 2, in 'Application of Heuristic (1-Opt Local Search) and Metaheuristic (Ant Colony Optimization) Algorithms for

Symbol Detection in MIMO Systems', *Communication and Network*, 2011, 3:200–209, www.researchgate.net/publication/221007721_Application_ of_ant_colony_optimization_based_algorithm_in_MIMO_detection, accessed 29 May 2021.

Kinlaw, Dennis, *Team Managed Facilitation: Critical Skills for Developing Self-Sufficient Teams* (San Diego, CA: Pfeiffer, 1993).

Klein, Brandon, 'What "Facilitation" Really Means and Why It's Key to the Future of Work', *Fast Company*, 15 September 2017, www.fastcompany. com/40467377/what-facilitation-really-means-and-why-its-key-to-the-future-of-work, accessed 29 May 2021.

Liu Changan, Yan Xiaohu, and Hua Wu, 'The Wolf Colony Algorithm and Its Application', *Chinese Journal of Electronics*, 2011, 20 (2):212–216, www. researchgate.net/publication/285935995_The_Wolf_Colony_Algorithm_ and_Its_Application, accessed 29 May 2021.

Lumer, Erik and Faieta, Baldo, 'Diversity and Adaptation in Populations of Clustering Ants', in *Proceedings of the Third International Conference on Simulation of Adaptive Behavior: From Animals to Animats* (Cambridge, MA: MIT Press, 1994) 501–508.

Martens, David, Baesens, Bart, and Fawcett, Tom, 'Editorial Survey: Swarm Intelligence for Data Mining', *Machine Learning*, 2011, 82 (1):1–42, https://link.springer.com/article/10.1007/s10994-010-5216-5, accessed 29 May 2021.

McQuate, Sarah, 'Researchers Create First Sensor Package That Can Ride Aboard Bees', *University of Washington News*, 11 December 2018, www. washington.edu/news/2018/12/11/sensor-bees/, accessed 29 May 2021.

Merritt, Tom, 'Top 5 Things to Know about Machine Vision', *Tech Republic*, 6 June 2017, www.techrepublic.com/article/top-5-things-to-know-about-machine-vision/, accessed 29 May 2021.

Miller, Peter, *The Smart Swarm: How Understanding Flocks, Schools, and Colonies, Can Make us Better at Communication, Decision Making and Getting Things Done* (New York, NY: Avery, 2010).

Navrat, Pavol, Jelinek, Tomas, and Jastrzembska, Lucia, 'Bee Hive at Work: A Problem Solving, Optimizing Mechanism', in *Conference Proceedings: Nature & Biologically Inspired Computing*, 2009, www.researchgate. net/publication/224105840_Bee_Hive_At_Work_A_Problem_Solving_ Optimizing_Mechanism, accessed 29 May 2021.

Okdem, Selcuk and Karaboga, Dervis, 'Routing in Wireless Sensor Networks Using an Ant Colony Optimization (ACO) Router Chip', *MDPI Sensors*, 2009, 9 (2):909–921, www.mdpi.com/1424-8220/9/2/909, accessed 29 May 2021.

Pham Duc Truong, Ghanbarzadeh, Ali, Koc, Ebubekir, Sameh, Otri, Shafqat Rahim, and Muhamed, Zaidi, 'The Bees Algorithm', *Technical Note*, Manufacturing Engineering Centre, Cardiff University, UK, 2005.

Pham, Duc Truong and Castellani, Marco, 'The Bees Algorithm: Modelling Foraging Behaviour to Solve Continuous Optimization Problems', *Sage Journals*, 2009, 223 (12):2919–2938, https://journals.sagepub.com/doi/abs/10.1243/09544062JMES1494, accessed 29 May 2021.

Pham, Duc Truong., Castellani, Marco, Le Ti, and Hoai An, 'Nature-Inspired Intelligent Optimisation Using the Bees Algorithm', *Lecture Notes in Computer Science*, January 2014, www.researchgate.net/publication/260230212_Nature-Inspired_Intelligent_Optimisation_Using_the_Bees_Algorithm, accessed 29 May 2021.

Prakash, Yadhu, Prabhu, Kahan, Kamtekar, Shruti, and Gade, Sainath, 'Incorporation of Swarm Intelligence in Autonomous Cars', *International Journal of Computer Science and Information Technologies (IJCSIT)*, 2014, 5 (5), https://pdfs.semanticscholar.org/490a/7f5263d43428c309cdad6a980377a1262e4d.pdf, accessed 29 May 2021.

Rajeswari, M., Amudhavel, Jayavel., Pothula, Sujatha, and Dhavachelvan, Ponnurangam, 'Directed Bee Colony Optimization Algorithm to Solve the Nurse Rostering Problem', *Computational Intelligence and Neuroscience*, 2017, www.ncbi.nlm.nih.gov/pmc/articles/PMC5394913/, accessed 29 May 2021.

Reynolds, Craig W., 'Flocks, Herds and Schools: A Distributed Behavioral Model', *Computer Graphics*, 21, 4, July 1987, 25–34.

Rizzoli, Andrea E., Casagrande, Norman, Donati, Alberto V., Gambardella, Luca M., Lepori, Daniele, Montemanni, Roberto, Pina, Piero, and Zaffalon, Marco, 'Planning and Optimisation of Vehicle Routes for Fuel Oil Distribution', Proceedings from *International Congress on Modelling and Simulation. Jupiters Hotel and Casino, Townsville, Australia.* Online: MODSIM 2003 International Congress on Modelling and Simulation. Modelling and Simulation Society of Australia and New Zealand, July 2003, https://mssanz.org.au/MODSIM03/Volume_04/C14/03_Rizzoli.pdf, edited by David A. Post.

Seeley, Thomas D., *The Wisdom of the Hive: The Social Physiology of Honey Bee Colonies* (Cambridge, MA: Harvard University Press, 1995).

Seeley, Thomas D., *Honeybee Democracy* (Princeton, NJ: Princeton University Press, 2010).

Sumpter, David J.T., 'The Principles of Collective Animal Behaviour', *Philosophical Transactions of the Royal Society B: Biological Sciences*, 2006, 361 (1465):5–22, https://royalsocietypublishing.org/doi/pdf/10.1098/rstb.2005.1733, accessed 29 May 2021.

Susskind, Lawrence, McKearnan, Sarah, and Thomasp-Larmer, Jennifer (eds.), *The Consensus Building Handbook: A Comprehensive Guide to Reaching Agreement* (Thousand Oaks, CA: Sage, 1999).

Talbi, El-Ghazali, *Metaheuristics: From Design to Implementation* (Hoboken, NJ: John Wiley & Sons, 2009).

Tautz, Jürgen, *The Buzz about Bees: Biology of a Superorganism* (Berlin and London: Springer, 2008).

Vince, Gaia, 'In Praise of Slime Molds', *The American Scholar*, 24 June 2015, https://theamericanscholar.org/in-praise-of-slime-molds/, accessed 29 May 2021.

Wheeler, William M., *The Social Insects: Their Origin and Evolution* (London, Kegan Paul & Co, 1928).

Wilson, Edward O., *The Insect Societies* (Cambridge, MA: The Belknap Press of Harvard University Press, 1971).

Woolley-Barker, Tamsin, *Teeming: How Superorganisms Work to Build Infinite Wealth in a Finite World* (Ashland, OR: White Cloud Press, 2017).

Wu, Husheng, Zang, Fengming, and Wu, Lushan, 'New Swarm Intelligence Algorithm – Wolf Pack Algorithm', *Journal of Systems Engineering and Electronics*, 2013, 35 (11), www.researchgate.net/publication/264928582_New_swarm_intelligence_algorithm-wolf_pack_algorithm, accessed 29 May 2021.

Xin-She, Yang, *Nature-Inspired Optimization* Algorithms (London: Elsevier, 2014).

Yadav, Neha D. and Mehta, Mohit, 'An Efficient Algorithmic Approach for Multicast Scheduling Using Ant Colony Optimization', *International Journal of Computing and Corporate Research*, 2013, 3 (4), www.semanticscholar.org/paper/AN-EFFICIENT-ALGORITHMIC-APPROACH-FOR-MULTICAST-ANT-Yadav-Mehta/9f8c9eea8fee239175e1bc5f7f295128c8a12c22, accessed 29 May 2021.

Yang, Jian, et al. 'Swarm Intelligence in Data Science: Applications, Opportunities and Challenges', in *Advances in Swarm Intelligence. ICSI 2020 Lecture Notes in Computer Science*, July 2020, Vol. 12145, eds. Ying Tan, Yuhui Shi, Milan Tuba (Cham: Springer), https://doi.org/10.1007/978-3-030-53956-6_1, accessed 29 May 2021.

Yang, Xin-She, Chien, Su-Fong, and Ting, Tiew On, *Bio-Inspired Computation in Telecommunications* (Burlington, MA: Morgan Kaufmann, 2015).

Yazdani, Maziar and Jolai, Fariborz, 'Lion Optimization Algorithm (LOA): A Nature-Inspired Metaheuristic Algorithm', *Journal of Computational Design and Engineering*, 2016, 3:24–36, www.sciencedirect.com/science/article/pii/S2288430015000524, accessed 29 May 2021.

Yuce, Baris, Packianather, Michael S., Mastrocinque, Ernesto, and Pham, Duc Truong, 'Honey Bees Inspired Optimization Method: The Bees Algorithm', *Insects*, 4 (4):646–662.

3

HUMAN WAGGLE DANCING IN THE AGE OF INTELLIGENCE AMPLIFICATION

In the original format of the popular game show, *Who Wants to be a Millionaire?*, contestants are offered three 'lifelines': 50/50 where the computer eliminates two wrong answers out of a possible four answers; phone a friend, where the contestants can phone somebody during the show for 30 seconds to seek their assistance; and ask the audience, where the question is passed to the audience who select an answer using voting pads. The audience response appears on a bar graph. In his excellent book, *The Wisdom of Crowds*, James Surowiecki reports that the audience gets the answer right 91% of the time compared to the other lifeline, 'phone a friend', where the 'expert' gets it right 65% of the time.[1] An electronic voting device augments the wisdom of the crowd in the studio. Meanwhile, people watching at home are Googling the answer before it appears on the screen. The show covers a broad spectrum of intelligence: mental processing, collaborative intelligence, crowd intelligence,[2] and intelligence amplification (IA)/augmented intelligence.

The core of this study is collective intelligence and collaboration in the workplace. Humans are going to need to work in a collective swarm environment and be as effective as honeybees at waggle dancing and arriving at an optimal solution. The reality is (based on previous experiences of humans working in collective environments such as teams and other

DOI: 10.4324/9781003215561-5

participatory formats) waggle dancing doesn't come naturally to humans. Swarm facilitation, based on a honeybee algorithm entitled 'The Swarm Flow Model' (Figure 2.4), seeks to provide a clear process for human waggle dancing within complex adaptive systems. In this chapter, I want to briefly explore the way we sense, process, and act both individually and in groups and how artificial intelligent systems will be able to help us to collaborate together more effectively to boost our swarm quotient.

Uniqueness and limitations of mental processes

This chapter explores mental processes in relation to machine and artificial intelligence (AI). Exploring the uniqueness and limitations of mental processing is important in the context of amplifying it.

Three human mental qualities

Before considering the limitations of mental processing, let's assess its uniqueness. Lance Whitney writes, 'humans hold the edge on tasks that machines simply can't perform'.[3] The human brain far outperforms machines in creativity, intuition, and natural sensemaking.

Let's look at each of these categories.

1. Creativity

According to research carried out by Salesforce, 73% of hiring managers believe human creativity and abstract thinking will be an important attribute in the future workplace.[4] In his recent book, *The Origins of Creativity*, the Entomologist Edward O. Wilson characterises creativity as an 'innate quest for originality'.[5] Humans outperform current machine intelligence because humans originate ideas. Later in this chapter, we will see how artificial systems are beginning to compete with humans in the creative field.

2. Intuition

Another thing that demarcates humans from machines is that humans have intuition or gut instinct. The role of intuition and gut feel has been discussed since antiquity. It manifests itself in physical reaction – gut instinct and intuition can quite literally arouse the skin and make our hands perspire. Neuroscientist, Antonio Damasio with Antoine Bechara et al., famously tested psychophysiological reactions of card players fitted with sensors to measure their sweat glands.[6] The University of Iowa experiment shows that most participants have a 'pre-hunch' known as a somatic marker during the card game leading Damasio and his colleagues to conclude that emotions such as increased heartbeat, anxiety, and nausea naturally guide behaviour and decision-making. Theories concerning intuition include suggestions that it relates to primitive brain physiology, that it is a subconscious reaction, that it is a predictive processing style, and that it is an anticipatory phenomenon.[7] Many commentators believe we should trust these gut feelings and instincts and use them to make quick decisions (something known as intuitive decision-making).[8] We will see in the next section the ways in which this perspective is challenged.

3. Natural sensemaking

Sensemaking, according to Klein et al., is 'a motivated, continuous effort to understand connections, which can be among people, places, and events, to anticipate their trajectories and act effectively'.[9] Sensemaking is about understanding the context. Weick says, 'Sensemaking is about contextual rationality. It is built out of vague questions, muddy answers, and negotiated agreements that attempt to reduce confusion'.[10] This is unique to humans because, as we shall see, machine and deep learning is still at an elementary phase of processing unstructured, unsupervised, and unlabelled data. Unlike current AI, the brain has a unique capacity to know what to pay attention to and what to ignore in non-linear and unpredictable and intangible situations. Natural sensemaking is about experience.[11] In *Descartes' Error: Emotion, Reason, and the Human Brain*, Antonio Damasio explores how brain-damaged patients lack contextual rationality.

The limitations of mental processing

Neuroscientists have conducted research for decades that have exposed the shortcomings and limitations of mental processing. Eric Bonabeau eloquently remarks,

The human brain is a magnificent instrument that has evolved over thousands of years to enable us to prosper in an impressive range of conditions. But it is wired to avoid complexity (not embrace it) and to respond quickly to ensure survival (not explore numerous options).[12]

Below are some classic studies that highlight mental processing limitations:

1. The executive function of our human brain has limited working memory capacity

In his classic 1955 paper, 'The Magical Number Seven, Plus or Minus Two: Some Limits on Our Capacity for Processing Information', George A. Miller exposes the limitations of human short-term memory where performance begins to decline after a certain amount of stimuli – Miller calculates it to be 'somewhere in the neighborhood of seven'.[13] On average, human brains take between 13 and 100 milliseconds to process an image; given the right algorithms, and in very specific parameters, computers are quicker and more efficient at processing images as a logical task.[14] With AI set to create much more data going forward (something we will explore later in the chapter) and our cognitive abilities limited only to being able to handle around seven parcels of data at a given time in our short-term memory, humans clearly need support from artificial intelligent systems to process this amount of data.

2. We make snap decisions that are plaintively wrong

Jean Charles de Menezes grew up on a farm in Minas Gerais in Brazil and was living and working in London as a student and electrician. On the morning of 22 July 2005, he left his apartment to go to work. He had to take a different commute than normal because the London transport system was operating a restricted service due to an ongoing security alert involving attempted suicide bombings at London underground stations. On the tube, three armed police officers grabbed him, pinned him to the seat, and shot him seven times in the head. The police thought Jean was a suicide bomber because his apartment block was linked to a gym membership card found at one of the crime scenes. When Jean left home, he was followed and his circuitous journey to the tube station aroused suspicion. Officers thought he had a concealed bomb strapped to him and they made a snap judgement to shoot him in the head before he could activate the suspected bomb. He was an innocent victim and the story remains one of the most notorious cases of mistaken shootings in UK police history. Here is an example where sensemaking led to the wrong judgement. Many commentators speak of the virtues of quick judgement and intuitive decision-making, but Daniel Kahneman in *Thinking, Fast and Slow* reminds us that we often make decisions based on a rule of thumb that can go terribly wrong.

3. We exercise cognitive bias

Cognitive bias, a term coined by Amos Tversky and Daniel Kahneman in their research published in 1974, concerns inherent shortcut biases that influence human perception, judgement, and decision-making.[15] Confirmation bias, for example, is where people actively select data to confirm their preconceived thinking. Most humans are not impartial when they sense and process information – they make inferences beyond the observable data. Behaviourist and data scientist Pragya Agarwal's latest book, *Sway: Unravelling Unconscious Bias*, published in 2020, contains interesting research on this topic about how unintended biases impact many aspects of our lives in negative ways, including decision-making. She also considers how humans can programme machines with unintentional bias.

4. We overanalyse and overthink things and this can lead to mistakes

Lengthy rational thought can quickly backfire and lead to mistakes. Cambridge Neurologists, Kristin Flegal and Michael Anderson, conducted a golfing experiment on university undergraduates and published their findings in 2008.[16] They randomly selected 40 participants with mixed golfing skills and divided them into two groups and asked them to putt in a series of trials from the same distance and conditions. During a five-minute break, one group was asked to analyse every aspect of their putt from the trials, whilst the other group undertook a distractor task that had no association with golfing. The group that analysed its performance significantly underachieved in the later test taking twice as many putts to achieve their initial trial results.

5. We fail to see the obvious

In the 1990s, two Harvard Professors, Christopher Chabris and Daniel Simons, conducted a simple psychological experiment called 'The Invisible Gorilla' that was a selective attention test. Subjects were asked to watch a short film of two teams dressed in black and white who were passing basketballs in their teams. They were given an instruction to count how many times the players wearing white passed the basketball. Midway through the video, a student wearing a gorilla costume walked into the frame, stopped in the middle of the players, faced the camera, thumped their chest, and walked off. The gorilla scene takes about nine seconds. Half the observers who were preoccupied counting the passes, failed to notice the gorilla. Without the preoccupation of counting passes, subjects saw the gorilla easily. The authors put this down to 'inattentional blindness'. This study shows that when we are preoccupied with many tasks, we can miss the obvious. The research was published in 2010 in *The Invisible Gorilla*.[17]

6. Our brains decay

Unlike machines, our brains are organic and can't easily be repaired or replaced. The problem with human mental processing is that human cognition has a limited capacity and is extremely fragile. The brain is organic, took millions of years to evolve, takes several decades to develop and mature, easily malfunctions when it is damaged or diseased, rapidly declines with old age,[18] and, according to Malcolm Gladwell in *Outliers: The Story of Success* (2008), takes up to 10,000 hours to perfect a skill. Research published in 2011 assessing brain disorder and mental illness in 30 European countries shows a staggering degree of brain disorders and mental illness – almost 38% of the total population of these 30 countries suffer from some form of mental illness.[19] Age factors are behind most common neurodegenerative diseases such as strokes and dementia.

7. Emotions can get in the way

The introduction started with the story of Apollo 11 and the historic lunar landing. The commander, Neil Armstrong, was an extremely capable and methodical professional who was highly respected by colleagues such as Buzz Aldrin who rated him as one of the best pilot he ever knew. James R. Hansen's biography of Neil Armstrong, *First Man: The Life of Neil A. Armstrong*, tells the story of a difficult time in his life when his second child, Karen, died of brain tumour in January 1962. Immediately after his daughter's death, he started experiencing technical difficulties and accidents which damaged research planes. It was attributed to pilot error and could have cost him his life. He acknowledged he was grieving for his daughter and that his judgement was clouded. Neil Armstrong's situational awareness was dulled by his emotional grief.

Group processing was seen as a fix to individual mental processing but brings more problems

Individualism and self-determination were core liberal values of the Enlightenment and persisted into the nineteenth century. The beginning of the twentieth century saw the rise of social psychology and group therapy which placed value on group work. Norman Triplett conducted various experiments on how people perform optimally in groups (something that Floyd Henry Allport later termed social facilitation). William McDougall published his seminal text, *The Group Mind*, which can be seen as a forerunner of the hive mind. Trigant Burrow, Jacob Levy Moreno, and Kurt Lewin were early pioneers in group processes through their work in group therapy. The concept of teamworking emerged out of the Hawthorne studies in the 1920s where Elton Mayo and Fritz Roethlisberger observed workers from the Hawthorne plant at the Western Electric Company. Group work was designed to counterbalance some of the limitations of individual mental processing outlined earlier. Group work, however, has brought its own challenges. These include the ant mill effect, the Ringelmann Effect/ social loafing, group polarisation, group think, and group hate.

- The ant mill effect occurs in the natural world when a circle of ants follow one another and form a continuous rotating tight circle until they experience a grizzly death from exhaustion.[20] Ant mills were first described by William Beebe in 1921 who observed a mill in Guyana that measured 1200 feet (370 metre) and took 2.5 hours for the ants to circuit the mill.[21] Groups can suffer from the ant mill effect by literally getting tied up in knots and suffering from group paralysis.

- The Ringelmann Effect is named after Max Ringelmann who observed that one person pulling on a rope will give 100% effort but that personal effort and contribution decrease as more people pull on the rope. This is akin to social loafing where studies show people put in less effort in teams than individually.[22]
- Group polarisation is common in groups where groups take more extreme decisions compared with individuals. One of the most compelling studies of group polarisation is related to a US federal court study in 1973.[23]
- Groupthink – a term widely believed to have been coined by William H. Whyte[24] – is defined by social psychologist Irving Janis, as 'a quick and easy way to refer to a mode of thinking that people engage in when they are deeply involved in a cohesive in-group, when the members' strivings for unanimity override their motivation to realistically appraise alternative courses of action'.[25] A classic case of groupthink occurred with the Space Shuttle Challenger disaster that happened in January 1986. Technical concerns raised by contract engineers were consistently ignored by management who, under pressure to launch, convinced themselves that conditions were safe. Groupthink is more likely to occur when there is a cohesive group of participants from similar backgrounds who are part of an in-group that pursue common goals.
- Susan Sorenson has researched a phenomenon known as 'group hate'. Four areas that generate group hate are to do with competition, interpersonal considerations, outcomes, and organisational factors. Alison Burke suggests people with preference for introversion can be overwhelmed in groups resulting in group resentment.[26]

What this opening context seeks to show is that humans have some unique mental processing qualities that machines can't replicate but have many mental processing flaws that can derail ideation and effective decision-making. The 'wisdom of crowds' can overcome some of these flaws – we saw this in 'Who Wants to be a Millionaire?' But formal group work brings its own unique set of challenges. The twentieth-century response to organising better group work and avoiding some of the pitfalls described earlier has been the rise of programme designers and group facilitators. But designers and facilitators steer and condition ideas – they are part of the traditional business operating system and, therefore, part of the problem. Honeybee colonies don't have designers or group facilitators. The proposed solution to this Catch-22 is swarm and swarm facilitation. The swarm flow model (Figure 2.4), inspired by house-hunting honeybees, brings some process and methodology to group work and collective decision-making that retains its complex adaptive system credentials but doesn't require alpha leaders, designers, or facilitators.

We will explore human swarms in Chapter 5. More ambitious forms of swarm will require a technological solution to waggle dancing. A digital waggle dance, if you will. We will see this play out in Chapters 6 and 7. The reminder of this chapter explores the background, current reality, and future possibilities for augmenting collective decision-making and facilitating swarmocracy using intelligent systems. It's time to bring human waggle dancing into the digital age.

Towards augmented intelligence

Over the years, we humans have tried many strategies to naturally enhance our mental capacity. These include initiatives around nutrition,[27] physical exercise,[28] and brain workouts.[29] There is also a sizeable amount of cognitive readiness tools available aimed to declutter the brain and enhance brain power so that better decisions can be made. These include cognitive load theory, mind maps, ambidextrous training,[30] attentional control, and reducing decision fatigue.[31] Some neuroscientists argue we have reached peak brain power capacity and that we simply cannot become more intelligent without impossible amounts of energy and oxygen.[32] Tech entrepreneurs Elon Musk and Ray Kurzweil both view augmented intelligence and cognitive enhancement as an inevitability. They see it as a continuation of human brain evolution (building on the tradition of Maclean's Triune brain).[33] The rest of this chapter explores the paradigm shift away from enhancing brain capacity towards using artificial intelligent systems to augment mental processing. Human intelligence, defined by Geoff Mulgan as 'our ability to use our brains to know which path to take, who to trust, and what to do or not do',[34] has taken millions of years to evolve and has many processing limitations. What we will see here is that AI has evolved over a period of just 70 years and is growing in capacity and application. Some believe that machine and AI will surpass human intelligence, a phenomenon known as singularity. This has huge implications for humankind. The rest of this chapter explores the key issues. The reason why this is important is although (as we shall see in Chapter 5) swarm and swarm facilitation can function in a human system (Swarm 1.0), its true potential lies in intelligence and decision augmentation where business intelligence and human ideation is digitised and processed through intelligent systems to support human and organisational decision-making (Swarm 2.0 and 3.0).

Background

Augmented intelligence is a derivation of AI. 'While the underlying technologies powering AI and IA are the same', writes Aaron Masih, 'the goals and applications are fundamentally different: AI aims to create systems that run without humans, whereas IA aims to create systems that make humans better'.[35] Understanding augmented intelligence means understanding the evolution of AI and its progress and forms.

Early AI

AI was for a long time a conceptual idea that was part of mythology, general fiction, and conceptual science. In Jewish folklore, for example, a human figure made from clay, Golem, comes to life when the rabbi inserts a piece of paper with God's name under its tongue. Jonathan Swift, Mary Shelly, and Samuel Butler all imagine artificial intelligent systems and beings. The developing genre of twentieth-century sci-fi in books and movies also explored AI. Huxley, Wells, and Asimov all wrote dystopian texts about the rise of autonomous thinking machines and their threat to humankind. Stanley Kubrick's *2001: A Space Odyssey* dealt with non-human intelligence threatening human life.

In the mid-fifties, the concept started to be developed at universities and research institutes. The term AI was coined by John McCarthy for a 1956 two-month conference at Dartmouth College in Hanover, New Hampshire, with an objective that 'every aspect of learning or any other feature of intelligence can in principle be so precisely described that a machine can be made to simulate it'.[36] From the 1960s onwards, AI started to move away from conceptuality to research and development and early AI programs, prototypes, and applications were developed. Influential research institutes in the field of cognitive science and AI started to form, and early AI applications materialised. The polymath MIT Professor, Herbert Simon, who excelled in economics, psychology, and computer science, came up with a concise definition as, 'finding ways of getting computers to do intelligent tasks, to do tasks which, if they were done by human beings, would call for our human intelligence'. [37] The following timeline (Figure 3.1) captures the early pioneering and game changing research that took place during active AI research and investment periods where AI began to have some very practical applications especially in the field of robotics, knowledge-based systems, natural language processing, search engine optimisation, and object detection/image processing.

The progress of AI

Since these early applications, AI-driven technology has become more sophisticated and has integrated into our everyday working and home lives. That said, the progression of AI has been patchy; it has had periods of inactivity due to lack of funding and interest.[38] These periods are known as AI winters. There are three important types of AI that have evolved over time that should be flagged in this background section.

1. Artificial narrow intelligence (ANI)

These early applications around knowledge-based systems, facial recognition, autonomous vehicles, and search optimisation featured in Figure 3.1 are rule-based systems that are based on specific predefined and labelled datasets. They are known as artificial narrow intelligence (ANI) which is a weak form of AI where artificial systems perform a very narrow/single application task. This technology extracts information from a specific predefined dataset and is merely following a basic IF-THEN-ELSE conditional algorithm rather than acting in a way that can be deemed smart or

Figure 3.1 Key technological breakthroughs in the early days of AI.

intelligent. Take, for example, autonomous vehicles, these devices have an extraordinary capacity to process configurations at lighting speed, but they are highly processed rather than strictly 'intelligent'.

2. Artificial general intelligence (AGI)

Artificial general intelligence (AGI) describes future machine capability where AI will match any intellectual task that mature humans perform. A recent study at Cornell University compared AI (in particular AlphaGo) to the average intelligence of school children. They discovered that the most advanced AI in general had the intelligence of a third-grade student.[39] The advancement in AGI is very much linked to the progress made in artificial systems being able to identify and process unlabelled datasets and learn and improve functioning without supervision. This will depend on the progress made in deep learning and unsupervised and reinforcement machine learning (something that will be discussed shortly). The point here is that AI is not programmed, but learns how to do complex tasks.

3. Artificial super intelligence (ASI)

Artificial super intelligence is the moment or tipping point when machines surpass and outperform humans in intelligent tasks. It is also known as technological singularity (or just singularity). The concept of singularity was first mentioned by Stanislaw Ulum recollecting a conversation with John von Neumann[40] and was popularised by Science Fiction author Vernor Vinge in his prescient 1993 paper, 'The Coming Technological Singularity'. Different expert commentators have differing views concerning singularity. Vernon Vinge speculated it would happen in the mid-2020s. Google's Director of Engineering, Ray Kurzweil, believes it will be in 2045.[41] Duke University Neuroscientist Miguel Nicolelis thinks singularity is 'a bunch of hot air'.[42] Some commentators are positive about it, viewing it in the context of augmented intelligence and a natural part of the mental evolution of homo sapiens, whilst others are more wary. In 2017, an open letter was produced by the *Future of Life Institute*, arguing for a more robust approach to AI research. Signatories included distinguished scientists and technology leaders, such as the late Stephen Hawking, Bill Gates, and Elon Musk.[43] Singularity and an increasing reliance on machines throws up some highly complex issues around job displacement and whether future technology will generate employment or displace it[44]; human value and identity, where we will be so digitised and dominated by intelligent systems that we will struggle to assert our own human identities[45]; and security and privacy issues.[46]

Machine intelligence and deep learning

Machine and deep learning are two technologies that have been behind the scenes evolving AI. It is important to be clear about a common misconception: AI, machine learning, and deep learning are not interchangeable terms. We have seen that AI is about understanding intelligent entities.[47] According to Sundar Pichai, the CEO of Google, machine learning is transformative and 'rethinking everything we're doing'.[48] It is a subset of AI and uses at least four variant algorithms: supervised, unsupervised, semi-supervised, and reinforcement. In her excellent blog, NVADIA (2018), Isha Salian uses a brilliant example of assembling IKEA furniture as a way of describing the key differentials of these algorithms.[49] If the package is opened with complete pieces and instructions, then it is a simple classification task (supervised machine learning). If we don't want to use the instructions because we have some experience assembling IKEA furniture, then we are building the furniture in an unclassified way based on our own system of detection (unsupervised machine learning used mainly in pattern detection and descriptive modelling). If some of the pieces are unlabelled or unclear in the instructions, we need to make some educated guesses to fill in the gaps (semi-supervised machine learning used mainly in medical images such as CT or MRI scans). If the instructions are missing and we have no experience of building IKEA furniture, we can learn as we go along using trial and error where we hopefully improve our skills along the way (reinforcement machine learning used in game applications such as AlphaGo). Conceptualised in 1965 by Grigoryevich Ivakhnenko and Valentin Lapa, deep learning relates to the unsupervised aspect of machine learning. Vandit Gupta defines deep learning as something that 'imitates the workings of the human brain in processing data and creating patterns for use in decision-making'.[50] It has artificial neural networks that connect like a web that can learn unsupervised from unlabelled, nonlinear, and unstructured data.

Where is AI?

The question concerning AI's status is tackled by John Launchbury from The US Defence Advanced Research Project Agency (DARPA). He neatly describes the progression of AI using a theory of AI waves which he outlines in a Technica Curiosa article (2017):

> To summarize, we see at DARPA that there have been three waves of AI, the first of which was handcrafted knowledge. It's still hot, it's still relevant, it's still important. The second wave, which is now very much in the mainstream for things like face recognition, is about statistical learning where we build systems that get trained on data. But those two waves by themselves are not going to be sufficient. We see the need to bring them together. And so, we're seeing the advent of a third wave of AI technology built around the concept of contextual adaption.[51]

This is conceptually close to Max Tegmark's *Life 3.0* who also looks at three stages of AI. He views Life 3.0 (the technological stage) as AI's ability to design its own hardware and software.

In the third wave, according to Launchbury, AI systems will understand meaning and context and learn and adapt very much like humans do.

In terms of measuring AI's progress, it seems we are constantly shifting the measurable parameters of what constitutes intelligent machines in relation to humans. The standard test to measure human versus AI was the Turing Test. This was an 'imitation game', created by Alan Turing in a seminal 1950 paper, 'Computing Machinery and Intelligence', involving human judges being able to differentiate between humans and machines. The broad consensus is that the Turing Test has been met and humans can be fooled by machine intelligence.[52] Another standard test of human versus machine intelligence was humans competing against machines in strategy games. To date, intelligent systems have beaten their human world champion counterparts in all of the major strategy games, including chess, backgammon, checkers, scrabble, Go, and Texas Hold 'em poker. Another human versus machine measure was the Lovelace Test in honour of Lady Lovelace who expressed in her memoirs about Babbage's Analytical Engine that machines will be deemed to have minds when they create and originate things. Recent developments in the creative arts where AI systems are producing original works of music, fiction, and art would also suggest that this criterion is being met.[53] New milestones are being suggested all the time, including a World Economic Forum piece, 'Can Machines Think? A New Turing Test May Have the Answer' by Carl Strathearn who looks at a multimodel Turing Test that judges a machines' appearance. Senior Vice President and Director of IBM research, John E. Kelly III, recently wrote in an IBM paper, 'The success of cognitive computing will not be measured by Turing tests or a computer's ability to mimic humans. It will be measured in more practical ways, like return on investment, new market opportunities, diseases cured and lives saved'.[54]

Current AI application in autonomous decision systems and decision augmentation

Since the 1950s, there have been some remarkable ANI innovations that have shaped our modern lives, especially in the field of robotics, nanobots, agritech, game applications, route finders, recommender systems, driverless cars, and medical diagnoses.[55] Decision and intelligence augmentation and autonomous decision systems (ADS), important technologies for the advancement of swarm, are pushing AI to the boundaries of Launchbury's third wave. Advanced algorithmic intelligent decision-making is already mainstream in some of the technologies cited earlier, including recommender systems and medical diagnosis, particularly clinical decision support systems (CDSS) such as CaDet and DXplain. It is also central to predictive analytics. Progress has also been made in augmenting organisational decision-making, which is key to the progression of organisational swarm. Technology used to support organisational decision-making has a long history. Decision support systems (DSS) are computer-based information and knowledge systems that were developed at the Carnegie Institute of Technology in the late 1950s and 1960s and used to help individuals within organisations to make more effective decisions. Group decision support systems (GDSS) are a subclass of DSS which supports group decision-making. DSS are still current and highly sophisticated systems for analysing vast amounts of business intelligence to inform business decisions.[56] Unanimous AI is showing the way in this field and has an established and commercially thriving artificial swarm intelligence (ASI) reputation. It is developing swarm intelligence algorithms to processes data in faster and more accurate ways in order to augment human intelligence and collective thinking. It has already developed tools that have overcome the technical challenge of pooling knowledge.[57] They use a platform called Swarm which it describes on its official website as an 'AI-powered collaboration platform that uses the biological principle of Swarm Intelligence to amplify the wisdom of any online team or group, quickly enabling more accurate forecasts, estimations, insights and evaluations'.[58] It should be pointed out that the advance of ADS and decision augmentation has been made possible because of the dramatic rise in processing power, advances in data (particularly in the field of cloud technology), developments in analytics, the migration of talent away from universities and research to industry, and an increasing societal acceptance of AI.[59] In the next section, we will assess how this all plays out in the workplace of the future.

Augmented intelligence and the workplace

The lengthy background was necessary because it provided crucial information for a better understanding of augmented intelligence. It was said that augmented intelligence is a derivation of AI. It is also known as assisted intelligence and IA. In a 2017 interview at Davos, former CEO of IBM, Ginni Rometty, explains why she favours the term augmented intelligence over AI. She views the future as an amplification of human intelligence.[60] The term amplify is derived from the Latin meaning to increase. It relates to outsourcing human thought using technology such as smartphones and computers to assist and amplify our natural intelligence and judgement. In augmented intelligence, humans still make decisions. Reaching for your smartphone and Googling information to check something that has come up in a casual conversation is technically a form of IA. Elon Musk considers the use of everyday smart electronics already characterises humans as cyborgs.[61] Augmented intelligence, then, complements rather than replaces our natural intelligence so that everyday tasks can be carried out quicker and smarter than mere reliance on human mental processing. Paul J.H. Schoemaker and Philip E. Tetlock have produced a useful four-box matrix that assesses the comparative advantages of human versus machines and shows that humans and computers collaborate well in low data density/routine tasks such as the digital process automation of insurance claims where the grunt work is eliminated by AI and in high data density/complex tasks such as autopilots where AI backs up human involvement.[62]

The coming years will see an unprecedented collaboration between humans and machines. Major companies that are investing in AI are doing so because they want to see practical value and return on their investment in the form of intelligent systems supporting human workers to optimise business performance and results. They are not interested in academic debates on the future of human versus machine intelligence.

Tech companies in general are investing in AI, with the AI market predicted to reach $309.6 billion by 2026.[63] Specific to augmented intelligence, Gartner predicted that AI augmentation would generate $2.9 trillion of business value in 2021 and that by 2030 'decision support/augmentation will surpass all other types of AI initiatives to account for 44% of the global AI-derived business value'.[64] It feels like it will be a golden decade for intelligent systems. We have been here before, of course, where AI summers have rapidly turned into AI winters, but this time, businesses are making substantial financial investments and they are seeking return in the form of producing more value-adding opportunities for human knowledge workers. This should transform employee roles and promote lifelong growth, learning, and opportunities and it could lead to more nimble and flexible enterprises with more collective organisational input and decision-making.

Augmented intelligence and the future of the workplace

This section explores two near-future scenarios: 2025 and 2035 which more or less correspond with the Swarm 2.0 and Swarm 3.0 phases where intelligent systems will be used to support swarm. In 2025, intelligent systems will play a greater role in predictive analytics and robotic process automation. It will support clusters of human collaboration and decision-making and help swarm communities make collective decisions. 2035 is where future technology can better deal with unlabelled data and will be able to assist humans make sense of intelligence by automating certain decision-making processes across the entire enterprise. Post-2035 is outside the scope of this study. It embraces the era of intelligent automation where intelligent systems will autonomously generate business intelligence and simultaneously implement swarm-based solutions without human intervention (the era of singularity).

Let's now look at the 2025 and 2035 scenarios and consider the intelligent systems likely to assist the swarmification of the business.

2025

We have tracked the sporadic rise of AI since the mid-twentieth century. We appear to be going through a golden age of AI where we are transitioning into its third wave because of progress made in machine intelligence and deep learning. Business, we have seen, is beginning to invest heavily in AI and seeks value from it in the form of augmented intelligence. This is starting to yield value to the business by cutting costs and raising efficiency and productivity. It is reported that 'by 2025, as many as 95 percent of all customer interactions will be through channels supported by artificial intelligence (AI) technology'.[65] These nascent technologies that will organise business intelligence, aid group collaboration, and digitise human experience, will be commonplace in the next few years. Trends include the following:

1. *Internet of Things (IoT) and embedded tech*

The Internet of Things (IOT), sensorization,[66] and embedded tech are set to expand rapidly in the next five years according to a Statista Report.[67] This will make our environment far more connected. Data and information will be more readily accessible and will advance AI. It will force companies to adapt their products, 'thereby creating the potential for new leaders and laggards to emerge across all industries'.[68] AI and IOT will revolutionise human and machine interface and promote instantaneous decision-making.

2. *Crowdsourcing platforms*

Crowdsourcing was a term first used by Jeff Howe in a *Wired* article in 2006 which looked at imaginative ways of outsourcing to individuals via a platform rather than to companies or countries. According to a 2015 eYeka report, 85% of the 2014 best global brands such as Gucci, IKEA, and FedEX had used crowdsourcing.[69] Many companies such as Starbucks, Procter and Gamble, and Lufthansa have established in-house crowdsourcing platforms and innovation hubs and many organisations, such as NASA, are using prize challenges to support internal innovation. Crowdsourcing is set to grow further and by 2025 will most likely be integrated into the internal organisational structure.[70] Permanent crowdsourcing platforms will eliminate R&D and innovation departments and overtake outsourcing as the major innovation strategy. The trend for third-party crowdsourcing companies such as InnoCentive is likely to grow.

3. Decision intelligence and decision augmentation

Earlier in the chapter, we explored the current trend in ADS and decision augmentation. Gartner predicts that by 2023, more than 33% of large organisations will have analysts actively practising decision intelligence and will employ decision intelligence analysts.[71] Decision augmentation and intelligence augmentation helps build context which positions it in the third wave of AI technology which John Launchbury characterises as contextual adaption. An excellent recent article by Michael Leyer and Sabrina Schneider entitled 'Decision Augmentation and Automation with Artificial Intelligence: Threat or Opportunity for Managers?' looks at practical ways this technology can be used in organisational decision-making. This technology will directly support the development of swarm and its progression to Swarm 2.0 and beyond.

4. Collaborative tools

There is now a developing trend of major organisations such as Twitter, Microsoft, Siemens, Spotify, Starbucks, Bank Standard Charter, and Lloyds revaluating presentism following the coronavirus pandemic. One of the things that has made homeworking possible is video conferencing from such services as Zoom, Microsoft Teams, and Slack. The team collaboration software market is set to be worth $35.71 billion by 2027 according to a *Fortune Business Insight* report that has factored in the Covid-19 effect.[72] According to Pew Research Center, the next five years will see more tech-driven solutions and integrated offerings between face time collaboration and remote collaboration and far more interactive tools such as swarm boards.[73] The next five years will see a rise in conversational AI to support and facilitate the collaborative experience. One developing application that is relevant to the future of swarm facilitation is autonomous facilitation using chatbots. This concept is now being discussed in scientific papers.[74]

5. Data and advanced analytics

The global digital datasphere (the amount of digital data generated) is doubling in size every two years and a *Cyber Security Ventures* study predicts that the world will store a staggering 200 zettabytes of data by 2025.[75] Collecting data has become cheaper in recent years with the increase in by-product generated data. New AI analytics, cloud technologies, and decision augmentation require high degrees of dataism and improved processing capacity and platforms. Commentators make the point that it is advances made in computer processing and storage and the development in Big Data and advanced algorithms that is enabling a new generation of AI-based decision-making.[76] Clearly, as superintelligent machines evolve they will require even more advanced dataism.

2035

By 2035, the 2025 trends outlined above will be well integrated into business processes and will contribute to the swarm-based organisation revolution that this study anticipates. By 2035, some additional paradigm-breaking trends that have already been conceptualised will be introduced into business that will transform the business landscape and will prove to be important technology that helps organisations shift towards becoming business superorganisms. Three key trends that will facilitate Swarm 3.0 include the following:

1. Spatial Web and immersive technology

Although universal Internet access is unlikely to happen until 2050,[77] the Internet will transform over the next 15 years and become more interactive and spatial. Web 2.0 was a more social and interactive experience than Web 1.0 which allowed for a greater collective experience.[78] Web 3.0 will be more spatial and will be able to accommodate more immersive technology such as IOT wearables.[79] Augmented reality, virtual reality and holograms will all have greater commercial application.[80] Tech forecaster, James Bellini, predicts that holograms will be commonplace in homes by 2030, stating, 'Advancements in technology and lightning-speed broadband mean that pioneering forms of connectivity, such as holograms, are now viable options for when we want to feel closer to those we're not physically able to be with'.[81] There are now university programmes about human computer interaction (HCI) which looks at the interface of computers and mobile technology with users. Computational AI such as virtual reality (VR) chatbots will be widely available and will optimise online human experience and presence. This all links to the brief discussion on human presence discussed in Chapter 1 in relation to the coronavirus pandemic.

2. Intelligent automation

Recalling John Launchbury's three AI waves, by 2035, AI should be well into its third wave where machines have the capacity to process more unlabelled and unstructured data and work with minimal supervision. According to a study by *Citrix Systems*, AI will make the majority of business decisions by 2035.[82] This could have all kinds of ramifications, including a reduction in leadership and management roles. Intelligent automation is dependent on the progression of singularity and most commentators anticipate full intelligent automation by 2050. That said, 2035 should see a significant amount of business processes using intelligent automation. More advanced intelligent systems will support swarm-based organisations, especially in advanced analytics, automated business intelligence, decision augmentation, and business process automation.

3. Empathetic AI and brain-computer interface

Research is actively taking place in the fields of emotional recognition systems and empathetic AI.[83] Emotional intelligence is a work in progress but has a great commercial potential. Technology is identifying and distinguishing humans from their heartbeats, walking gaits, and microbial traces.[84] Research by Rincon et al. (2016) promotes the idea of using intelligent wristbands/wearables to detect biosignals and emotional states. There exists controversy to what degree recognition systems truly represent inner emotion.[85] Recognition systems will be an important component of human digitisation strategy as the market in smart wearables is expected to hit 648.4 million units by 2025.[86] Another important technology that is currently being developed is brain-computer interface and neurotech. This could have possible application by 2035 and contribute to the digitisation of human experience in the form of thought and feeling recognition. Current research and development includes brain/cranial implants, visualising thoughts, neuro-nanorobotics, brain net, thought recognition, mind loading, and neurostimulation. Elon Musk and Dmitry Itskov are dominant in this field. This is human digitalism taken to the level of human thought and perception. Wearables, inplants, and neural lace technology will be bio assisted and will make the connectivity and navigation easier. This is an age where humans will be literally (physically) connected to the web which will enhance collaboration and the processing of personal thoughts and emotions. The digitisation of human experience is at the heart of advanced forms of swarm. Implants and wearables that facilitate and augment decision-making across the enterprise will be key to building a business superorganism. Obviously, this raises some ethical concerns about the advanced digitalisation of the individual. Some researchers are calling for more work to be conducted in this area and for there to be a clear framework.[87]

Chapter 1 presented the case for upgrading the business operating system. Chapter 2 introduced a methodology to facilitate swarm (based on a swarm flow model inspired by relocating honeybees). This chapter has detailed the limitations of mental and group processing to achieve effective ideation and decision-making. It appraised how artificial intelligent systems – now and in the future – could augment swarm facilitation and help the organisation transform from local human swarm communities to becoming a business superorganism.

This chapter concludes Part 1 of the book. It has covered some theoretical ground. It articulated a transformational vision for the business in the guise of a new business operating system and explored two key progressors of swarm: swarm facilitation and augmented intelligence. Part 2 of the book is a practical exposition that clearly sets out three levers that drive the business transformation from BOS 1.0 to BOS 3.0. It dedicates a chapter to each of the three swarm transformation phases. The conclusion provides a clear and practical route map for a successful business transformation.

Notes

1   James Surowiecki, *The Wisdom of Crowds* (New York: Anchor Books, 2005), 4.

2   The concept of crowd intelligence has been around for centuries. It was the Marquis de Condorcet in 1785 who argued in *Essai sur l'application de l'analyse à la probabilité des décisions rendues à la pluralité des voix* that the majority opinion on a yes/no question is most likely to be correct. In 1906 statistician Francis Galton observed a competition where people had to guess the weight of an ox at a country fair. He published his findings in *Nature* in 1907. This experiment was replicated by Jack Treynor in 1987 in *Financial Analysts Journal*. The wisdom of the crowd is even more relevant in popular culture and social media.

3   Lance Whitney, 'Are Computers Already Smarter Than Humans?', *Time*, 29 September 2017, https://time.com/4960778/computers-smarter-than-humans/, accessed 29 May 2021.

4   Source: 'The Future of Workforce Development', Salesforce, www.salesforce.com/content/dam/web/en_us/www/documents/research/market/future-of-workforce-development-salesforce-research.pdf, accessed 29 May 2021, 6.

5   Edward O. Wilson, *The Origins of Creativity* (New York, NY: Liveright, 2017), 13.

6   Source: Antoine Bechara et al., 'Deciding Advantageously before Knowing the Advantageous Strategy', *Science*, New Series, Vol 275, No. 5304, February 1997, 1293–1295.

7   For intuition related to brain theory see Daniel Goleman, *Emotional Intelligence: Why It Can Matter More than IQ* (New York, NY: Bantam Books, 1997); for intuition related to subconscious reaction see Malcolm Gladwell, *Blink: The Power of Thinking without Thinking* (New York, NY: Back Bay Books, 2007); for intuition related to predictive processing style see Valerie Van Mulukom, 'Is it Rational to Trust Your Gut Feelings? A Neuroscientist Explains', *The Conversation*, 16 May 2018; for intuition related to anticipatory phenomenon see Gary Klein and David Snowden, 'Anticipatory Thinking', in Informed by Knowledge Expert Performance in Complex Situations, January 2011. Klein.

8 Good source: Kurt Matzler et al., 'Intuitive Decision Making', *MIT Sloan Management Review*, 1 October 2007, https://sloanreview.mit.edu/article/ intuitive-decision-making/, accessed 29 May 2021.

9 Gary Klein, et al., 'Making Sense of Sensemaking 1: Alternative Perspectives', *Intelligent Systems*, 21, 4, 2006, 70–73, www.researchgate.net/publication/ 3454348_Making_Sense_of_Sensemaking_1_Alternative_Perspective, accessed 29 May 2021, 71.

10 K.E. Weick, 'The Collapse of Sensemaking in Organizations: The Mann Gulch Disaster', in *Administrative Science Quarterly*, 38, 4, 1993, 628–652, 636.

11 Sensemaking has been defined by Maureen Duffy as 'how people make sense out of their experience in the world', Maureen Duffy, 'Sensemaking in Classroom Conversations', in Ilja Maso et al. (eds.), *Openness in Research: The Tension between Self and Other* (Assen: Van Gorcum, 1995), 119–132.

12 Eric Bonabeau, 'Decisions 2.0: The Power of Collective Intelligence', *MIT Sloan Management Review*, 9 January 2009, https://sloanreview.mit.edu/ article/decisions-20-the-power-of-collective-intelligence/, accessed 29 May 2021.

13 G.A. Miller, 'The Magical Number Seven, Plus or Minus Two: Some Limits on Our Capacity for Processing Information', *Psychological Review*, 63, 2, 1956, 81–97, 90. Miller's findings was challenged by Richard Shiffrin and Robert Nosofsky, 'Seven Plus or Minus Two: A Commentary on Capacity Limitations', *Psychological Review*, 2, 101 (Centennial), 1994, 357–361.

14 Source: Anne Trafton, 'In the Blink of an Eye', *MIT News*, 16 January 2014, https://news.mit.edu/2014/in-the-blink-of-an-eye-0116, accessed 29 May 2021.

15 Amos Tversky and Daniel Kahneman, 'Judgment under Uncertainty: Heuristics and Biases', *Science*, 185, 4157, 1974, 1124–1131.

16 Kristin Flegal and Michael Anderson, 'Overthinking Skilled Motor Performance: Or Why Those Who Teach Can't Do', *Psychonomic Bulletin & Review*, 15, 5, 2008, 927–932.

17 Christopher Chabris and Daniel Simons, *The Invisible Gorilla: And Other Ways Our Intuition Deceives Us* (London: HarperCollins, 2010). Daniel Simons posted the original experiment online. 'Selective Attention Test', posted by David Simons, *YouTube*, 10 March 2010, www.youtube.com/ watch?v=vJG698U2Mvo, accessed 29 May 2021.

18 Source: R. Peters, 'Ageing and the Brain', *Postgraduate Medical Journal*, 82, 964, 2006, 84–88.

19 Source: 'Brain Burdens', *Nature*, 477, 2011, 132, www.nature.com/articles/ 477132a, accessed 29 May 2021. Some diseases and damage are not so physically obvious but create profound personality disorders. See, for example, the case studies about Phineas Gage and Elliot in Antonio R. Damasio, *Descartes' Error*.

20 A film was taken of this spectacle. Source: 'Ant Death Spiral – Costa Rica', *YouTube*, posted as 'Ant Mill' on 5 December 2013 by BrodinNets, www. youtube.com/watch?v=3Rup3EdAokw&feature=youtu.be, accessed 5 November 2020.

21 William Beebe, *Edge of the Jungle* (New York, NY: Henry Holt and Co., 1921).

22 Social loafing is a term coined by Latané et al., 'Many Hands Make Light the Work: The Causes and Consequences of Social Loafing', *Journal of Personality and Social Psychology*, 37, 6, 1979, 822–832. The concept existed much earlier in the work of M. Ringelmann, 'Recherches sur les moteurs animés: Travail de l'homme' [Research on Animate Sources of Power: The Work of Man]', *Annales de l'Institut National Agronomique*, 2nd series, 12, 1913, 1–40.

23 E.C. Main and T.G. Walker, 'Choice Shifts and Extreme Behavior – Judicial Review in the Federal Courts', *Journal of Social Psychology*, 91, 1973, 215–221.

24 William H. Whyte, 'Group Think', *Fortune Magazine*, 1952, republished online on 22 July 2012, http://fortune.com/2012/07/22/groupthink-fort une-1952/, accessed 29 May 2021.

25 Irving Janis, *Victims of Groupthink: A Psychological Study of Foreign-Policy Decisions and Fiascoes* (Boston: Houghton, Mifflin, 1972), 9.

26 Susan M. Sorenson, 'Group-Hate: A Negative Reaction to Group Work', *Annual Meeting of the International Communication Association, Minneapolis, MN*, 21–25 May 1981, https://eric.ed.gov/?id=ED204821, accessed 29 May 2021; Alison Burke, 'Group Work: How to Use Groups Effectively', *The Journal of Effective Teaching*, 11, 2, 2011, 87–95, https://eric.ed.gov/?id= EJ1092109, accessed 29 May 2021.

27 Source: Jo Lewin, '10 Foods to Boost Your Brainpower', *BBC Good Food*, www.bbcgoodfood.com/howto/guide/10-foods-boost-your-brainpower, accessed 29 May 2021.

28 Source: Ben Martynoga, 'How Physical Exercise Makes Your Brian Work Better', *The Guardian*, 18 June 2016, www.theguardian.com/educa- tion/2016/jun/18/how-physical-exercise-makes-your-brain-work-better, accessed 29 May 2021.

29 Source: Gary Small, 'Mind Games: A Mental Workout to Help Keep Your Brain Sharp', *The Guardian*, 13 October 2018, www.theguardian.com/lifeandstyle/2018/oct/13/mental-exercises-to-keep-your-brain-sharp, accessed 29 May 2021.

30 Source: Mo Costandi, 'Can You Boost Your Brain Power by Making Yourself Ambidextrous?', *The Guardian*, 3 September 2016, www.theguardian.com/education/2016/sep/03/can-you-boost-your-brain-power-by-making-yourself-ambidextrous, accessed 29 May 2021.

31 Source: Drake Baer, 'The Scientific Reason Why Barack Obama and Mark Zuckerberg Wear the Same Outfit Everyday', *Business Insider*, 28 April 2015, www.businessinsider.com/barack-obama-mark-zuckerberg-wear-the-same-outfit-2015-4?r=US&IR=T, accessed 29 May 2021.

32 David Robson, 'Has Humanity Reached "Peak Intelligence"?', *BBC Future*, 10 July 2019, www.bbc.com/future/article/20190709-has-humanity-reached-peak-intelligence, accessed 29 May 2021.

33 Source Olivia Solon, 'Elon Musk Says Humans Must Become Cyborgs to Stay Relevant. Is He Right?', *The Guardian*, 15 February 2017, www.theguardian.com/technology/2017/feb/15/elon-musk-cyborgs-robots-artificial-intelligence-is-he-right, accessed 29 May 2021. Also Sarah Marsh, 'Neurotechnology, Elon Musk and the Goal of Human Enhancement', *The Guardian*, 1 January 2018, www.theguardian.com/technology/2018/jan/01/elon-musk-neurotechnology-human-enhancement-brain-computer-interfaces, accessed 29 May 2021. In this interview Ray Kurzweil also considers augmented intelligence as an evolution of brain function – he calls it a 'synthetic neocortex' and he believes that by the 2030s we will have a synthetic neocortex connected to the cloud. Ray Kurzweil, 'Ray Kurzweil on What the Future Holds Next', The Ted Interview, interviewed by Chris Anderson, December 2018, www.ted.com/talks/the_ted_interview_ray_kurzweil_on_what_the_future_holds_next, accessed 29 May 2021.

34 Geoff Mulgan, *Big Mind: How Collective Intelligence Can Change Our World* (Princeton, New Jersey and Oxford: Princeton University Press, 2018), 14. Intelligence category definitions include such things as intelligence testing such as Boring (1923) and cognitive ability such as Herrnstein and Murray (1996). Intelligence is a controversial term because there is no consistent definition and there exists much debate on how it evolved, its physiology, and how it is measured. Standard dictionaries use terms such as understand, reason, think, learn and acquire skills/knowledge. These descriptions fall into loose categories around sense, process and act and

include the ability to learn from past experience and influence the environment with this newly acquired insight; adapt to new situations; and process abstract concepts and ideas.

35 Aaron Masih, 'Augmented Intelligence, Not Artificial Intelligence, Is the Future', *Data Driven Investor*, 2 January 2019, https://medium.datadriveni nvestor.com/augmented-intelligence-not-artificial-intelligence-is-the-fut ure-fo7ada7d4815, accessed 29 May 2021.

36 J. McCarthy, et al., 'A Proposal for the Dartmouth Summer Research Project on Artificial Intelligence', *Stanford Education Website*, 31 August 1955, http://jmc.stanford.edu/articles/dartmouth.html, accessed 29 May 2021.

37 Herbert A. Simon, 'The Theory of Scientific Discovery' in Johann Gőtschl (ed.), *Revolutionary Changes in Understanding Man and Society* (Dordrecht: Springer Science + Business Media, 1995), 55–75, 55.

38 There are modern commentators who still maintain AI is a hype. See Mike Lloyd, 'Don't Believe the Hype: AI is No Silver Bullet', *Computer Weekly*, 7 August 2020, www.computerweekly.com/opinion/Dont-believe-the-hype-AI-is-no-silver-bullet, accessed 29 May 2021.

39 Source: Feng Liu, et al., 'Intelligence Quotient and Intelligence Grade of Artificial Intelligence', *Annals of Data Science*, 4, 2, 2017, 179–191, https://arxiv.org/abs/1709.10242, accessed 29 May 2021. Researchers from Machine Learning Lab Open AI managed to fool intelligent systems with handwritten notes. James Vincent, 'OpenAI's State-of-the-Art Machine Vision AI Is Fooled by Handwritten Notes', *The Verge*, 8 March 2021, www.theverge.com/2021/3/8/22319173/openai-machine-vision-adversarial-typographic-attacka-clip-multimodal-neuron, accessed 29 May 2021.

40

One conversation centered on the ever accelerating progress of technology and changes in the mode of human life, which gives the appearance of approaching some essential singularity in the history of the race beyond which human affairs, as we know them, could not continue.

Stanislaw Ulam, 'John von Neumann 1903–1957',
Bulletin of the American Mathematical Society, 64, 3, 1958, 1–49,
www.ams.org/journals/bull/1958-64-03/ (free pdf access
www.ams.org/journals/bull/1958-64-03/S0002-9904-
1958-10189-5/S0002-9904-1958-10189-5.pdf), 5

41 Source: Ed Lauder, 'Ray Kurzweil Predicts That the Singularity Will Take Place by 2045', *AI Business*, 17 March 2017, https://aibusiness.com/docum ent.asp?doc_id=760200#:~:text=During%20a%20Facebook%20Live%20 stream,human%2Dlevel%20intelligence%20by%202029.&text=I%20h ave%20set%20the%20date,created%2C%22%20wrote%20Ray%20Kurzw eil, accessed 29 May 2021.

42 Source: Antonio Regalado, 'The Brain is Not Computable', *MIT Technology Review*, 18 February 2013, www.technologyreview.com/2013/02/18/180012/ the-brain-is-not-computable/, accessed 29 May 2021.

43 'An Open Letter: Research Priorities for Robust and Beneficial Artificial Intelligence', *Future of Life Institute*, https://futureoflife.org/ai-open-letter, accessed 29 May 2021.

44 A well-respected Forrester report in 2017 asserts that by 2027 AI will displace 24.7 million jobs and create 14.9 million new ones. Source: P. Gownder, et al., 'The Future of Jobs 2027: Working Side By Side With Robots', *Forrester*, 3 April 2017, www.forrester.com/report/The+Future+Of+Jobs+ 2025+Working+Side+By+Side+With+Robots/-/E-RES119861#, accessed 29 May 2021. This is countered by the World Economic Forum (WEF) that believes 60 million jobs will be created by the new technology. Source: Saheli Roy Choudhury, 'A.I. and Robotics Will Create Almost 60 Million More Jobs than They Destroy By 2022, Report Says', *CNBC*, 17 September 2018, www.cnbc.com/2018/09/17/wef-machines-are-going-to-perform-more-tasks-than-humans-by-2025.html, accessed 29 May 2021. A balanced view can be found in the latest MIT, The Work of the Future report. Source: David Autor, et al., 'The Work of the Future: Building Better Jobs in an Age of Intelligent Machines', *MIT Work of the Future*, 17 November 2020, https://workofthefuture.mit.edu/research-post/the-work-of-the-future-building-better-jobs-in-an-age-of-intelligent-machines/, accessed 29 May 2021. Brynjolfsson and McAfee (2017) also give a pragmatic view in their Harvard Business Review Article when they say, 'Over the next decade, AI won't replace managers, but managers who use AI will replace those who don't'. Erik Brynjolfsson and Andrew McAfee, 'The Business of Artificial Intelligence', *Harvard Business Review*, 18 July 2017, https://hbr.org/2017/ 07/the-business-of-artificial-intelligence, accessed 29 May 2021. The impli-cation for mass job displacement by technology could be universal basic income or robot taxes.

45 Sarah Lindenfeld Hall (2019) raises the issue of young children growing up under the influence of smart speakers where kid's first words are 'OK Google'. Sarah Lindenfeld Hall, 'Does Your Kid Think Your Smart Speaker is Just Another Family Member?', *Mashable UK*, 30 November 2019, https://mashable.com/article/kids-and-smart-speakers/?europe=true, accessed 29 May 2021. Professor Frank Gunn-Moore, Director of Research in the School of Biology, University of St Andrews, opines that over-reliance on smart technology could harm our cognitive capacity (source: John Jeffay, 'Using Google Instead of Our Brains Could Increase Our Chances of Getting Dementia, Expert Warns', *Mirror*, 3 December 2017, www.mirror.co.uk/lifestyle/health/using-google-instead-brains-could-11633452, accessed 29 May 2021.

46 Cyberattacks such as the notorious ILOVEYOU computer worm in 2000 caused billions in damages worldwide. Moreover, data analytics and recognition systems based on our predicted health, sexual orientation, lifestyle and political beliefs is already causing privacy concerns. There are growing calls to legislate and curb mass surveillance.

47 Good resource: Stuart Russell and Peter Norvig, *Artificial Intelligence: A Modern Approach* (Hoboken, NJ: Prentice Hall, 1995).

48 Source: James Niccolai, 'Google Says It's 'Rethinking Everything' Around Machine Learning', *PC World*, 23 October 2015, www.pcworld.com/article/2996620/google-reports-strong-profit-says-its-rethinking-everything-around-machine-learning.html, accessed 29 May 2021.

49 Salian, Isha, 'Supervize me: What's the Difference Between Supervised, Unsupervised, Semi-supervised, and Reinforcement Learning', *NVIDIA Blog*, 2 August 2018, https://blogs.nvidia.com/blog/2018/08/02/supervised-unsupervised-learning/, accessed 14 November 2021.

50 Vandit Gupta, 'COVID-19 Detection Using Deep Learning', *International Journal for Modern Trends in Science and Technology*, 6, 12, 421-425, 2020, https://www.researchgate.net/publication/354269856_COVID-19_Detection_using_Deep_Learning, accessed 27 November 2021.

51 John Launchbury, 'A DARPA Perspective of Artificial Intelligence', *Technica Curiosa*, 19 March 2017, https://machinelearning.technicacuriosa.com/2017/03/19/a-darpa-perspective-on-artificial-intelligence/, accessed 29 May 2021.

52 Director of Engineering at Google, Ray Kurzweil, opined that a computer would pass the legendary Turing Test in 2029. In fact, a chatbot, posed as a 13-year old Ukrainian teenager, Eugene Goostman, in June 2014 in a

five-minute chat and fooled 33% of a panel of judges into thinking that he was a real kid. Source: Doug Aamoth, 'Interview with Eugene Goostman, the Fake Kid Who Passed the Turing Test', *Time*, 9 June 2014, https://time.com/2847900/eugene-goostman-turing-test/, accessed 29 May 2021.

53 AIVA (Artificial Intelligence Virtual Artist) is an AI programme that has created original music. See Bartu Kaleagasi, 'A New AI Can Write Music as Well as a Human Composer', *Futurism*, 3 September 2017, https://futurism.com/a-new-ai-can-write-music-as-well-as-a-human-composer, accessed 29 May 2021. There is a rise of AI authors. See Steven Poole, 'The Rise of Robot Authors: Is the Writing on the Wall for Human Novelists?', *The Guardian*, 25 March 2019, www.theguardian.com/books/2019/mar/25/the-rise-of-robot-authors-is-the-writing-on-the-wall-for-human-novelists, accessed 29 May 2021. The University of Tokyo has created a machine that produces original works of art. See Jennifer Kite-Powell, 'This AI Robot Will Paint a Canvas at SXSW 2021', *Forbes*, 10 March 2021, www.forbes.com/sites/jenniferhicks/2021/03/10/this-ai-robot-will-paint-a-canvas-at-sxsw-2021/?sh=37a15a72b449, accessed 29 May 2021.

54 John E. Kelly III, 'Computing, Cognition and the Future of Knowing: How Humans and Machines are Forging a New Age of Understanding', *IBM Corporation*, 2015, www.academia.edu/24586152/Computing_cognition_and_the_future_of_knowing_How_humans_and_machines_are_forging_a_new_age_of_understanding, accessed 29 May 2021, 2.

55 In China, for example, AI defeated a team of elite doctors in both speed and accuracy rate, in a neuroimaging recognition contest. Source: Wang Xiaodong, 'AI Defeats Top Doctors in Competition', *China Daily*, 2 July 2018, http://usa.chinadaily.com.cn/a/201807/02/WS5b397076a31033491 41e006b.html, accessed 29 May 2021.

56 Good source: Thor Olavsrud, 'Decision Support Systems: Sifting Data for Better Business Decisions', *CIO*, 29 May 2020, www.cio.com/article/3545813/decision-support-systems-sifting-data-for-better-business-decisions.html, accessed 29 May 2021.

57 CEO of Unanimous AI, Louis Rosenberg recently co-authored an article in California Management Review where it is argued that 'ASI also automatically captures extensive real-time data about individual and swarm behavior as the group converges upon a decision. These data can be used to provide rapid feedback to swarm participants'. Lynn Metcalf, et al., 'Keeping Humans in the Loop: Pooling Knowledge through Artificial Swarm Intelligence to Improve Business Decision Making', *2019, California*

Management Review, 1–26, 18. This technology is further described in conference proceedings Gregg Willcox, et al., 'Analysis of Human Behaviors in Real-Time Swarms', in *10th Annual Computing and Communication Workshop and Conference (CCWC)*, 2020, www.semanticscholar.org/paper/ Analysis-of-Human-Behaviors-in-Real-Time-Swarms-Willcox-Rosenberg/ aec4cf3886d15c8c6450db05418bd196883dde65, accessed 29 May 2021.

58 'Swarm: Get Smarter Together', Unanimous AI, https://unanimous.ai/ swarm/, accessed 29 May 2021.

59 Salesforce research, for example, discovered that 62% of customers said they would consider using AI to improve their experience. 'State of the Connected Customer', in *Salesforce Report*, 2019, https://c1.sfdcstatic. com/content/dam/web/en_us/www/assets/pdf/salesforce-state-of-the- connected-customer-report-2019.pdf, accessed 29 May 2021, 16.

60 'Davos 2017 – An Insight, An Idea with Ginni Rometty', Interview, *You Tube*, interviewed by Fareed Zakaria, posted by *World Economic Forum*, 16 January 2017, www.youtube.com/watch?v=mNEQsl1-iZs, accessed 29 May 2021.

61 Thomas Ricker, 'Elon Musk: We're Already Cyborgs', *The Verge*, 2 June 2016, www.theverge.com/2016/6/2/11837854/neural-lace-cyborgs-elon-musk, accessed 29 May 2021.

62 Paul J.H. Schoemaker and Philip E. Tetlock, 'Building a More Intelligent Enterprise', *MIT Sloan Management Review*, 2017, Spring, 58/3.

63 'Artificial Intelligence (AI) Market worth $306.6 Billion by 2026', *Markets and Markets*, Press Release, www.marketsandmarkets.com/PressReleases/ artificial-intelligence.asp%20.asp, accessed 29 May 2021.

64 'Gartner Says AI Augmentation Will Create $2.9 Trillion of Business Value in 2021', *Gartner*, Press Release, 5 August 2019, www.gartner.com/en/ newsroom/press-releases/2019-08-05-gartner-says-ai-augmentation- will-create-2point9-trillion-of-business-value-in-2021, accessed 29 May 2021.

65 'Powering the Future of the Customer Experience', *Microsoft Features*, 8 November 2017, https://news.microsoft.com/europe/features/ai-power ing-customer-experience/, accessed 29 May 2021.

66 Benedict Dellot et al. argue 'Sensors may one day be so small and cheap that they become ubiquitous, meaning everything from what we eat, to the way we work, to how we shop can be monitored and analysed'. Benedict Dellot, Rich Mason, and Fabian Wallace-Stephens, 'The Four Futures of Work', March 2019, www.thersa.org/globalassets/pdfs/reports/rsa_four- futures-of-work.pdf, accessed 29 May 2021, 33.

67 Source: 'Forecast End-User Spending on IOT Solutions Worldwide from 2017 to 2025', *Statista*, www.statista.com/statistics/976313/global-iot-market-size/, accessed 29 May 2021.

68 'Leveraging the Upcoming Disruptions from AI and IOT', *PWC*, 2017, www.pwc.com/gx/en/industries/communications/assets/pwc-ai-and-iot.pdf, accessed 29 May 2021, 14.

69 'eYeka Releases "The State of Crowdsourcing in 2015 Trend Report"', *eYeka*, 9 April 2015, https://eyeka.pr.co/99215-eyeka-releases-the-state-of-crowdsourcing-in-2015-trend-report, accessed 29 May 2021.

70 Influenced on this point by 'Defining Workforce 2025', *Vodafone Blog*, www.vodafone.com/business/news-and-insights/blog/gigabit-thinking/defining-workforce-2025, accessed 29 May 2021.

71 Source: Laurence Goasduff, 'Gartner: Top 10 Trends in Data and Analytics for 2020', 19 October 2020, www.gartner.com/smarterwithgartner/gartner-top-10-trends-in-data-and-analytics-for-2020/, accessed 29 May 2021.

72 'Team Collaboration Software Market to Reach USD 35.71 Billion by 2027; Trend of BYOD among Small & Medium-Sized Companies to Aid Growth', *Fortune Business Insights/Intrado GlobeNewswire*, 9 October 2020, www.globenewswire.com/news-release/2020/10/09/2106440/0/en/Team-Collaboration-Software-Market-to-Reach-USD-35-71-Billion-by-2027-Trend-of-BYOD-among-Small-Medium-sized-Companies-to-Aid-Growth.html, accessed 29 May 2021.

73 Janna Anderson, et al. 'Experts Say the "New Normal" in 2025 Will Be Far More Tech-Driven, Presenting More Big Challenges', *Pew Research Center*, 18 February 2021, www.pewresearch.org/internet/2021/02/18/experts-say-the-new-normal-in-2025-will-be-far-more-tech-driven-presenting-more-big-challenges/, accessed 29 May 2021.

74 For example, Navid Tavanapour and Eva Bittner, 'Automated Facilitation for Idea Platforms: Design and Evaluation of a Chatbot Prototype', in *Conference Proceedings at San Francisco: Thirty Ninth International Conference on Information Systems (ICIS)*, October 2018, www.researchgate.net/publication/328145863_Automated_Facilitation_for_Idea_Platforms_Design_and_Evaluation_of_a_Chatbot_Prototype, accessed 29 May 2021. They see chatbot facilitators as providing greater steer and direction on idea platforms. Other good resources chatbot facilitators include Soomin Kim, et al., 'Bot in the Bunch: Facilitating Group Chat Discussion by Improving Efficiency and Participation with a Chatbot', in *Proceedings of the 2020 CHI*

Conference on Human Factors in Computing Systems, April 2020, https:// dl.acm.org/doi/fullHtml/10.1145/3313831.3376785, accessed 29 May 2021, 1–13; Eva Bittner and Omid Shoury, 'Designing Automated Facilitation for Design Thinking: A Chatbot for Supporting Teams in the Empathy Map Method', in *Proceedings of the 52nd Hawaii International Conference on System Sciences*, 2019, https://scholarspace.manoa.hawaii.edu/bitstream/ 10125/59463/0023.pdf, accessed 29 May 2021.

75 Source: Steve Morgan, 'The World Will Store 200 Zettabytes of Data By 2025', *Cybercrime Magazine*, 8 June 2020, https://cybersecurityventures. com/the-world-will-store-200-zettabytes-of-data-by-2025/, accessed 29 May 2021.

76 See Y.R. Shrestha, et al., 'Organizational Decision-Making Structures in the Age of Artificial Intelligence', *California Management Review*, 61, 4, 2019, 66–83, https://journals.sagepub.com/doi/abs/10.1177/0008125619862 257?journalCode=cmra, accessed 29 May 2021. Also, Yanqing Duan, et al., 'Artificial Intelligence for Decision Making in the Era of Big Data – Evolution, Challenges and Research Agenda', *International Journal of Information Management*, 48, 2019, 63–71, www.sciencedirect.com/science/article/ abs/pii/S0268401219300581, accessed 29 May 2021.

77 Source: Ian Sample, 'Universal Internet Access Unlikely until At Least 2050, Experts Say', *The Guardian*, 10 January 2019, www.theguardian.com/tech-nology/2019/jan/10/universal-internet-access-unlikely-until-2050-experts-say-lack-skills-investment-slow-growth, accessed 29 May 2021.

78 Good source: Daniel Nations, 'What Does "Web 2.0" Even Mean?', *Lifewire*, 24 February 2020, www.lifewire.com/what-is-web-2-0-p2-3486624, accessed 29 May 2021.

79 Good source: Mayur Shewale, 'What Is the Spatial Web and How It Will Transform the Internet?', *MirrorReview*, www.mirrorreview.com/what-is-the-spatial-web-and-how-it-will-transform-the-internet/, accessed 29 May 2021.

80 An IMEC piece considered how augmented reality glasses will be com-monplace by 2035. This is the part-inspiration for Chapter 7's use of smart glasses. Source: 'Will We Be Trading in Our Smartphone for Augmented Reality Glasses by 2035?', *IMEC*, www.imec-int.com/en/imec-turns-35-in-2019/augmented-reality-glasses, accessed 29 May 2021.

81 James Bellini cited in Sian Traynor, 'Hologram Pizza Restaurant to Open in Edinburgh to Connect Loved Ones Apart Due to Covid', *EdinburghLive*, 15

April 2021, www.edinburghlive.co.uk/best-in-edinburgh/hologram-pizza-restaurant-open-edinburgh-20396613, accessed 29 May 2021.

82 'Work 2035: Citrix Research Reveals a More Intelligent Future', *Business Wire*, 21 September 2020, www.businesswire.com/news/home/20200 921005041/en/Work-2035-Citrix-Research-Reveals-a-More-Intelligent-Future, accessed 29 May 2021.

83 Good source: Jesus Mantas, 'Empathic AI Could Be the Next Stage in Human Evolution – If We Get It Right', *World Economic Forum*, 2 July 2019, www.weforum.org/agenda/2019/07/empathic-ai-could-be-the-next-stage-in-human-evolution-if-we-get-it-right/, accessed 29 May 2021.

84 Source: Aaron Holmes, 'Facial Recognition Is on the Rise, but Artificial Intelligence Is Already Being Trained to Recognize Humans in New Ways – Including Gait Detection and Heartbeat Sensors', *Business Insider*, 29 October 2019, www.businessinsider.com/ai-training-beyond-facial-recognition-gait-detection-heartbeat-sensors-2019-10?r=US&IR=T, accessed 29 May 2021.

85 Source: James Vincent, 'AI "Emotion Recognition" Can't Be Trusted', *The Verge*, 25 July 2019, www.theverge.com/2019/7/25/8929793/emotion-recognition-analysis-ai-machine-learning-facial-expression-review, accessed 29 May 2021.

86 'Global Smart Wearables Market Outlook 2025: COVID-19, Opportunities, Future Trends and Investment Analysis', *Research and Markets/Intrado GlobalNewswire*, 17 November 2020, www.globenewswire.com/news-release/2020/11/17/2128183/0/en/Global-Smart-Wearables-Market-Outlook-2025-COVID-19-Opportunities-Future-Trends-and-Investment-Analysis.html, accessed 29 May 2021.

87 Christian Matt, et al., 'The Digitization of the Individual: Conceptual Foundations and Opportunities for Research', *Electron Markets*, 29, 2019, 315–322.

Bibliography

Aamoth, Doug, 'Interview with Eugene Goostman, the Fake Kid Who Passed the Turing Test', *Time*, 9 June 2014, https://time.com/2847900/eugene-goostman-turing-test/, accessed 29 May 2021.

Agarwal, Pragya, *Sway: Unravelling Unconscious Bias* (London: Bloomsbury Sigma, 2020).

Allport, Flloyd H., 'The Influence of the Group upon Association and Thought', *Journal of Experimental Psychology*, 1920, 3, 3:159–182.

Anderson, Janna, Raine, Lee, and Vogels, Emily A., 'Experts Say the 'New Normal' in 2025 Will Be Far More Tech-Driven, Presenting More Big Challenges', *Pew Research Center*, 18 February 2021, www.pewresearch.org/internet/2021/02/18/experts-say-the-new-normal-in-2025-will-be-far-more-tech-driven-presenting-more-big-challenges/, accessed 29 May 2021.

Autor, David, Mindell, David, and Reynolds, Elisabeth, 'The Work of the Future: Building Better Jobs in an Age of Intelligent Machines', *MIT Work of the Future*, 17 November 2020, https://workofthefuture.mit.edu/research-post/the-work-of-the-future-building-better-jobs-in-an-age-of-intelligent-machines/, accessed 29 May 2021.

Baer, Drake, 'The Scientific Reason Why Barack Obama and Mark Zuckerberg Wear the Same Outfit Everyday', *Business Insider*, 28 April 2015, www.businessinsider.com/barack-obama-mark-zuckerberg-wear-the-same-outfit-2015-4?r=US&IR=T, accessed 29 May 2021.

Bechara Antoine, Damasio Hanna, Tranel Daniel, and Damasio Antonio R., 'Deciding Advantageously Before Knowing the Advantageous Strategy', *Science*, New Series, Vol 275, No. 5304, February 1997, 1293–1295.

Beebe, William, *Edge of the Jungle* (New York, NY: Henry Holt and Co., 1921).

Bittner, Eva A. and Shoury, Omid, 'Designing Automated Facilitation for Design Thinking: A Chatbot for Supporting Teams in the Empathy Map Method', in *Proceedings of the 52nd Hawaii International Conference on System Sciences*, 2019, https://scholarspace.manoa.hawaii.edu/bitstream/10125/59463/0023.pdf, accessed 29 May 2021.

Bonabeau, Eric, 'Decisions 2.0: The Power of Collective Intelligence', *MIT Sloan Management Review*, 9 January 2009, https://sloanreview.mit.edu/article/decisions-20-the-power-of-collective-intelligence/, accessed 29 May 2021.

Boring, Edwin G., 'Intelligence as the Tests Test It', *New Republic*, 1923, 36:35–37.

Brynjolfsson, Erik and McAfee, Andrew, 'The Business of Artificial Intelligence', *Harvard Business Review*, 18 July 2017, https://hbr.org/2017/07/the-business-of-artificial-intelligence, accessed 29 May 2021.

Burke, Alison, 'Group Work: How to Use Groups Effectively', *The Journal of Effective Teaching*, 2011, 11 (2):87–95, https://eric.ed.gov/?id=EJ1092109, accessed 29 May 2021.

Burrow, Trigant, *The Social Basis of Consciousness. A Study in Organic Psychology Based upon a Synthetic and Societal Concept of the Neuroses* (New York, NY: Harcourt, Brace & Co. Inc., 1927) Preface, XV–XVIII.

Chabris, Christopher and Simons, Daniel, *The Invisible Gorilla: And Other Ways Our Intuition Deceives Us* (London: HarperCollins, 2010).

Choudhury, Saheli R., 'A.I. and Robotics Will Create Almost 60 Million More Jobs Than They Destroy By 2022, Report Says', *CNBC*, 17 September 2018, www.cnbc.com/2018/09/17/wef-machines-are-going-to-perform-more-tasks-than-humans-by-2025.html, accessed 29 May 2021.

Costandi, Mo, 'Can You Boost Your Brain Power by Making Yourself Ambidextrous?', *The Guardian*, 3 September 2016, www.theguardian.com/education/2016/sep/03/can-you-boost-your-brain-power-by-making-yourself-ambidextrous, accessed 29 May 2021.

Damasio, Antonio R., *Descartes' Error: Emotion, Reason and the Human Brain* (New York, NY: G.P. Putman, 1994).

de Condorcet, Marquis, *Essai sur l'application de l'analyse à la probabilité des décisions rendues à la pluralité des voix* [*Essay on the Application of Analysis to the Probability of Majority Decisions*] (Paris: De L'Imprimerie Royale, 1785).

Dellot, Benedict, Mason, Rich, and Wallace-Stephens, Fabian, *The Four Futures of Work*, March 2019, www.thersa.org/globalassets/pdfs/reports/rsa_four-futures-of-work.pdf, accessed 29 May 2021.

Duan, Yanqing, Edwards, John S., and Dwivedi, Yogesh K., 'Artificial Intelligence for Decision Making in the Era of Big Data – Evolution, Challenges and Research Agenda', *International Journal of Information Management*, 2019, 48:63–71, www.sciencedirect.com/science/article/abs/pii/S0268401219300581, accessed 29 May 2021.

Duffy, Maureen Whelehan, 'Sensemaking in Classroom Conversations', in *Openness in Research: The Tension between Self and Other*, eds. Ilja Maso, Paul A. Atkinson, and Sara Delamont (Assen: Van Gorcum, 1995) 119–132.

Flegal, Kristin and Anderson, Michael. 'Overthinking Skilled Motor Performance: Or Why Those Who Teach Can't Do', *Psychonomic Bulletin & Review*, 2008, 15, 5:927–932.

Gabora, Liane and Russon, Anne, 'The Evolution of Intelligence', in *The Cambridge Handbook of Intelligence*, eds. Robert Sternberg and Scott Kaufman (Cambridge: Cambridge University Press, 2011) 328–350.

Galton, Francis, 'Vox Populi', *Nature*, 1907, Volume 75, 450–451.

Gardner, Howard, *Frames of Mind: The Theory of Multiple Intelligences* (London: Fontana, 1993).

Gierer, Alfred, 'Human Brain Evolution, Theories of Innovation, and Lessons from the History of Technology', *Journal of Bioscience*, 2004, 29:235–244.

Gladwell, Malcolm, *Blink: The Power of Thinking without Thinking* (New York, NY: Little Brown Company, 2007).

Gladwell, Malcolm, *Outliers: The Story of Success* (London: Penguin Books, 2008).

Goasduff, Laurence, *Gartner: Top 10 Trends in Data and Analytics for 2020*, 19 October 2020, www.gartner.com/smarterwithgartner/gartner-top-10-trends-in-data-and-analytics-for-2020/, accessed 29 May 2021.

Goleman, Daniel, *Emotional Intelligence: Why It Can Matter More than IQ* (New York, NY: Bantam Books, 1997).

Gownder, JP., Koetzle, Laura, Condon, Cliff, McNabb, Kyle, Voce, Christopher, Bartels, Andrew, Goetz, Michele, Hoar, Andy, Garberg, Clare, and Lynch, Diane, 'The Future of Jobs 2027: Working Side By Side With Robots', *Forrester*, 3 April 2017, www.forrester.com/report/The+Future+Of+Jobs+2025+Working+Side+By+Side+With+Robots/-/E-RES119861#, accessed 29 May 2021.

Gregory, Richard L., *The Oxford Companion to the Mind. Oxford University Press* (Oxford: Oxford University Press, 1998).

Gupta, Vandit, 'COVID-19 Detection Using Deep Learning', *International Journal for Modern Trends in Science and Technology*, 6, 12, 421–425, 2020, https://www.researchgate.net/publication/354269856_COVID-19_Detection_using_Deep_Learning, accessed 29 May 2021.

Hansen, James R., *First Man: The Life of Neil A. Armstrong* (New York, NY: Simon & Schuster, 2005).

Herrnstein, Richard J. and Murray, Charles, *The Bell Curve: Intelligence and Class Structure in American Life* (New York, NY: Free Press, 1996).

Holmes, Aaron, 'Facial Recognition is on the Rise, But Artificial Intelligence is Already Being Trained to Recognize Humans in New Ways – Including Gait Detection and Heartbeat Sensors', *Business Insider*, 29 October 2019, www.businessinsider.com/ai-training-beyond-facial-recognition-gait-detection-heartbeat-sensors-2019-10?r=US&IR=T, accessed 29 May 2021.

Howe, Jeff, 'The Rise of Crowdsourcing', *Wired*, 1 June 2006, www.wired.com/2006/06/crowds/, accessed 29 May 2021.

Janis, Irving, *Victims of Groupthink: A Psychological Study of Foreign-Policy Decisions and Fiascoes* (Boston: Houghton, Mifflin, 1972).

Jeffay, John, 'Using Google Instead of our Brains Could Increase Our Chances of Getting Dementia, Expert Warns', *Mirror*, 3 December 2017, www.mirror.co.uk/lifestyle/health/using-google-instead-brains-could-11633452, accessed 29 May 2021.

Kahneman, Daniel, *Thinking, Fast and Slow* (New York, NY: Farrar, Straus and Giroux, 2011).

Kaleagasi, Bartu, 'A New AI Can Write Music as Well as a Human Composer', *Futurism*, 3 September 2017, https://futurism.com/a-new-ai-can-write-music-as-well-as-a-human-composer, accessed 29 May 2021.

Kelly, John E. III, 'Computing, Cognition and the Future of Knowing: How Humans and Machines Are Forging a New Age of Understanding', *IBM Corporation*, 2015, www.academia.edu/24586152/Computing_cognition_and_the_future_of_knowing_How_humans_and_machines_are_forging_a_new_age_of_understanding, accessed 29 May 2021.

Kim, Soomin, Eun, Jinsu, Oh, Changhoon, Suh, Bongwon, and Lee, Joonhwan, 'Bot in the Bunch: Facilitating Group Chat Discussion by Improving Efficiency and Participation with a Chatbot', in *Proceedings of the 2020 CHI Conference on Human Factors in Computing Systems*, April 2020, https://dl.acm.org/doi/fullHtml/10.1145/3313831.3376785, accessed 29 May 2021, 1–13.

Kite-Powell, Jennifer, 'This AI Robot Will Paint a Canvas at SXSW 2021', *Forbes*, 10 March 2021, www.forbes.com/sites/jenniferhicks/2021/03/10/this-ai-robot-will-paint-a-canvas-at-sxsw-2021/?sh=37a15a72b449, accessed 29 May 2021.

Klein, Gary, Moon, Brian, and Hoffman, Robert, 'Making Sense of Sensemaking 1: Alternative Perspectives', *Intelligent Systems*, 2006, 21, 4:70–73, www.researchgate.net/publication/3454348_Making_Sense_of_Sensemaking_1_Alternative_Perspectives, accessed 29 May 2021.

Klein, Gary and Snowden, David, 'Anticipatory Thinking', in *Informed by Knowledge Expert Performance in Complex Situations*, January 2011, www.researchgate.net/publication/228953044_Anticipatory_Thinking, accessed 29 May 2021.

Latané, Bibb, Williams, Kipling, and Harkins, Stephen, 'Many Hands Make Light the Work: The Causes and Consequences of Social Loafing', *Journal of Personality and Social Psychology*, 1979, 37 (6):822–832.

Lauder, Ed, 'Ray Kurzweil Predicts That the Singularity Will Take Place by 2045', *AI Business*, 17 March, 2017, https://aibusiness.com/document.asp?doc_id=760200#:~:text=During%20a%20Facebook%20Live%20stream,human%2Dlevel%20intelligence%20by%202029.&text=I%20have%20set%20the%20date,created%2C%22%20wrote%20Ray%20Kurzweil, accessed 29 May 2021.

Launchbury, John, 'A DARPA Perspective of Artificial Intelligence', *Technica Curiosa*, 19 March 2917, https://machinelearning.technicacuriosa.com/2017/03/19/a-darpa-perspective-on-artificial-intelligence/, accessed 29 May 2021.

Lewin, Jo, '10 Foods to Boost Your Brainpower', *BBC Good Food*, 21 January 2020, www.bbcgoodfood.com/howto/guide/10-foods-boost-your-brain-power, accessed 29 May 2021.

Lewin, Kurt, Lippit, Ronald, and White, Ralph K., 'Patterns of Aggressive Behavior in Experimentally Created Social Climates', *Journal of Social Psychology*, 1939, 10:271–301.

Leyer, Michael and Schneider, Sabrina, 'Decision Augmentation and Automation with Artificial Intelligence: Threat or Opportunity for Managers?', *Business Horizons*, 4 February 2021, www.sciencedirect.com/science/article/abs/pii/S0007681321000288?via%3Dihub, accessed 29 May 2021.

Lindenfeld Hall, Sarah, 'Does Your Kid Think Your Smart Speaker is Just Another Family Member?', *Mashable UK*, 30 November 2019, https://mashable.com/article/kids-and-smart-speakers/?europe=true, accessed 29 May 2021.

Liu, Feng, Shi, Yong, and Liu, Ying, 'Intelligence Quotient and Intelligence Grade of Artificial Intelligence', *Annals of Data Science*, 2017, 4 (2):179–191, https://arxiv.org/abs/1709.10242, accessed 29 May 2021.

Lloyd, Mike, 'Don't Believe the Hype: AI is No Silver Bullet', *Computer Weekly*, 7 August 2020, www.computerweekly.com/opinion/Dont-believe-the-hype-AI-is-no-silver-bullet, accessed 29 May 2021.

Main, Eleanor C. and Walker, Thomas G., 'Choice Shifts and Extreme Behavior – Judicial Review in the Federal Courts', *Journal of Social Psychology*, 1973, 91:215–221.

Mantas, Jesus, 'Empathic AI Could Be the Next Stage in Human Evolution – If We Get it Right', *World Economic Forum*, 2 July 2019, www.weforum.org/agenda/2019/07/empathic-ai-could-be-the-next-stage-in-human-evolution-if-we-get-it-right/, accessed 29 May 2021.

Marsh, Sarah, 'Neurotechnology, Elon Musk and the Goal of Human Enhancement', *The Guardian*, 1 January 2018, www.theguardian.com/technology/2018/jan/01/elon-musk-neurotechnology-human-enhancement-brain-computer-interfaces, accessed 29 May 2021.

Martynoga, Ben, 'How Physical Exercise Makes Your Brian Work Better', *The Guardian*, 18 June 2016, www.theguardian.com/education/2016/jun/18/how-physical-exercise-makes-your-brain-work-better, accessed 29 May 2021.

Masih, Aaron, 'Augmented Intelligence, Not Artificial Intelligence, is the Future', *Data Driven Investor*, 2 January 2019, https://medium.datadriveninvestor.com/augmented-intelligence-not-artificial-intelligence-is-the-future-f07ada7d4815, accessed 29 May 2021.

Maso, Ilja, Atkinson, Paul, Delamont, Sara, and Verhoeven, Jef, *Openness in Research: The Tension between Self and Other* (Assen: Van Gorcum, 1995).

Matt, Christian, Trenz, Manuel, Cheung, Christy M.K., and Turel, Ofir. 'The Digitization of the Individual: Conceptual Foundations and Opportunities for Research', *Electron Markets*, 2019, 29:315–322.

Matzler, Kurt, Bailom, Franz, and Mooradian, Todd A., 'Intuitive Decision Making', *MIT Sloan Management Review*, 1 October 2007, https://sloanreview.mit.edu/article/intuitive-decision-making/, accessed 29 May 2021.

Mayo, Elton, *The Human Problems of an Industrial Civilization*, Volume 6, The Early Sociology of Management and Organisations (New York, NY: The Macmillan Co., 1933).

McCarthy, John, Minsky, Marvin L., Rochester, Nathanial, and Shannon, Claude E., 'A Proposal for the Dartmouth Summer Research Project on Artificial Intelligence', *Stanford Education Website*, 31 August 1955, http://jmc.stanford.edu/articles/dartmouth.html, accessed 20 November 2021.

McDougal, William, *The Group Mind. A Sketch of the Principles of Collective Psychology, with Some Attempt to Apply Them to the Interpretation of National Life and Character* (Cambridge: Cambridge University Press, 1920).

Metcalf, Lynn, Askay, David A., and Rosenberg, Louis B., 'Keeping Humans in the Loop: Pooling Knowledge through Artificial Swarm Intelligence to Improve Business Decision Making', 2019, *California Management Review*, Volume 61, Issue 4, 84–109.

Miller, George A. 'The Magical Number Seven, Plus or Minus Two: Some Limits on Our Capacity for Processing Information', *Psychological Review*, 1956, 63(2):81–97.

Moreno, Jacob L., *Who Shall Survive: A New Approach to the Problem of Human Interrelations* (Washington, DC: Nervous and Mental Disease Publishing Co., 1934).

Morgan, Steve, 'The World Will Store 200 Zettabytes of Data By 2025', *Cybercrime Magazine*, 8 June 2020, https://cybersecurityventures.com/the-world-will-store-200-zettabytes-of-data-by-2025/, accessed 29 May 2021.

Mulgan, Geoff, *Big Mind: How Collective Intelligence Can Change Our World* (Princeton, NJ: Princeton University Press, 2018).

Nations, Daniel, 'What Does "Web 2.0" Even Mean?', *Lifewire*, 24 February 2020, www.lifewire.com/what-is-web-2-0-p2-3486624, accessed 29 May 2021.

Nave Gideon, Jung, Wi Hoon, Karlsson Linnér, Richard , Kable, Josoph W., and Koellinger, Philipp D., 'Are Bigger Brains Smarter? Evidence from a Large-Scale Preregistered Study', *Science of Psychology*, 2019, 30 (1): 43–54, https://journals.sagepub.com/doi/full/10.1177/0956797618808470, accessed 29 May 2021.

Niccolai, James, 'Google Says It's 'Rethinking Everything' Around Machine Learning', *PC World*, 23 October 2015, www.pcworld.com/article/2996620/google-reports-strong-profit-says-its-rethinking-everything-around-machine-learning.html, accessed 29 May 2021.

Olavsrud, Thor, 'Decision Support Systems: Sifting Data for Better Business Decisions', *CIO*, 29 May 2020, www.cio.com/article/3545813/decision-support-systems-sifting-data-for-better-business-decisions.html, accessed 29 May 2021.

Paulus, Paul B. and Nijstad, Bernard A., *Group Creativity: Innovation through Collaboration* (Oxford: Oxford University Press, 2003).

Peters Ruth, 'Ageing and the Brain', *Postgraduate Medical Journal*, 2006, 82 (964):84–88.

Poole, Steven, 'The Rise of Robot Authors: Is the Writing on the Wall for Human Novelists?', *The Guardian*, 25 March 2019, www.theguardian.com/books/2019/mar/25/the-rise-of-robot-authors-is-the-writing-on-the-wall-for-human-novelists, accessed 29 May 2021.

Regalado, Antonio, 'The Brain is not Computable', *MIT Technology Review*, 18 February 2013, www.technologyreview.com/2013/02/18/180012/the-brain-is-not-computable/, accessed 29 May 2021.

Ricker, Thomas, 'Elon Musk: We're Already Cyborgs', *The Verge*, 2 June 2016, www.theverge.com/2016/6/2/11837854/neural-lace-cyborgs-elon-musk, accessed 29 May 2021.

Rincon, Jaime Andres, Costa, Angelo, Novais, Paulo, Julián, Vicente, and Carrascosa, Carlos, 'Using Non-Invasive Wearables for Detecting Emotions with Intelligent Agents', in *Conference: 11th International Conference on Soft Computing Models in Industrial and Environmental Applications at San Sebastian, Spain*, Vol. 527, October 2016, www.researchgate.net/publication/309380085_Using_Non-invasive_Wearables_for_Detecting_Emotions_with_Intelligent_Agents, accessed 29 May 2021.

Ringelmann, Max, 'Recherches sur les moteurs animés: Travail de l'homme' [Research on Animate Sources of Power: The Work of Man]', *Annales de l'Institut National Agronomique*, 1913, 2nd series, 12:1–40.

Robson, David, 'Has Humanity Reached "Peak Intelligence"?', *BBC Future*, 10 July 2019, www.bbc.com/future/article/20190709-has-humanity-reached-peak-intelligence, accessed 29 May 2021.

Russell, Stuart and Norvig, Peter, *Artificial Intelligence: A Modern Approach* (Hoboken, NJ: Prentice Hall, 1995).

Sagan, Carl, *Dragons of Eden: Speculations on the Evolution of Human Intelligence* (New York, NY: Ballantine Books, 1977).

Salian, Isha, 'SuperVize Me: What's the Difference between Supervised, Unsupervised, Semi-Supervised and Reinforcement Learning?', *NVIDIA Blog*, 2 August 2018, https://blogs.nvidia.com/blog/2018/08/02/supervised-unsupervised-learning/, accessed 29 May 2021.

Sample, Ian, 'Universal Internet Access Unlikely until At Least 2050, Experts Say', *The Guardian*, 10 January 2019, www.theguardian.com/technology/2019/jan/10/universal-internet-access-unlikely-until-2050-experts-say-lack-skills-investment-slow-growth, accessed 29 May 2021.

Schoemaker, Paul J.H. and Tetlock, Philip E., 'Building a More Intelligent Enterprise', *MIT Sloan Management Review*, 2017, Spring (58/3), https://sloanreview.mit.edu/article/building-a-more-intelligent-enterprise/, accessed 21 October 2021.

Seeley, Thomas D., *Honeybee Democracy* (Princeton, NJ: Princeton University Press, 2010).

Shewale, Mayur, 'What Is the Spatial Web and How It Will Transform the Internet?', *Mirro R*, 2021, www.mirrorreview.com/what-is-the-spatial-web-and-how-it-will-transform-the-internet/, accessed 29 May 2021.

Shiffrin, Richard and Nosofsky, Robert, 'Seven Plus or Minus Two: A Commentary on Capacity Limitations', *Psychological Review*, 1994, 2 (101 (Centennial)):357–361.

Shrestha, Yash Raj, Ben-Menahem, Shiko M., and von Krogh, Georg, 'Organizational Decision-Making Structures in the Age of Artificial Intelligence', *California Management Review*, 2019, 61 (4): 66–83, https://journals.sagepub.com/doi/abs/10.1177/0008125619862257?journalCode=cmra, accessed 29 May 2021.

Simon, Herbert A., 'The Theory of Scientific Discovery', in *Revolutionary Changes in Understanding Man and Society*, ed. Johann Gőtschl (Dordrecht: Springer Science + Business Media, 1995) 55–75.

Small, Gary, 'Mind Games: A Mental Workout to Help Keep Your Brain Sharp', *The Guardian*, 13 October 2018, www.theguardian.com/lifeandstyle/2018/oct/13/mental-exercises-to-keep-your-brain-sharp, accessed 29 May 2021.

Sorenson, Susan M., 'Group-Hate: A Negative Reaction to Group Work', in Annual Meeting of the International Communication Association *Minneapolis, MN*, 21–25 May 1981, https://eric.ed.gov/?id=ED204821, accessed 29 May 2021.

Strathearn, Carl, 'Can Machines Think? A New Turing Test May Have the Answer', *World Economic Forum*, 2 August 2019, www.weforum.org/agenda/2019/08/our-turing-test-for-androids-will-judge-how-lifelike-humanoid-robots-can-be/, accessed 29 May 2021.

Surowiecki, James, *The Wisdom of Crowds* (New York: Anchor Books, 2015).

Tavanapour, Navid and Bittner, Eva, 'Automated Facilitation for Idea Platforms: Design and Evaluation of a Chatbot Prototype', in *Conference Proceedings at San Francisco: Thirty Ninth International Conference on Information Systems (ICIS)*, October 2018, www.researchgate.net/publication/328145863_Automated_Facilitation_for_Idea_Platforms_Design_and_Evaluation_of_a_Chatbot_Prototype, accessed 29 May 2021.

Tegmark, Max, *Life 3.0: Being Human in the Age of Artificial Intelligence* (London: Allen Lane, 2017).

Trafton, Anne, 'In the Blink of an Eye', *MIT News*, 16 January 2014, https://news.mit.edu/2014/in-the-blink-of-an-eye-0116, accessed 29 May 2021.

Traynor, Sian, 'Hologram Pizza Restaurant to Open in Edinburgh to Connect Loved Ones Apart Due to Covid', *EdinburghLive*, 15 April 2021, www.edinburghlive.co.uk/best-in-edinburgh/hologram-pizza-restaurant-open-edinburgh-20396613, accessed 29 May 2021.

Treynor, Jack, 'Market Efficiency and the Bean Jar Experiment', *Financial Analysts Journal*, 1987, 43 (3), 50–53.

Triplett, Norman, 'The dynamogenic factors in pacemaking and competition.' *The American Journal of Psychology*, 1898, 9 (4), 507–533, https://www.jstor.org/stable/pdf/1412188.pdf, accessed 23 August 2021.

Turing, Alan M., 'Computing Machinery and Intelligence', *Mind*, 1950, LIX (236):433–460.

Tversky, Amos and Kahneman, Daniel, 'Judgment under Uncertainty: Heuristics and Biases', *Science*, 1974, 185 (4157):1124–1131.

Van Mulukom, Valerie, 'Is It Rational to Trust Your Gut Feelings? A Neuroscientist Explains', *The Conversation*, 16 May 2018, https://theconversation.com/is-it-rational-to-trust-your-gut-feelings-a-neuroscientist-explains-95086, accessed 29 May 2021.

Vincent, James, 'AI "Emotion Recognition" Can't Be Trusted', *The Verge*, 25 July 2019, www.theverge.com/2019/7/25/8929793/emotion-recognition-analysis-ai-machine-learning-facial-expression-review, accessed 29 May 2021.

Vinge, Vernor, 'The Coming Technological Singularity', in Vision-21: Interdisciplinary Science & Engineering in the Era of CyberSpace, Proceedings of a Symposium Held at NASA Lewis Research Center (NASA Conference Publication *CP-10129*), March 1993, 30–31.

Wang, Xiaodong, 'AI Defeats Top Doctors in Competition', *China Daily*, 2 July 2018, http://usa.chinadaily.com.cn/a/201807/02/WS5b397076a31033491 41e006b.html, accessed 29 May 2021.

Weick, Karl E., 'The Collapse of Sensemaking in Organizations: The Mann Gulch Disaster', in *Administrative Science Quarterly*, 1993, 38 (4):628–652.

Whitney, Lance, 'Are Computers Already Smarter Than Humans?', *Time*, 29 September 2017, https://time.com/4960778/computers-smarter-than-humans/, accessed 29 May 2021.

Whyte, William H., 'Group Think', *Fortune Magazine*, 1952, republished online on July 22, 2012, http://fortune.com/2012/07/22/groupthink-fortune-1952/, accessed 29 May 2021.

Willcox, Gregg, Rosenberg, Louis B., and Domnauer, Colin, 'Analysis of Human Behaviors in Real-Time Swarms', in 10th Annual Computing and Communication Workshop and Conference (CCWC), 2020, www.semanticscholar.org/paper/Analysis-of-Human-Behaviors-in-Real-Time-Swarms-Willcox-Rosenberg/aec4cf3886d15c8c6450db05418bd1968 83dde65, accessed 29 May 2021.

Wilson, Edward O., *The Origins of Creativity* (New York, NY: Liveright, 2017).

Wurman, Richard S., *Information Anxiety 2, 1989* (Indianapolis, IN: QUE, 2000).

Part 2

APPLICATION

4

SWARM TRANSFORMATION

THREE LEVERS THAT ENABLE THE BUSINESS TO SWARM

Can you imagine a scenario where every year a large thriving commercial enterprise undergoes a major business transformation where two-thirds of the company (up to 10,000 workers) spontaneously leave the parent group, relocate premises, and set themselves up as a new enterprise? We saw in Chapter 2 that honeybees (*Apis mellifera*) do precisely this every year around late spring/early summer to propagate the species; and moreover, they do it with minimum fuss and in a self-organising way. This chapter is about swarm transformation – or business transformation expediated by swarm. We discussed in Chapter 1 that most organisations have a poor track record of getting business transformations off the ground.[1] It would appear nature, as ever, has the answers to some of our seemingly complex organisational challenges.

Chapter 1 provided a business transformation vision; Chapter 2 introduced the 'swarm flow model'; and Chapter 3 considered how nascent technology can augment human decision-making to make human swarming more efficient and practical. This chapter brings these strands

DOI: 10.4324/9781003215561-7

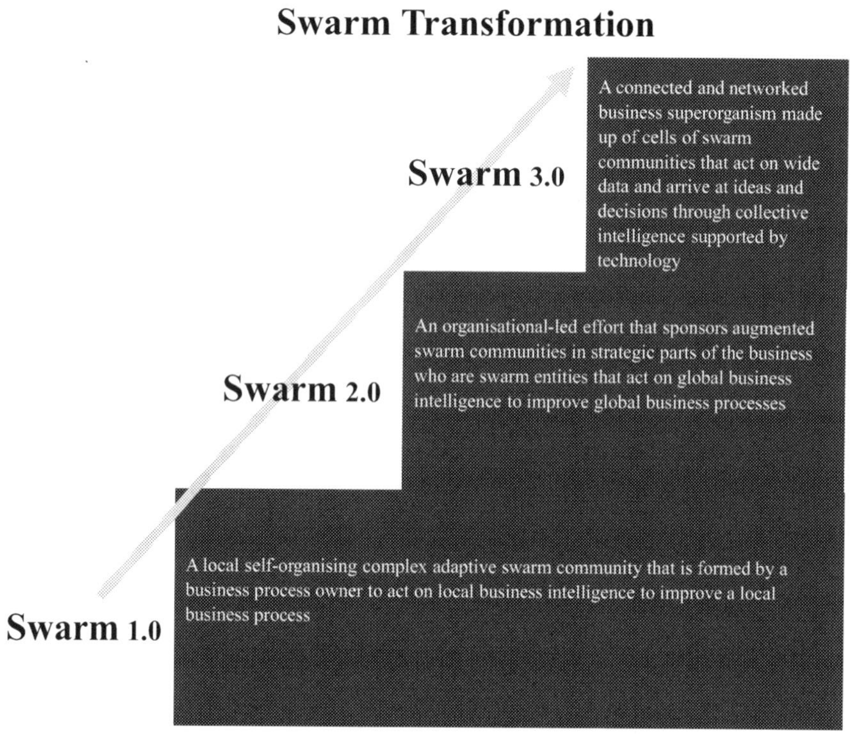

Swarm Transformation

A connected and networked business superorganism made up of cells of swarm communities that act on wide data and arrive at ideas and decisions through collective intelligence supported by technology

Swarm 3.0

An organisational-led effort that sponsors augmented swarm communities in strategic parts of the business who are swarm entities that act on global business intelligence to improve global business processes

Swarm 2.0

A local self-organising complex adaptive swarm community that is formed by a business process owner to act on local business intelligence to improve a local business process

Swarm 1.0

Figure 4.1 The three building blocks of swarm transformation.

together under a process called 'swarm transformation'. Swarm transformation, a term briefly introduced in Chapter 2, describes the end-to-end change process from a single emergent swarm community to a business superorganism. Figure 4.1 visualises the three distinct swarm phases that make up the building blocks of swarm transformation.

For each building block, there are three expediating levers. Lever 1 is a systems transformation where structures, technology, and mindsets need to be reviewed and reconfigured to support swarm. Lever 2 relates to the organisational change and development strategy that supports the swarm transformation. Lever 3, inspired by the swarm flow model in Chapter 2, relates to facilitating swarm through collective decision-making rather than executive decision makers. Let's look at each of these levers in turn.

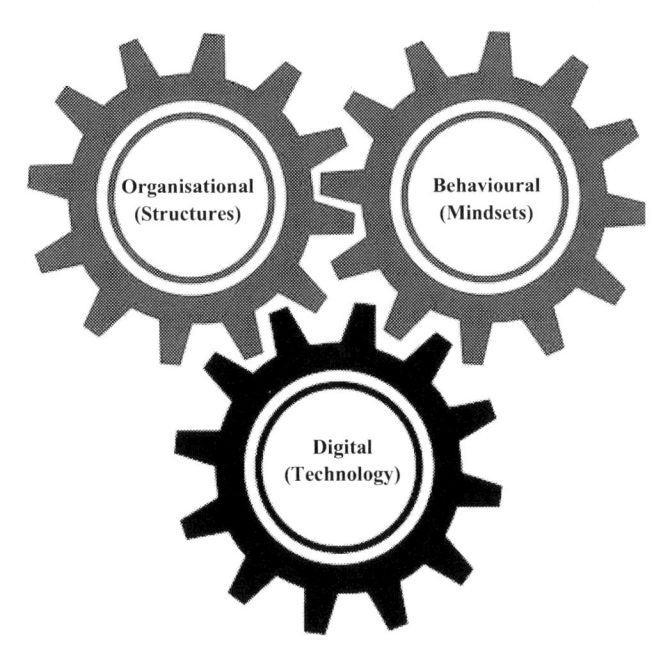

Figure 4.2 Three coactive system transformations.

Lever 1: system transformation

The first lever is a system transformation and is linked to how structures, digital technologies, and behaviours coactively define and shape organisational culture and how these systems need to evolve if the organisation is to progress to a self-organising complex adaptive system that sustains swarm. Figure 4.2 illustrates the three coactive (total) system transformations: organisational (relating to structure), digital (relating to technology), and behavioural (relating to mindsets).

Let's look at each of these system cogs.

Organisational transformation

Swarm thrives in agile and organic environments. Organisational transformation is a strategic evolution of structures and business processes that move away from hierarchy towards an organic complex adaptive system. A 2020 CISCO 'Future of Work' series believes that agile and borderless workplaces encapsulates the future of organisational structures.[2] This structural component of swarm transformation involves reconfiguring environments away from ego-led executive decision makers forcing ideas and directives down narrow hierarchies and scaler chains to a new paradigm where ideas and decisions emerge from the swarm community. This represents a significant shunt from a closed to an open system, from hierarchical egostructures to complex adaptive systems. Let's look in detail now at the organising structure that will support swarm and its phased journey towards becoming a business superorganism.

Honeycomb organisational structure

The organisational structure that will best accommodate such a swarm-based transformation is the honeycomb organisational structure. This is a grid-like structure that supports organic growth. Organic structures were first described by Tom Burns and Graham Stalker in their 1961 publication, *The Management of Innovation.* They differentiated between mechanistic and organic structures. The mechanistic structure includes the hierarchical organisation that still prevails in contemporary corporate sectors such as 3M and US Steel and is characterised as top-down, subordinate, and ranked. This type of structure has origins in classical management theory. The antithesis to this, according to Burns and Stalker, is the organic organisational structure. The organic structure is characterised as a lateral, decentralised, connectivist structure rather than a scaler chain of command. Organic organisations are best suited for a swarm environment because, just as in a honeybee colony, swarm organisations are complex adaptive systems with limited contralised control. 'Honeycomb' and 'organic' are synonymous, but I prefer the term honeycomb because it links to the theme of honeybees. More importantly, it facilitates the kind of phased and emergent swarm acceleration that is being promoted in this book. The online survey organisation, Typeform, uses a honeycomb structure to support its swarm transformation.[3] Let's explore the honeycomb structure as it relates to the three phases of swarm.

1. Swarm 1.0

At this level, the organisational swarm structure resembles a single honeycomb cell. Figure 4.3 shows an intact swarm community allied with a business process owner within a formal structure.

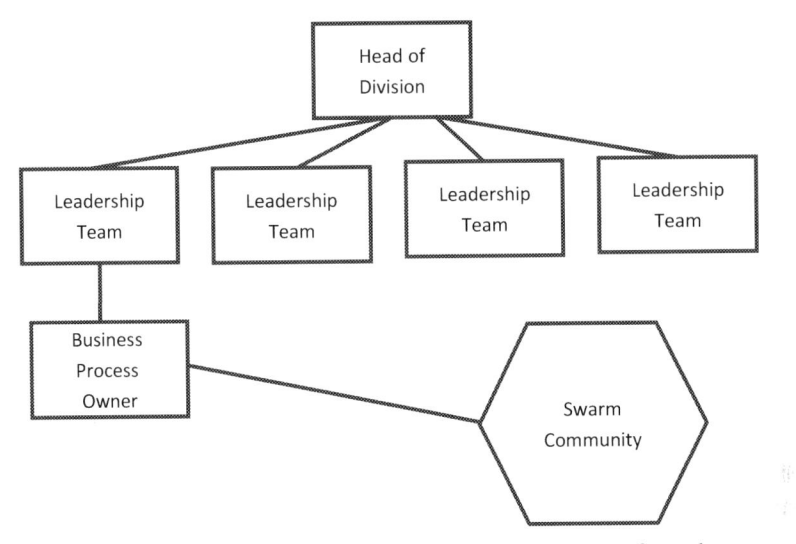

Figure 4.3 Swarm 1.0. A single honeycomb cell within a more formal structure.

Chapter 5 contains a case study based on this scenario. Here, an intact and independent swarm community is bivouacked outside of the formal structure and operates as a complex adaptive cell which serves the business process owners and makes sense of local business intelligence and challenges. More detail will emerge in Chapter 5.

2. Swarm 2.0

Swarm 2.0 builds on and replicates the swarm communities established in Swarm 1.0. It extends across a part of the honeycomb structure. Figure 4.4 shows how the honeycomb structure begins to take shape. Executive leaders, known as swarm mentor leaders (SMLs), are directly associated with the swarm communities. This is a hybrid between a more formal structure and a business superorganism.

Swarm 2.0 is more planned and organised across the enterprise with senior executives directly mentoring swarm communities, which will reduce the need for middle management. The self-organising swarm communities are nested in the broader hierarchy where global services such as HR, finance, IT, marketing, sales, etc. provide functional support to them. Swarm communities look to technology to harness business intelligence

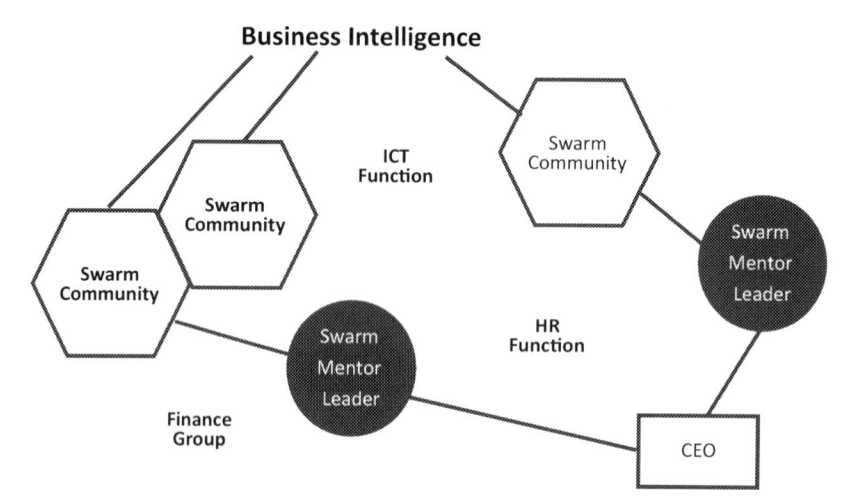

Figure 4.4 Swarm 2.0. A more developed honeycomb structure within a supporting functional and mentoring network.

and support ideation and decision-making. We will go into greater detail of this in Chapter 6.

3. Swarm 3.0

At this level, the organisational structure is a fully organic structure, a complete honeycomb model that functions as a business superorganism where business intelligence is distributed along digital conduits and networked highways (see Figure 4.5).

As in a honeybee colony, there is no formal leadership or management, just interconnected swarm communities. Within the structure is a supersedure cell, which in honeybee colonies is a suspended cell where the queen bee resides. In this configuration, there is a CEO or Collective Enterprise Optimiser who, like the queen bee, serves the community, optimises it, and represents the enterprise but has no decision-making authority. We will go into greater detail in Chapter 7.

The benefit of this organic approach is that it will grow and evolve experientially with the growth of swarm in the organisation and the rise of technology and intelligent systems. Details will be covered in later sections.

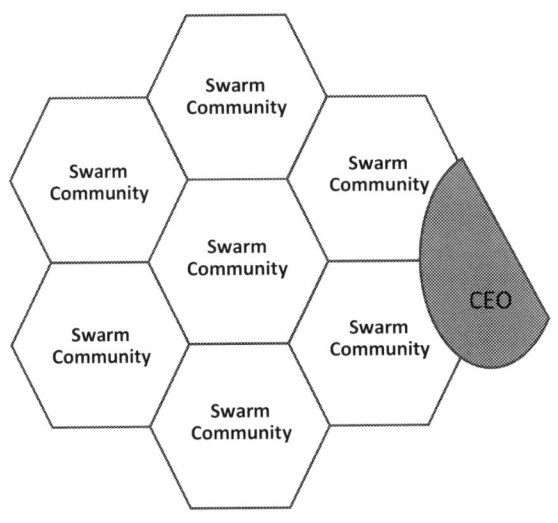

Figure 4.5 Swarm 3.0. A fully developed honeycomb structure with an integrated support system.

Some key properties of a honeycomb organisational structure

We have talked about single swarm cells in Swarm 1.0 that replicate in Swarm 2.0 and evolve into a business superorganism by Swarm 3.0. Here are some key properties of the honeycomb structure.

1. It is protean

The honeycomb organisational structure is an organic and evolving system that adapts with the swarm transformation. The structure flexes on demand.

2. It is connectivist

Connectivism is where 'knowledge is distributed across a network of connections'[4] that is based on 'rapidly altering foundations'.[5] We saw in Chapter 2 that natural swarm behaviour occurs through stigmergy and allelomimesis as opposed to centralised control. The honeycomb structure is networked rather than hierarchical. Here connections are not imposed as they are in traditional networks but are self-organising, cross-functional, and evolving.

3. It is wirearchical

Wirearchy is a term coined by Jon Husband to mean 'the power and effectiveness of people working together through connection and collaboration... taking responsibility individually and collectively rather than relying on traditional hierarchical status'.[6] It is an organising principle that connects people and technology. Effectively, organisations are wired together through the interconnections of people and technology rather than through alpha leadership and hierarchy. As we move deeper into artificial intelligence (AI) workplaces, where ideation and decision-making is augmented by technology, organisations will need to be wired differently. The physical edges of the honeycomb cells are the digital conduits or veins that run between the swarm communities. Ideas and decisions flow in and out of the swarm communities and across the enterprise via these highways, transporting the ideas and decisions that come out of the swarm communities to humans and machines across the enterprise.

4. It is intelligence-led

Formal organisations are knowledge-led; honeycomb organisational structures are intelligence-led and thrive on connectivity. This is why so much emphasis is being placed on swarm clusters and business intelligence networks. In formal organisations, knowledge is about power and control through micromanaging systems and workforces. Swarm, distributed through honeycomb structures, is all about emergent intelligence managed through collective human and machine resources. For this to happen, organisations need to be wired in a certain way to allow the free flow of intelligence, ideas, and decisions that emerge from the collective and not from alpha leaders.

5. It is deformalised

This traditional hierarchy and egostructure was built to supervise, control, and condition workers. Things like job grades, salary scales, executive perks, performance appraisals, bonuses, fixed working days and hours, goal setting, and personal scorecards have no place in an organic honeycomb structure. Traditional companies have been built on negative and positive reinforcement. This kind of operant conditioning simply reinforces alpha leader behaviour and employee supplication.[7] In a swarm-based organisation, these old conditioning legacies, which took seed in the industrial revolution, need to be eliminated.

6. It is generative

The word generative is from Latin *generare* meaning to beget. Honeycomb structures are organic and, like DNA, replicate through the enterprise. We discovered in Chapter 2 that 'generativity' was coined by Erik Erikson meaning to mentor and guide future generations. This phased swarm transformation approach that is facilitated by the honeycomb structure echoes Donald Schön's learning system theory which he developed in his 1971 publication *Beyond the Stable State. Public and Private Learning in a Changing Society*. More will be said about this in Chapter 7.

Future chapters will show in detail how this all plays out at different phases of the swarm transformation.

Digital transformation

Conceptually, digital transformation goes back to the mid-twentieth century but has become a more widely-used term in recent years. It is, yet another, ill-defined term. Some see it through the lens of business performance[8]; some see it as a strategic business model[9]; others see it in the context of technology adoption.[10] Brian Solis views it more holistically as embracing all of these perspectives.[11] Its progress was slow leading up to the coronavirus pandemic with organisations being quite backward in adopting digital transformation.[12] Now it is a trending topic in a pandemic era that has witnessed a narrowing of the digital divide and a general acceptance of working through remote networks and embracing technology to keep homeworkers connected.[13] According to a recent McKinsey digital analysis,

> If the pace of the pre-coronavirus world was already fast, the luxury of time now seems to have disappeared completely. Businesses that once mapped

digital strategy in one-to-three-year phases must now scale their initiatives in a matter of days or weeks.[14]

This is reflected in the global spend on digital transformation where direct investments in digital transformation between 2020 and 2024 are projected to reach $7.8 trillion.[15]

Some basic digital transformation general principles include:

1. It is more than just a systems upgrade

There is a procurement and development component to digital transformation, but it would be a mistake to believe that this is the main purpose of it. A successful digital transformation is broader than simply introducing new systems and technology; it is about creating efficiencies and overseeing the digital facilitation of the business. This isn't just about procuring the latest tech but futureproofing and transforming organisational structure and behaviours. George Westerman opines,

> The real value of digital transformation comes not from the initial investment, but from continuously reenvisioning how you can extend your capabilities to increase revenue, cut costs, or gain other benefits. Initial investments become the foundation upon which you can make additional strategic investments.[16]

2. A good digital transformation strategy mitigates disruption that can come about when introducing new technology and innovation in the workplace

Historically, organisations have had to handle all manner of disruptive change that has come about through the adoption of new and disruptive technologies. As George Westerman remarks, 'The last time there was this much technological innovation hitting the business world was the first time. It was the Industrial Revolution, when new machines bent the curve of commerce, capitalism, and, indeed, human history'.[17] Michael Beer and Nitin Nohria go further in 'Cracking the Code of Change' in 2020 and argue, 'Not since the Industrial Revolution have the stakes of dealing with change been so high'.[18] It is important to have a strategy and

THE SIX STAGES OF DIGITAL TRANSFORMATION

BUSINESS AS USUAL:
Organizations operate with a familiar legacy perspective of customers, processes, metrics, business models, and technology, believing that it remains the solution to digital relevance.

PRESENT AND ACTIVE:
Pockets of experimentation are driving digital literacy and creativity, albeit disparately, throughout the organization while aiming to improve and amplify specific touch-points and processes.

FORMALIZED:
Experimentation becomes intentional while executing at more promising and capable levels. Initiatives become bolder and, as a result, change agents seek executive support for new resources and technology.

STRATEGIC:
Individual groups recognize the strength in collaboration as their research, work, and shared insights contribute to new strategic roadmaps that plan for digital transformation ownership, efforts, and investments.

CONVERGED:
A dedicated digital transformation team forms to guide strategy and operations based on business and customer-centric goals. The new infrastructure of the organization takes shape as roles, expertise, models, processes, and systems to support transformation are solidified.

INNOVATIVE AND ADAPTIVE:
Digital transformation becomes a way of business as executives and strategists recognize that change is constant. A new ecosystem is established to identify and act upon technology and market trends in pilot and, eventually, at scale.

ALTIMETER

Figure 4.6 The six stages of digital transformation by Brian Solis with illustration by Jim MacLeod, Altimeter, 2016.

plan to deal with new technology and innovation. Brian Solis, working for Altimeter in 2016, came up with an excellent model outlining six stages of digital transformation that can help organisations embrace and integrate new innovation which Jim MacLeod made into a visual (Figure 4.6).

This will prove to be a useful digital transformation model for swarm.

3. It is a long-term strategy and needs a vision

This book explores the adoption of swarm over a phased period, spanning from the present to 2035. Digital transformation is part of this story. It is a long-term strategy that is both emergent and planned that embraces digitalisation, digitism, and digital process automation. Daniel Newman discusses the importance of building a cohesive strategy that develops infrastructure, data, and talent.[19] All of this takes time and needs vision.

4. Key to digital transformation success is to recruit the right people

To be effective in the digital space, organisations will need to build their digital expertise. The digital transformation effort is going to be different for each swarm phase and will require bespoke recruitment strategies. This may include recruiting Chief Information Officers, Chief Data Officers, data scientists, data detectives, AI business development specialists, AI procurement specialists, and network analysts. The next three chapters will carefully detail the digital transformation talent required for each phase.

Behavioural transformation

There is a broad consensus that getting people to accept new cultures is critical to the success of business transformation.[20] Behavioural transformation is about shifting employees' willingness and abilities from an existing way of doing business to a future possibility. In the context of swarm, Garrett Jones, Louis Rosenberg, and others refer to this as developing a 'hivemind'. Garrett Jones views hive minds as a 'nation's collective intelligence'.[21] Louis Rosenberg adroitly links hive minds to augmented intelligence:

> The interfaces and algorithms to connect people into real time swarms also exist already and are referred to as 'artificial swarm intelligence'. Governed by AI algorithms, these combine the knowledge, wisdom, insights and intuitions of real people and in real time, enabling large groups of networked humans to quickly converge upon optimised decisions, predictions, solutions and evaluations.[22]

Mike Bentley, Strategic Advisor and Global Change Leader of Deloitte, explores the differentiation between willingness and ability:

> Organisational Ability can be thought of as making sure that the workforce understands *What* to do, and *How* to do it. Organisational Willingness is best thought of as building an understanding of *Why* the workforce needs to do something a new way.[23]

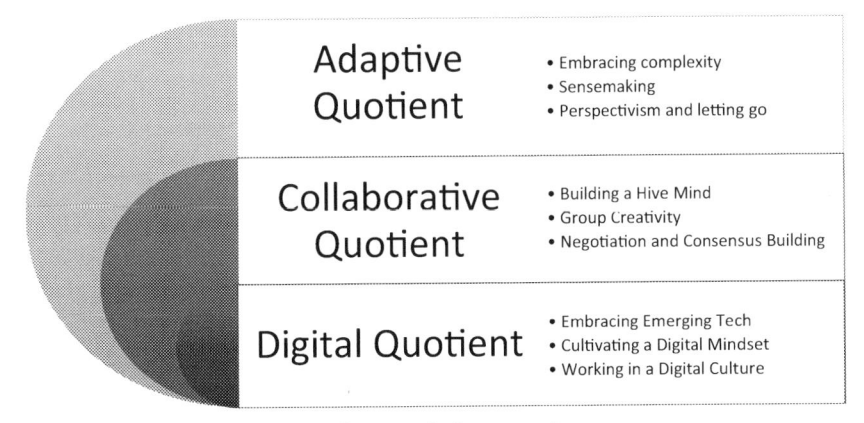

Figure 4.7 Three mindset quotients and nine core themes.

We have established that to change the business operating system to support a swarm-based organisation and business superorganism, a significant organisational and digital transformation effort will be required. But it will come to nothing if people retain a hierarchical mindset that is closed to the idea of the organisation embracing this swarm approach. There are three mindset quotients (adaptive, collaborative, and digital) for developing a hivemind. Each quotient has three core themes (nine in total) that can be worked into any educational content aimed at raising the ability and willingness to work in a swarm environment. Figure 4.7 represents this dynamic.

These quotients and themes support behavioural transformation (the willingness and ability to embrace swarm) and cultivate a hivemind. As we shall see in the coming chapters, the content, depth, ability/willingness equation, and methodologies will be different for each phase of the swarm transformation. Here are some generic descriptions of the three quotients and themes.

Raising adaptive quotient (AQ)

An essential behavioural component of swarm is being able to adapt. We saw in Chapter 2 that swarm is part of a complex adaptive system and that honeybees are highly adaptive. Agility is key to thriving in any kind of complex adaptive system. Here are three swarm themes that cultivate adaptiveness and an agile mindset.

1. *Embracing complexity*

   An important quality to help individuals thrive in swarm environments is to understand and navigate complexity. There is a vast amount of literature on complexity, particularly coming out of the complexity science movement briefly explored in Chapter 1. *Embracing Complexity* by Jean Boulton et al. published in 2015 is a good general text on the subject. In practical terms, organisations should focus on cultivating diversity and encouraging individuals to take on challenging assignments. A test and learn culture that views mistakes as learning opportunities will reinforce adaptive behaviours. Systemic thinking and mental models are useful tools to help navigate complexity and develop an experimental mindset. A useful psychometric for understanding complexity and change is the Change Style Indicator (CSI) which helps us understand our attitudes to change.

2. *Sensemaking*

   Sensemaking is an important element of swarm theory. It has many applications but is widely applied in a business context, through the work of Karl Weick. Weick and Sutcliffe capture the spirit of organisational sensemaking when they say, 'Sensemaking is not about truth and getting it right. Instead, it is about continued redrafting of an emerging story so that it becomes more comprehensive, incorporates more of the observed data, and is more resilient in the face of criticism'.[24] In swarm theory, sensemaking is about making collective sense of business intelligence and arriving at a group perspective that takes into account the entire groups' input. Sensemaking involves curiosity, optimisation, and emergence of ideas and decisions rather than blindly following processes and preconceived truths. Swarm clusters and swarm teams are sensemaking entities and should be diverse, collaborative, and challenging. They should embrace swarmocracy, avoid groupthink, and celebrate differing perspectives. Scenario planning and the Cynefin framework are all useful sensemaking frameworks and tools. Any of the personality psychometrics such as Myers Briggs can help create diverse teams and avoid some of the group processing pitfalls outlined in Chapter 3.

3. *Perspectivism/letting go*

    Author Laurens Van der Post said in *The Lost World of the Kalahari* that 'Human beings are perhaps never more frightening than when they are convinced beyond doubt that they are right'.[25] An important mindset of swarm is perspectivism, curiosity, and the ability to let go of fixed assumptions and to openly engage with ideas in swarm teams and clusters. Open thinking and a willingness to embrace new ideas is vital to swarm. In the natural world, the individual agent always embraces the collective view. Donald Schön and Reid Martin's 'frame reflection' and Claus Otto Scharmer's 'Theory U' are both useful tools for letting go of entrenched ideas and encouraging open thinking.[26] Any of the self-awareness tools will help build a sense of perspective (particularly social and emotional intelligence). Tools such as systemic thinking can help us see the bigger picture.

Building collaborative quotient (CQ)

Another key behavioural component of swarm is the art of collaboration. We observed that an essential element of swarm intelligence in the natural world concerns how superorganisms act collectively and how individual agents are less important in relation to the overall colony. It was noted that to function in a swarm environment, swarm communities need to be deformalised, self-organising, and have the ability to work together for the greater good. The next three themes raise collaborative quotient within organisations so that individuals can be effective in a swarm environment.

4. Cultivating a hive mind

    Honeybees think for the good of the colony. Collective mindsets in organisations are about considering the 'we' rather than the 'me', to have social intelligence, and to build shared understanding and con-sensus through self-organising means. We saw in earlier chapters that collective intelligence is one of the core properties of the new business operating system and is key to swarm intelligence in the natural world. Building a collective mindset is linked to structure because an open ecosystem will encourage a hive mind. That said, there are some powerful extant tools that encourage collectivism through dialogue. David Bohm's *On Dialogue* (1996) and William *Isaacs Dialogue and the Art of Thinking Together* (1999) are both good resources. Kaizen (改善) is an excellent group improvement method. Peer feedback tools are a good way to build trust, community spirit, and togetherness. Belbin is a useful psychometric for understanding team dynamic and the Thomas-Kilmann Conflict Mode Instrument helps individuals appreciate how they deal with conflict in groups. Fons Trompenaars and Charles Hampden-Turner's 1997 *Riding the Waves of Culture* presents some good insights into collectivist cultures.

5. Group creativity

   Group creativity and collaborative creativity is central to swarm and swarm-based organisations. Swarm and swarm facilitation is a group ideation and decision-making activity. Group creativity in business was formally acknowledged and theorised by Alex Osborn through his pioneering 'brainstorming' theory that was developed in 1939 but popularised in his 1953 book, *Applied Imagination*. Publications on group creativity have been voluminous. Many studies on group creativity make the compelling case that some of the world's iconic ideas, inventions, and creations from relativity theory to the invention of the telephone have come about through group collaboration. We have already discussed in Chapter 3 how group work can be messy. The important factor in working in creative teams is having a clear approach to team objectives/processes, characteristics, and dynamics. Having a good model for teamworking, such as Richard Beckhard's GRPI model that he introduced in 1972 in *Optimizing Team Building Effort. Journal of Contemporary Business*, is imperative. Also, having a good process helps (that's why the swarm facilitation model is so important). Creating a shared vision is an important tool in group creativity. Design thinking, a design bespoke problem-solving approach, is becoming popular as a solution-based tool that can help the group shape the business challenge. Team dynamic psychometrics are also useful tools here.

6. Negotiation and consensus building

   One of the important things that we discovered about house-hunting honeybees is that they are individual sensemakers that return to the nest and broadcast their discoveries to the rest of the colony. This is known as the waggle dance. Honeybees negotiate consensus around best fit. These are especially important attributes in a swarm cluster environment. Technology at Swarm 2.0 and 3.0 does not displace decision-making; it augments and assists it. Humans at this level are still part of the creative decision-making process. Just as we empower people to work with ideas and reach group decisions, we must also raise their ability to be collaborative negotiators, consensus-driven problem solvers, and idea generators. There are a vast amount of tools in the interpersonal field concerning influencing, engaging, and negotiating that can be recycled here to include in learning interventions. Such tools include multiple intelligences, dialoguing, listening, consulting, managing conflict, and contributing to a learning and feedback culture. Self-awareness is also part of this mix. Psychometrics can help us build self and community understanding. I value Robert Thomas' 'The Three Essential Ingredients of Great Collaborations' in which he looks at three conditions of collaborating.[27] This informs a swarm approach around collectivism and self-organising complex adaptive systems.

Building digital quotient (DQ)

Another key behavioural component of advanced swarm is digital quotient (DQ). Organisations are complex entities and human swarming requires a lot of manual effort to distil and consolidate information. Advanced data analytics and decision augmentation will identify business intelligence and support humans to process information. It will be necessary to raise organisational ability and understanding around existing and future technology in addition to developing people to work in AI-augmented environments. Here are the final three themes relating to DQ:

7. Embracing emerging tech
   Business leaders should revamp their corporate training and development programmes to include tech-savviness and an appreciation of how emerging technologies can support ideation and decision-making and help the enterprise on its swarm journey. This initiative will benefit existing employees who need to understand the

tech opportunities, but also for new resources who must embrace the digital culture. Since every employee may not be tech-savvy, personalised learning should be a priority for organisations. Organisations should use employee data to analyse their current skillsets, qualifications, and experience for developing personalised learning solutions. The learning and development programmes should help employees appreciate how emerging technologies can augment their intelligence. There are, of course, other ways to raise the technical DQ abilities of the organisation. A modern recruiting practice for developing intact talented teams is acquihiring, a portmanteau of 'acquisition' and 'hiring'. This relates to the acquisition of a company in order to access its talent. This is particularly useful for raising DQ and technical ability. Online e-learning is an excellent tool for technical training. The organisation should also think about tech-buddies and mentors to work with colleagues to help them build understanding of emerging tech. Kate Smaje of McKinsey suggests in a 2015 HBR Ideacast that an effective way to help colleagues raise their digital literacy is by demystifying AI through teaching simple coding to help people understand what drives the technology that they are being asked to use.[28]

8. Cultivating a digital mindset

    We have seen that swarm facilitation is going to be increasingly supported by digital technologies and especially decision augmentation. This will require advance digitisation, information transparency, navigationalism, and digital security. Humans will need to change their habits and mindsets to make this a success. For Swarm 2.0 and 3.0 to be effective in ideation and decision-making, all forms of human reaction and experiences should be dataised. Systems such as wearables, implants, and recognition technology will increasingly be able to assist digitisation, but humans need to cultivate a knowledge sharing mindset. Part of any learning intervention about digital culture needs to press home the importance of digitising and dataising everyday situations and collaborations. Information transparency is all about open cultures and knowledge transparency. Studies on knowledge retention highlight how creativity within organisations is negatively impacted when employees hoard information.[29] Tom Brown calls this navigationism, where learners self-navigate through open systems.[30] Again, learning interventions need to address this and encourage open, random, and supportive mindsets. Digital security is also something that needs to be part of a learning intervention on building a digital culture and mindset.

9. Working in a digital culture

One of the challenges of recent times has been remote collaborative working and working with digital networks. The coronavirus pandemic has accelerated the need for remote collaborative working since many now find themselves working from home and collaborating online. Although there are now lots of online collaborative tools that help us to have a better online experience (some of which have already been profiled in Chapter 3 and will be further explored in Chapter 6), there is a need for organisations to develop healthier mindsets and abilities relating to working. Erica Dhawan and Tomas Chamorro-Premuzic provide some good working practices in their 2018 HBR article, 'How to Collaborate Effectively if Your Team is Remote'. Jared Spataro, Corporate Vice President for Microsoft 365, shares some excellent insights concerning collaborating remotely.[31] In a recent Wall Street Journal feature, Leigh Thompson, professor of management and organisation at Northwester University, talks about e-charisma and cultivating an online presence.[32] Raising network perspective is also key to remote collaborative working. Digital etiquette is important when working with online networks. The issue around the use of collaborative tools, planning collaborative meetings, and cultivating e-charisma and digital etiquette was not a priority before the coronavirus pandemic. It is a crucial mindset going forward. Using digital networks to get things done is considerably different from using traditional networks and any learning intervention needs to reflect this. The levels of swarm outlined in this book are increasingly moving away from face-to-face human collaboration towards remote human and machine collaboration. As we saw in Chapter 3, the technology is getting better in terms of digital presence and human mindsets need to catch up.

Learning intervention

The type and frequency of learning interventions are also significant. Sometimes learning interventions are part of a transition to future reality (I call this pre-swarm development). This would be the case for individuals who are developing for a next role or for the entire organisation going through a cultural transition. Other forms of learning interventions are made in-role or on the job (I call this in-swarm development). This would be the case for individuals who are seeking to develop their abilities to improve their performance or to adjust to a new cultural reality in their current role. These two interventions are reflected in future chapters. Whatever the level of swarm, swarm participants will need both pre-swarm and in-swarm development to increase their willingness and ability, raise their performance, and reinforce their new behaviours. The pre-swarm interventions raise willingness and ability to work in swarm clusters. This will include formal programmes to raise awareness and skills to be effective in transitioning to a swarm environment. The in-swarm interventions sharpen ability and include peer-to-peer development during the swarm cluster activity. These learning interventions and their methodological application will be set out in future chapters.

Lever 2: organisational change and development

Organisational change can be defined as a shift from one state to another (usually a desired future state).[33] Rosabeth Moss Kanter et al. argues,

> Change involves the crystallization of new action possibilities (new policies, new behaviors, new patterns, new methodologies, new products or new market ideas) based on the reconceptualized patterns in the organization. The architecture of change involves the design and construction of new patterns, or the reconceptualization of old ones, to make new, and hopefully more productive, actions possible.[34]

Organisational development is widely considered as a total system approach to organisational change.[35] This notion of new possibilities through emergence and a total system transformation through planned change is a good hybrid and one that occurs in the natural world.

House-hunting honeybees have a clear transformational change strategy that it is both planned (preparations such as rearing of new queens, getting the mother queen ready for flight, and monitoring the weather conditions) and self-organising and adaptive (the swarm relocates to a temporary bivouac, scout bees search for appropriate accommodation, other bees are recruited during the waggle dance and contribute to the decision-making). Adopting a swarm approach for the enterprise is best executed through a hybrid approach to transformational change. Both planned and emergent approaches mitigate some of the challenges of business transformation, especially around organisational disruption and momentum. Let's briefly explore the three change scenarios.

Planned change effort

A planned change initiative involves a programmatic, top-down imposed change. Popularised by Kurt Lewin, whom some call the father of planned change, a planned approach to effecting change within organisations was widespread in the 1940s and the postwar period. Lewin's classic 1947 article published in the year of his death, 'Frontiers in Group Dynamics: Concept, Method and Reality in Social Science; Equilibrium and Social Change', produces a practical three step framework known as the Ice model. Its central idea of unfreeze, move, and freeze inspired many researchers who champion planned organisational change.[36] Burnes argues, 'the planned approach to change has been, and still is, highly influential... Even today, it is still far and away the best developed, documented and supported approach to change'.[37]

Emergent change effort

Planned change works well if you need the entire organisation to shift in a managed way. The problem with the planned approach to change is that it can be disruptive, it can create resistance that needs to be managed, and it tends to react to change rather than evolve with it. There is a growing consensus from theorists and practitioners working in the organisational change and development field that Lewin's 'quaintly linear and static conception'[38] is not suitable for Industry 4.0 and its volatile/uncertain/complex/ambiguous (VUCA) environment and fails to grasp the complex nature of the modern world. Emergent change addresses this. Karl Weick, a leading player in emergent change, says, 'Emergent change consists of ongoing accommodations, adaptations, and alterations that produce fundamental change without a priori intentions to do so'.[39] Chapter 1, you recall, described emergence using the example of desire paths and bootleg trails. Emergence works best in non 'burning platform' environments where there is a high degree of complexity and non-predictive behaviour and a cultural resistance to planned/implemented change initiatives. Here, sensemaking the system and building change around emerging patterns is deemed to be more successful and lasting than a top-down programmatic initiative. Emerging change is less researched and developed than planned change. Major influences on emergent change include the contingency theory[40] self-organising theory,[41] processual theory,[42] and the chaos theory.[43]

Hybrid change model

We have seen that a planned change creates an organisational-wide momentum but has several limitations. Emergent change is good for phased change and embedding behaviours and evolving the organisation from grassroots up, but also has limitations. Emergent change is a long-term change effort that can lack strategic alignment and momentum and is certainly not a change plan to use in a burning platform scenario. Luckily, relocating honeybees have shown the way. The phased approach to change and development is a hybrid of managed and emergent change (Figure 4.8).

Dexter Dunphy and Doug Stace comprehensively set out the case for a hybrid approach:

> A more comprehensive approach to organizational change management and consultancy is needed which finds a place for transformation as well as incrementalism and which accommodates the use of directive/coercive as well as participative means of achieving change. [44]

The hybrid approach integrates top-down and bottom-up traditions in organisational change and development. It allows for a more bespoke business process change to emerge where the planned change can be adopted and adapted by the business and change recipients.[45] Successful

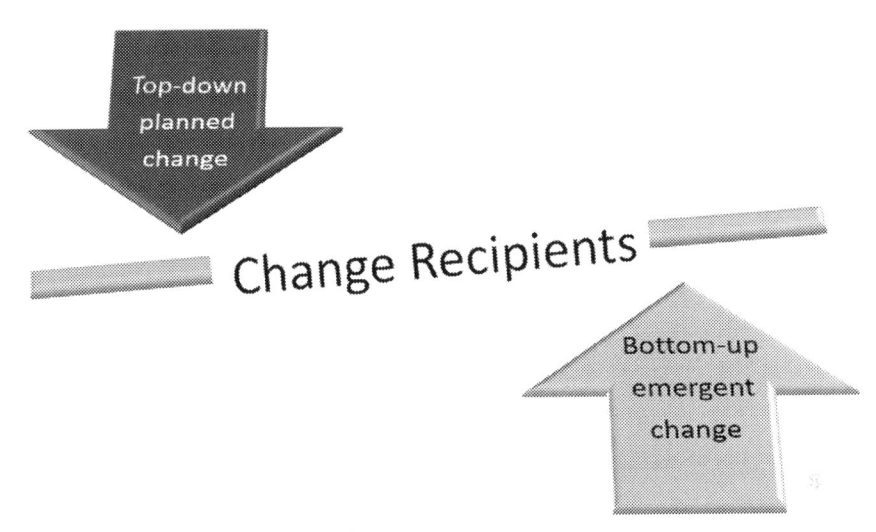

Figure 4.8 Hybrid model for change.

change always considers recipient's needs. Jean Bartunek et al. convincingly argue the case for the change recipients' active role in the organisational change process.[46] Furthermore, Michael Beer and Nitan Nohria suggest a synthesis of planned and emergent change allows for a more adaptive approach to change – 'Through this process leaders create managers capable of leading change and organizations that are adaptive – the one capability most needed for survival in a fast-changing world'.[47] There are some good case studies from the small group of researchers who promote the idea of a hybrid approach. Miguel Cunha and Rita Cunha in their 2003 piece, 'The interplay of planned and emergent change in Cuba', give a fascinating account of how Cuba successfully mixed top-down planned change and bottom-up emergent change via focus groups to create social innovation in the country.

John Kotter, a highly influential leading change specialist, whom I have purposefully avoided mentioning until now, has produced several models that consider sponsored change and episodic change. His recent book, *Accelerate: Building Strategic Agility for a Faster-moving World* (2014), directly speaks to the idea of a dual approach to change. In a 2012 HBR article, 'Accelerate!', Business as usual is taken care of by traditional hierarchies and management processes, explains Kotter, but a second process can run in parallel that has an 'agile, networklike structure' that seeks to create new opportunities and innovations:

> It complements rather than overburdens the traditional hierarchy, thus freeing the latter to do what it's optimized to do. It actually makes enterprises easier to run and accelerates strategic change. This is not an 'either or' idea. It's 'both and'. I'm proposing two systems that operate in concert.[48]

Swarm transformation is a hybrid change approach that evolves over three distinct phases. There are four critical considerations for adopting this hybrid approach:

1. Swarm transformation requires a total-system/phased structural, digital, and behavioural change. A hybrid approach of planned and emergent change is effective for this type of total-system change that is phased over time.
2. Progression towards business superorganism status is going to require a technology that is still under development and therefore a hybrid approach makes sense as it allows for a phased adoption once the technology becomes available.
3. The change is part of an organisational learning system. A slow-burn hybrid change that accelerates when the organisation is ready and one that supports continuous learning.
4. The hybrid approach is phased and avoids an organisational big bang and follows principles of change and adaption from the natural world.

We have seen that the business transformation requires a total system approach across structures, technologies, and behaviours and that a hybrid organisational change and development strategy supports a phased technology-led change that mitigates disturbance and feels more natural and organic.

Lever 3: swarm facilitation based on the swarm flow model

We saw in Chapter 2 that honeybee colonies are complex adaptive systems that follow a distinct algorithm when looking for new accommodation.

This is known as the swarm flow model and was represented in Figure 2.4. When it comes to searching for a new home, honeybees follow a cycle of preparation, clustering, sensemaking, acting, and regeneration. Specific characteristics include that they involve the entire system, split into diverse self-organising clusters, embrace diversity, focus on live issues that strengthens the colony, use mechanisms to filter information, unify and act around common purpose, and rebuild and regenerate the colony. This natural algorithm has been adopted to demonstrate the swarm stages that take place within organisations during the ideation and decision-making of swarm communities – a process known as swarm facilitation.

In this model, business challenges are identified through business intelligence networks. Swarm communities and clusters are formed to make sense of this intelligence and come up with ideas and recommendations. Crucially, it is a regenerative process because it contributes to the business process outcome. The assertion of this book is that swarm facilitation can occur in human swarms (Swarm 1.0) which use open non-digital technologies to facilitate and organise the collective view; it further considers that swarm facilitation will come into its own by adopting emerging technology such as collaborative tools, advanced analytics, and decision augmentation to optimise human ideation and decision-making (Swarm 2.0 and 3.0). The practical use of the model will be explored for each swarm level in the next three chapters.

General principles, benefits, and pitfalls of swarm facilitation

The swarm flow model was substantially detailed in Chapter 2 and will be expanded upon in the next three chapters. I wish to give some thought to the swarm facilitation process by reflecting on some general principles, benefits, and pitfalls. Figure 4.9 provides five general principles of swarm facilitation.

These principles should be a central consideration for each phase of swarm facilitation.

It would be useful to briefly consider the benefits and pitfalls of swarm facilitation to further elucidate its functionality. Tables 4.1 and 4.2 outline some of the issues.

This chapter has defined three important levers that expedite the business transformation in each of the swarm phases and is a key route

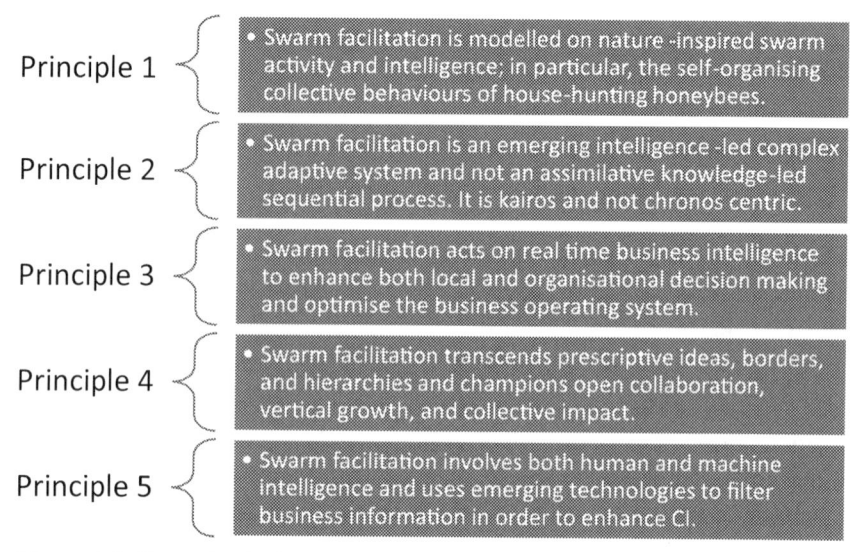

Principle 1
- Swarm facilitation is modelled on nature -inspired swarm activity and intelligence; in particular, the self-organising collective behaviours of house-hunting honeybees.

Principle 2
- Swarm facilitation is an emerging intelligence -led complex adaptive system and not an assimilative knowledge-led sequential process. It is kairos and not chronos centric.

Principle 3
- Swarm facilitation acts on real time business intelligence to enhance both local and organisational decision making and optimise the business operating system.

Principle 4
- Swarm facilitation transcends prescriptive ideas, borders, and hierarchies and champions open collaboration, vertical growth, and collective impact.

Principle 5
- Swarm facilitation involves both human and machine intelligence and uses emerging technologies to filter business information in order to enhance CI.

Figure 4.9 General principles of swarm facilitation.

Table 4.1 Benefits of swarm facilitation

Why adopt it?	Because…
It is natural	Swarm facilitation is nature's way of optimising intelligence and decision-making.
It promotes reflection	We saw in Chapter 2 that introverts sometimes don't flourish in groups leading to feelings of group-hate. Swarm facilitation is an emergent and self-organising complex adaptive system in which individuals can contribute (personal best) for the benefit of the group (group best). Swarm becomes part of an organisational learning system.
It is collaborative	Swarm facilitation is a collective intelligence theory and embraces open collaboration and collective impact.
It can drive up productivity	Swarm facilitation maximises group motivation and energy. It is truly a self-actualising experience that requires limited leadership and supervision. Global companies have major problems with productivity.[49] Collective working and shared leadership can dramatically raise productivity and motivation levels.[50]
It is inclusive	Every idea counts in swarm facilitation. Ideas and decisions are not manufactured by executives but through the group. Swarm facilitation is a whole-system approach to generating ideas and decisions. It actively breaks down barriers.

Table 4.1 Cont.

Why adopt it?	Because...
It is practical and scalable	Unlike Holacracy, which requires an upfront system-wide reorganisation effort to implement and has complicated rules and processes (something we will explore in Chapter 5), swarm facilitation is scalable and follows simple rules. As we shall see in Chapter 5, it is possible to implement swarm facilitation within months for a single meeting or workshop.
It promotes collective responsibility	Swarm facilitation is a collective phenomenon where decision-making and innovation is shared. It moves away from the cult of the superhero and the idea of the individual singlehandedly making all the decisions.
It is relevant	We are heading towards Industry 4.0 which embraces augmented and artificial intelligence. The old business operating system which supported a more linear business approach is no longer fit for purpose. Swarm facilitation heralds a new era of collectivism and adaptiveness.

Table 4.2 Pitfalls of swarm facilitation

Why resist it?	Because...
Some people need structure	Studies such as Lewin et al. (1939) signal that structureless working environments can lead to disinterest and demotivation. Some people need structure. The late CEO, Tony Hsieh, discovered this when he converted Zappos to Holacracy and 18% of the workforce abandoned the organisation.[51]
It can tie you up in knots	We looked at the Ant Mill Effect in Chapter 3 and how following neighbours in swarms can literally tie you up in knots. Given that swarm facilitation has simple rules and is self-organising and emergent, there is always a chance that the group can follow each other down dead ends.
Human ego can get in the way	The truth of the matter is, humans are not social insects or swarming fish. We have superior intelligence and human consciousness.[52] Centuries of human achievement shows a species that has historically been driven by individual rather than collective achievement. Some individuals are naturally territorial.
The full adoption of Swarm Facilitation will take time and investment.	Building an organisational swarm culture will take time, investment, and an incremental reorganisation of structures, networks, and and behaviours to achieve the full implication of swarm facilitation and self-organising collective intelligence. Its progress is phased and its full success is dependent on emerging technology.

map for the next three chapters. Lever 1 concerns system transformation which is the organisational (structures), digital (technology), and behavioural (mindsets) transformations. Lever 2 is the organisational change and development model which is a hybrid emergent/planned approach that will accelerate or scale through each phase of swarm. Lever 3 is the swarm facilitation approach based on the algorithm identified in Chapter 2 as the swarm flow model (Figure 2.4). The next three chapters will take a deep dive into the three swarm phases (human swarm, swarm-based organisation, and business superorganism) based on the blueprint outlined in this chapter. We start with human swarms.

Notes

1 A McKinsey Global Survey into business transformations signal a continuous trend of business transformational failure. Only 26% of surveyed executives report that their business transformation succeeded. Source: 'How to Beat the Transformational Odds', *McKinsey & Company*, 1 April 2015, Survey, www.mckinsey.com/business-functions/organization/our-insights/how-to-beat-the-transformation-odds, accessed 29 May 2021. Nitin Nohria and Michael Beer rightly appraise, 'The brutal fact is that about 70% of all change initiatives fail'. Nitin Nohria and Michael Beer, 'Cracking the Code of Change', *Harvard Business Review*, May–June 2020, https://hbr.org/2000/05/cracking-the-code-of-change, accessed 29 May 2021. Most business transformations fail because they are not clear on outcomes or definitions. For a good appraisal of this view, see Scott Anthony, 'What Do You Really Mean by Business "Transformation"'?, *Harvard Business Review*, 29 February 2016, https://hbr.org/2016/02/what-do-you-really-mean-by-business-transformation, accessed 29 May 2021.

2 'The Future of Work Is Coming. It Is Borderless, Lightning-Fast, Highly Creative', *CISCO*, 2020, www.cisco.com/c/en_uk/solutions/executive-perspectives/strategic-technology-trends/the-future-of-work-is-coming.html, accessed 29 May 2021.

3 Source: Eleonara Zucconi, 'Toby Oliver (CTO @ Typeform) on Hiring, Managing, and Scaling Engineering Teams', *Medium*, 15 January 2018, https://medium.com/@eleonorazucconi/toby-oliver-cto-typeform-on-hiring-managing-and-scaling-engineering-teams-86bef9e5a708, accessed 29 May 2021.

4 Stephen Downes, 'What Connectivism Is', *Half an Hour Blog*, 3 February 2007, https://halfanhour.blogspot.com/2007/02/what-connectivism-is.html, accessed 16 June 2020.

5 George Siemens, 'Connectivism: A Learning Theory for the Digital Age', 2004, *Elearningspace*, 5 April 2005, https://pdfs.semanticscholar.org/a25f/84bc55488d01bd5f5acac4eed0c7d8f4597c.pdf, accessed 29 May 2021.

6 Jon Husband, 'What Is Wirearchy?', *Wirearchy* (blog), 16 February 2013, http://wirearchy.com/what-is-wirearchy/, accessed 29 May 2021.

7 These are terms used by B.F. Skinner set out in Skinner (1937). Operant means a strengthening if behaviour; positive and negative reinforcement concerns the degree to which an action is likely to be repeated. B.F. Skinner, 'Two Types of Conditioned Reflex: A Reply to Konorski and Miller', *Journal of General Psychology*, 16, 1937, 272–279.

8 Sources: G.C. Westerman, et al., 'Digital Transformation: A Roadmap for Billion-Dollar Organizations', *MIT Center for Digital Business and Capgemini Consulting*, 17 November 2011, www.capgemini.com/resources/digital-transformation-a-roadmap-for-billiondollar-organizations/, accessed 29 May 2021; Clint Boulton, ' "What is Digital Transformation?' A Necessary Disruption', *CIO*, 17 September 2020, www.cio.com/article/3211428/what-is-digital-transformation-a-necessary-disruption.html, accessed 29 May 2021.

9 Source: D.M. Mazzone, *Digital or Death: Digital Transformation—The Only Choice for Business to Survive Smash and Conquer* (Mississauga: Smash Box Consulting Inc., 2014).

10 Herbert Lindsey, *Digital Transformation: Build Your Organization's Future for the Innovation Age* (London and New York, NY: Bloomsbury Business, 2017).

11 'Digital transformation is the evolving pursuit of innovative and agile business and operational models—fueled by evolving technologies, processes, analytics, and talent—to create new value and experiences for customers, employees, and stakeholders'. Brian Solis, 'Definition of Digital Transformation', 23 January 2017, www.briansolis.com/2017/01/definition-of-digital-transformation/, accessed 29 May 2021.

12 Mark Jones (2019) wrote a pre-Covid article which reflects this hesitancy. Mark Jones, 'Most Employers Don't Get Digital Transformation', 9 April 2019, https://techhq.com/2019/04/most-employees-dont-get-digital-transformation/, accessed 29 May 2021.

13 An excellent *World Economic Forum* paper (Xiao et al., 2020) on technology trends in Covid-19 shows emerging technology is coming of age in this pandemic including online shopping, contactless payment, homeworking aided by collaborative technology, distance learning for our children and telehealth apps that are booking Covid-19 tests and vaccines.

14 Simon Blackburn, et al., 'Digital Strategy in a Time of Crisis', *McKinsey*, 22 April 2020, www.mckinsey.com/business-functions/mckinsey-digital/our-insights/digital-strategy-in-a-time-of-crisis, accessed 29 May 2021.

15 Source: Kimberly Mlitz, 'Digital Transformation Spending Worldwide 2017–2024', *Statista*, 31 Mar 2021, www.statista.com/statistics/870924/worldwide-digital-transformation-market-size/, accessed 29 May 2021.

16 George Westerman, *Leading Digital: Turning Technology into Business Transformation* (Boston, MA: Harvard Business Review Press, 2014), 170–171.

17 George Westerman, *Leading Digital*, 2.

18 Michael Beer and Nitin Nohria, 'Cracking the Code of Change', *Harvard Business Review*, May/June 2000, https://hbr.org/2000/05/cracking-the-code-of-change, accessed 29 May 2021.

19 Daniel Newman, 'Six Reasons Why We Haven't Seen Full AI Adoption', *Forbes*, 12 March 2019, www.forbes.com/sites/danielnewman/2019/03/12/6-reasons-why-we-havent-seen-full-ai-adoption/?sh=46c6e3e53e99, accessed 29 May 2021.

20 See, for example: Mike Bentley, 'Behavioural Design Is Key to Successful Business Transformation', *Financial Director*, 11 September 2018, www.financialdirector.co.uk/2018/09/11/behavioural-design-is-key-to-successful-business-transformation/, accessed 29 May 2021; Tony O'Driscoll, 'People Are the Key to Business Transformation', *Duke Corporate Education*, December 2019, www.dukece.com/insights/people-driven-transformation/, accessed 29 May 2021; Nadim Matta and Ron Ashkenas, 'Why Good Projects Fail Anyway', *Harvard Business Review*, September 2003, https://hbr.org/2003/09/why-good-projects-fail-anyway, accessed 29 May 2021. McKinsey notoriously observed in 2015 that 70% of organisational change programmes fail to achieve their goals due to 'employee resistance and lack of management support'. Ewenstein, Boris, Smith, Wesley, and Sologar, Ashvin, 'Changing Change Management', *McKinsey*

& Company, 1 July 2015, www.mckinsey.com/featured-insights/leadership/changing-change-management, accessed 29 May 2021.

21 Garett Jones, *Hive Mind: How Your Nation's IQ Matters So Much More Than Your Own* (Stanford, CA: Stanford University Press, 2016), 22.

22 Louis Rosenberg, 'The Rise of the Human Hive Mind', *Foundry4*, 8 October 2017, https://foundry4.com/the-rise-of-the-human-hive-mind, accessed 29 May 2021.

23 Mike Bentley, 'Behavioural Design Is Key to Successful Business Transformation'.

24 Karl E. Weick and Kathleen M. Sutcliffe, 'Organizing and the Process of Sensemaking', *Organization Science*, 2005, 16, 4, 409–421, 415.

25 Lauren Van der Post, *The Lost World of Kalahari, 1958* (London: Vintage, 2002), 57.

26 Donald Schön and Reid Martin, *Frame Reflection: Toward the Resolution of Intractable Policy Controversies* (New York, NY: Basic Books, 1994) and C. Otto Scharmer, *Theory U: Leading from the Future As It Emerges* (Oakland, CA: Berrett-Koehler, 2009).

27 Robert Thomas, 'The Three Essential Ingredients of Great Collaborations', *Harvard Business Review*, 1 June 2011, https://hbr.org/2011/06/the-three-essential-ingredient, accessed 29 May 2021.

28 Kate Smaje, 'What's Your Digital Quotient?', *Harvard Business Review*, Ideacast, Episode 483, 3 September 2015, https://hbr.org/podcast/2015/09/whats-your-digital-quotient.html?registration=success, accessed 29 May 2021.

29 Good source: Matej Černe, et al., 'What Goes Around Comes Around: Knowledge Hiding, Perceived Motivational Climate, and Creativity', *Academy of Management*, 57, 1, 4 January 2013, https://journals.aom.org/doi/full/10.5465/amj.2012.0122, accessed 29 May 2021.

30 Tom Brown, 'Beyond Constructivism: Navigationism in the Knowledge Era', *On the Horizon*, 14, 2006, 108–120, www.researchgate.net/publication/228340946_Beyond_constructivism_Navigationism_in_the_knowledge_era, accessed 29 May 2021.

31 Jared Spataro, 'How Remote Work Impacts Collaboration: Findings from our Team', *Microsoft*, 22 April 2020, www.microsoft.com/en-us/microsoft-365/blog/2020/04/22/how-remote-work-impacts-collaboration-findings-team/, accessed 29 May 2021.

32 Source: Ray A. Smith, 'Do You Have E-Charisma on Zoom? Here's How to Get It', *Wall Street Journal*, 29 November 2020, www.wsj.com/articles/do-you-have-e-charisma-on-zoom-heres-how-to-get-it-11606651200, accessed 29 May 2021.

33 A good literature review of organisational change can be found in Paolo Quattrone and Trevor Hopper, 'What Does Organizational Change Mean? Speculations on a Taken for Granted Gategory', *Management Accounting Research*, 12, 4, 2011, 403–435.

34 R.M. Kanter, *The Change Masters: Innovation and Entrepreneurship in the American Corporation* (New York, NY: Simon & Schuster, 1982), 279.

35 Thomas Cummings and Christopher Worley opine, 'OD is oriented to improving the total system—the organization and its parts in the context of the larger environment that affects them'. Thomas G. Cummings and Christopher G. Worley, *Organization Development & Change 2005* (Mason, OH/London: South-Western/Cengage Learning, 2009), 1.

36 The idea of change as a three-stage structure was not a seminal idea – the French-Dutch cultural anthropologist, Arnold Vann Gennep, formulated a three-stage transition in 1909 in the context of a study called *The Rites of Passage*. Commentators who have gone on to build on Lewin's model include Lippitt et al. (1958), Beckhard and Harris (1977), Bullock and Batten (1985).

37 Bernard Burnes, *Managing Change: A Strategic Approach to Organisational Dynamics*, 1992 (Harlow: Pearson, 2000), 281.

38 R.M. Kanter, et al., *The Challenge of Organizational Change: How Companies Experience It and Leaders Guide It* (New York, NY: Free Press, 1992). 10.
    This is not a unique perspective. Planned change began to attract criticism from the 1980s onwards such as: Thomas Peters and Robert Waterman, *In Search of Excellence: Lessons from America's Best-Run Companies* (New York, NY: Harper & Row, 1982); David Charles Wilson, *A Strategy of Change: Concepts and Controversies in the Management of Change* (London: Routledge, 1992).

39 Karl Weick, 'Emergent Change as a Universal in Organizations', in Michael Beer and Nitin Nohria (eds.), 2000, 223–241, 237.

40 See Tom Burns and Graham M. Stalker, *The Management of Innovation* (London: Tavistock, 1961).

41 See Erich Jantsch, *The Self-Organizing Universe: Scientific and Human Implications of the Emerging Paradigm of Evolution* (Oxford: Pergamon Press, 1980).

42 See Andrew M. Pettigrew, 'What Is a Processual Analysis?', *Scandinavian Journal of Management*, 13, 4, 1997, 337–348; Patrick Dawson, *Reshaping Change: A Processual Approach* (London: Routledge, 2003).

43 See Ikujio Nonaka, 'Creating Organizational Order Out of Chaos: Self-Renewal in Japanese Firms', *California Management Review*, 30, 3, 1988, 57–73; Ralph D. Stacey, *Managing Chaos: Dynamic Business Strategies in an Unpredictable World* (London: Kogan Page, 1992); Stephen J. Guastello, *Chaos, Catastrophe and Human Affairs: Applications of Nonlinear Dynamics to Work, Organisations and Social Evolution* (Mahwah, NJ: Lawrence Erlbaum Associates, 1995).

44 Dexter Dunphy and Doug Stace, 'The Strategic Management of Corporate Change', *Human Relations*, 46, 8, 1993, 905–920, 916.

45 This is inspired by McKinsey's 'Axes of Change' model in Steven F. Dichter, et al., 'Leading Organizational Transformations', *McKinsey & Company: McKinsey Quarterly*, 1 February 1993, www.mckinsey.com/business-functions/organization/our-insights/leading-organizational-transformations, accessed 29 May 2021.

46 Jean Bartunek, Denise Rousseau, Jenny Rudolph, and Judith Depalma, 'On the Receiving End: Sensemaking, Emotion, and Assessments of an Organizational Change Initiated by Others', *The Journal of Applied Behavioral Science*, 42, 2, 2006, 182–206, www.researchgate.net/publication/250959684_On_the_Receiving_EndSensemaking_Emotion_and_Assessments_of_an_Organizational_Change_Initiated_by_Others.

47 Michael Beer and Nitin Nohria (eds.), Introduction, *Breaking the Code of Change* (Boston, MA: Harvard Business School Press, 2000, 27.

48 John Kotter, 'Accelerate!', *Harvard Business Review*, November 2012, https://hbr.org/2012/11/accelerate, accessed 29 May 2021.

49 The global aggregate from Gallup data collected in 2014, 2015, and 2016 across 155 countries indicates that just 15% of employees worldwide are engaged in their job. Source: 'State of the Global Workforce', *GALLUP*, 2017, www.gallup.com/workplace/238079/state-global-workplace-2017.aspx#formheader, accessed 29 May 2021.

50 Source: Adi Gaskell, 'New Study Finds that Collaboration Drives Workplace Performance', *Forbes*, 22 June 2017, www.forbes.com/sites/adigaskell/2017/06/22/new-study-finds-that-collaboration-drives-workplace-performance/#57cd58da3d02, accessed 29 May 2021.

51 Source: Jena McGregor, 'Zappos Says 18 Percent of the Company Has Left Following Its Radical "No Bosses" Approach', *The Washington Post*,

14 January 2016, www.washingtonpost.com/news/on-leadership/wp/2016/01/14/zappos-says-18-percent-of-the-company-has-left-following-its-radical-no-bosses-approach/, accessed 29 May 2021.

52 That said, an interesting new University of Otago study suggests that human brains and honeybee brains are similar. Mark Hathaway, 'Study Reveals Similarities between Bee Brains and Human Brains', *Phys.org*, 26 February 2020, https://phys.org/news/2020-02-reveals-similarities-bee-brains-human.html, accessed 29 May 2021.

Bibliography

Anthony, Scott D., 'What Do You Really Mean by Business "Transformation"?', *Harvard Business Review*, 29 February 2016, https://hbr.org/2016/02/what-do-you-really-mean-by-business-transformation, accessed 29 May 2021.

Bartunek, Jean, Rousseau, Denise, Rudolph, Jenny, and Depalma, Judith, 'On the Receiving End: Sensemaking, Emotion, and Assessments of an Organizational Change Initiated by Others', *The Journal of Applied Behavioral Science*, 42, 2, 2006, 182–206, www.researchgate.net/publication/250959684_On_the_Receiving_EndSensemaking_Emotion_and_Assessments_of_an_Organizational_Change_Initiated_by_Others, accessed 23 August 2021.

Beckhard, Richard, 'Optimizing Team Building Effort', *Journal of Contemporary Business*, 1972, 1 (3):23–32.

Beckhard, Richard and Harris, Reuben T., *Organisational Transitions: Managing Complex Change* (Reading, MA/London: Addison-Wesley, 1977).

Beebe, William, *Edge of the Jungle* (New York, NY: Henry Holt and Co., 1921).

Beer, Michael and Nohria, Nitin (eds.), *Breaking the Code of Change* (Boston, MA: Harvard Business School Press, 2000).

Beer, Michael and Nohria, Nitin, 'Cracking the Code of Change', *Harvard Business Review*, May/June 2000, https://hbr.org/2000/05/cracking-the-code-of-change, accessed 29 May 2021.

Bentley, Mike, 'Behavioural Design is Key to Successful Business Transformation', *Financial Director*, 11 September 2018, www.financialdirector.co.uk/2018/09/11/behavioural-design-is-key-to-successful-business-transformation/, accessed 29 May 2021.

Blackburn, Simon, LaBerge, Laura, O'Toole, Clayton, and Schneider, Jeremy, 'Digital Strategy in a Time if Crisis', *McKinsey*, 22 April 2020, www.mckinsey.com/business-functions/mckinsey-digital/our-insights/digital-strategy-in-a-time-of-crisis, accessed 29 May 2021.

Bohm, David, *On Dialogue* (London: Routledge, 1996).

Boulton, Clint, '"What is Digital Transformation?" A Necessary Disruption', *CIO*, 17 September 2020, www.cio.com/article/3211428/what-is-digital-transformation-a-necessary-disruption.html, accessed 29 May 2021.

Boulton, Jean G., Allen, Peter M., and Bowman, Cliff, *Embracing Complexity: Strategic Perspectives for an Age of Turbulence* (Oxford: Oxford University Press, 2015).

Brown, Tom, 'Beyond Constructivism: Navigationism in the Knowledge Era', *On the Horizon*, 2006, 14:108–120, www.researchgate.net/publication/228340946_Beyond_constructivism_Navigationism_in_the_knowledge_era, accessed 29 May 2021.

Bullock, R.J. and Batten, Donde, 'It's Just a Phase We're Going through: A Review and Synthesis of OD Phase Analysis', *Group & Organization Studies*, 1985, 10 (4):383–412.

Burns, Tom and Stalker, George Macpherson, *The Management of Innovation* (London: Tavistock, 1961).

Burnes, Bernard, *Managing Change: A Strategic Approach to Organisational Dynamics*, 1992 (Harlow: Pearson, 2004).

Černe, Matej, Nerstad, Christina G.L., Dysvik, Anders, and Škerlavaj, Miha, 'What Goes Around Comes Around: Knowledge Hiding, Perceived Motivational Climate, and Creativity', *Academy of Management*, 57, 1, 4 January 2013, https://journals.aom.org/doi/full/10.5465/amj.2012.0122, accessed 29 May 2021.

Cummings, Thomas G. and Worley, Christopher G., *Organization Development & Change 2005* (Mason, OH/London: South-Western/Cengage Learning, 2009).

Cunha, Migueland Cunha, Rita, 'The Interplay of Planned and Emergent Change in Cuba', *International Business Review*, 2003, 12, 4:445–459.

Dawson, Patrick, *Reshaping Change: A Processual Approach* (London: Routledge, 2003).

Dhawan, Erica and Chamorro-Premuzic, Tomas, 'How to Collaborate Effectively if Your Team Is Remote', *Harvard Business Review*, 27 February 2018, https://hbr.org/2018/02/how-to-collaborate-effectively-if-your-team-is-remote, accessed 29 May 2021.

Dichter, Steven F., Gagnon, Chris and Alexander, Ashok, 'Leading Organizational Transformations', *McKinsey & Company: McKinsey Quarterly*, 1 February 1993, www.mckinsey.com/business-functions/organization/our-insights/leading-organizational-transformations, accessed 29 May 2021.

Downes, Stephen, 'What Connectivism Is', *Half an Hour Blog*, 3 February 2007, https://halfanhour.blogspot.com/2007/02/what-connectivism-is.html, accessed 29 May 2021.

Dunphy, Dexter and Stace, Doug, "The Strategic Management of Corporate Change", *Human Relations*, 1993, 46 (8):905–920.

Erikson, Erik, *Childhood and Society* (New York: W.W. Norton, 1950).

Ewenstein, Boris, Smith, Wesley, and Sologar, Ashvin, 'Changing Change Management', *McKinsey & Company*, 1 July 2015, www.mckinsey.com/featured-insights/leadership/changing-change-management, accessed 29 May 2021.

Gaskell, Adi, 'New Study Finds that Collaboration Drives Workplace Performance', *Forbes*, 22 June 2017, www.forbes.com/sites/adigaskell/2017/06/22/new-study-finds-that-collaboration-drives-workplace-per-formance/#57cd58da3d02, accessed 29 May 2021.

Guastello, Stephen J., *Chaos, Catastrophe and Human Affairs: Applications of Nonlinear Dynamics to Work, Organisations and Social Evolution* (Mahwah, NJ: Lawrence Erlbaum Associates, 1995).

Gloor, Peter A., *Swarm Creativity: Competitive Advantage through Collaborative Innovation Networks* (Oxford: Oxford University Press, 2006).

Hathaway, Mark, 'Study Reveals Similarities between Bee Brains and Human Brains', *Phys.org*, 26 February 2020, https://phys.org/news/2020-02-reveals-similarities-bee-brains-human.html, accessed 29 May 2021.

Heyden, Mariano, Fourné, Sebastian, Koene, Bas, Werkman, Renate, and Ansari, Shaz, 'Rethinking 'Top-Down' and 'Bottom-Up' Roles of Top and Middle Managers in Organizational Change: Implications for Employee Support', *Journal of Management Studies*, 2016, 54 (7), 961-985.

Husband, Jon, 'What Is Wirearchy?', *Wirearchy* (blog), 16 February 2013, http://wirearchy.com/what-is-wirearchy/, accessed 29 May 2021.

Isaacs, William, *Dialogue and the Art of Thinking Together: A Pioneering Approach to Communicating in Business and in Life* (New York, NY: Currency, 1999).

Jantsch, Erich, *The Self-Organizing Universe: Scientific and Human Implications of the Emerging Paradigm of Evolution* (Oxford: Pergamon Press, 1980).

Jones, Garett, *Hive Mind: How Your Nation's IQ Matters So Much More Than Your Own* (Stanford, CA: Stanford University Press, 2016).

Jones, Mark, 'Most Employers Don't Get Digital Transformation', 9 April 2019, https://techhq.com/2019/04/most-employees-dont-get-digital-transformation/, accessed 29 May 2021.

Kania, John and Kramer, Mark, 'Collective Impact', *Stanford Social Innovation Review*, 2011, https://ssir.org/articles/entry/collective_impact, accessed 29 May 2021.

Kanter, Rosabeth Moss, *The Change Masters: Innovation and Entrepreneurship in the American Corporation* (New York, NY: Simon & Schuster, 1982).

Kanter, Rosabeth Moss, Stein, B., and Jick, T.D., *The Challenge of Organizational Change: How Companies Experience It and Leaders Guide It* (New York, NY: Free Press, 1992).

Kotter, John, 'Accelerate!', *Harvard Business Review*, November 2012, https://hbr.org/2012/11/accelerate, accessed 29 May 2021.

Kotter, John P., *Accelerate: Building Strategic Agility for a Faster-Moving World* (Boston, MA: Harvard Business Press Books, 2014).

Lewin, Kurt, 'Frontiers in Group Dynamics: Concept, Method and Reality in Social Science; Equilibrium and Social Change', *Human Relations*, 1947, 1 (1):5–41.

Lewin, Kurt, Lippit, Ronald, and White, Ralph K., 'Patterns of Aggressive Behavior in Experimentally Created Social Climates', *Journal of Social Psychology*, 1939, 10:271–301.

Lindsey, Herbert, *Digital Transformation: Build Your Organization's Future for the Innovation Age* (London and New York, NY: Bloomsbury Business, 2017).

Lippitt Ronald., Watson, Jeanne, and Westley, Bruce, *Dynamics of Planned Change* (New York, NY: Harcourt, Brace & World, 1958).

Matta, Nadim and Ashkenas, Ron, 'Why Good Projects Fail Anyway', *Harvard Business Review*, September 2003, https://hbr.org/2003/09/why-good-projects-fail-anyway, accessed 29 May 2021.

Mazzone, Dominic M., *Digital or Death: Digital Transformation—The Only Choice for Business to Survive Smash and Conquer* (Mississauga: Smash Box Consulting Inc., 2014).

McGregor, Jena, 'Zappos Says 18 Percent of the Company Has Left Following Its Radical "No Bosses" Approach', *The Washington Post*, 14 January 2016, www.washingtonpost.com/news/on-leadership/wp/2016/01/14/zappos-says-18-percent-of-the-company-has-left-following-its-radical-no-bosses-approach/, accessed 29 May 2021.

Mlitz, Kimberly, 'Digital Transformation Spending Worldwide 2017-2024', *Statista*, 31 Mar 2021, www.statista.com/statistics/870924/worldwide-digital-transformation-market-size/, accessed 29 May 2021.

Newman, Daniel, 'Six Reasons Why We Haven't Seen Full AI Adoption', *Forbes*, 12 March 2019, www.forbes.com/sites/danielnewman/2019/03/12/6-reasons-why-we-havent-seen-full-ai-adoption/?sh=46c6e3e53e99, accessed 29 May 2021.

Nohria, Nitin and Beer, Michael, 'Cracking the Code of Change', *Harvard Business Review*, May–June 2020, https://hbr.org/2000/05/cracking-the-code-of-change, accessed 29 May 2021.

Nonaka, Ikujiro, *Creating Organizational Order Out of Chaos: Self-Renewal in Japanese Firms. California Management Review*, 1988, 30 (3):57–73.

O'Driscoll, Tony, 'People Are the Key to Business Transformation', *Duke Corporate Education*, December 2019, www.dukece.com/insights/people-driven-transformation/, accessed 29 May 2021.

Osborn, Alexander, *Applied Imagination. Principles and Procedures of Creative Thinking* (New York, NY: Charles Scribner's Sons, 1953).

Peters, Thomas and Waterman, Robert, *In Search of Excellence: Lessons from America's Best-Run Companies* (New York, NY: Harper & Row, 1982).

Pettigrew, Andrew M., 'What is a Processual Analysis?', *Scandinavian Journal of Management*, 1997, 13 (4):337–348.

Quattrone, Paolo and Hopper, Trevor, 'What Does Organizational Change Mean? Speculations on a Taken for Granted Gategory', *Management Accounting Research*, 2011, 12 (4):403–435.

Rosenberg, Louis, 'The Rise of the Human Hive Mind', *Foundry4*, 8 October 2017, https://foundry4.com/the-rise-of-the-human-hive-mind, accessed 29 May 2021.

Scharmer, Claus O., *Theory U: Leading from the Future As It Emerges* (Oakland, CA: Berrett-Koehler, 2009).

Schön, Donald A., *Beyond the Stable State. Public and Private Learning in a Changing Society* (London: Temple Smith, 1971).

Schön, Donald and Reid, Martin, *Frame Reflection: Toward the Resolution of Intractable Policy Controversies* (New York, NY: Basic Books, 1994).

Siemens, George, 'Connectivism: A Learning Theory for the Digital Age, 2004', *Elearningspace*, 5 April 2005, https://pdfs.semanticscholar.org/a25f/84bc55488d01bd5f5acac4eed0c7d8f4597c.pdf, accessed 29 May 2021.

Skinner, Burrhus Frederic, 'Two Types of Conditioned Reflex: A Reply to Konorski and Miller', *Journal of General Psychology*, 1937, 16:272–279.

Smaje, Kate, 'What's Your Digital Quotient?', *Harvard Business Review*, Ideacast, Episode 483, 3 September 2015, https://hbr.org/podcast/2015/09/whats-your-digital-quotient.html?registration=success, accessed 20 May 2021.

Smith, Ray A., 'Do You Have E-Charisma on Zoom? Here's How to Get It', *Wall Street Journal*, 29 November 2020, www.wsj.com/articles/do-you-have-e-charisma-on-zoom-heres-how-to-get-it-11606651200, accessed 29 May 2021.

Solis, Brian, 'Definition of Digital Transformation', 23 January 2017, www.briansolis.com/2017/01/definition-of-digital-transformation/, accessed 29 May 2021.

Spataro, Jared, 'How Remote Work Impacts Collaboration: Findings from our Team', *Microsoft*, 22 April 2020, www.microsoft.com/en-us/microsoft-365/blog/2020/04/22/how-remote-work-impacts-collaboration-findings-team/, accessed 29 May 2021.

Stacey, Ralph D., *Managing Chaos: Dynamic Business Strategies in an Unpredictable World* (London: Kogan Page, 1992).

Thomas, Robert J., 'The Three Essential Ingredients of Great Collaborations', *Harvard Business Review*, 1 June 2011, https://hbr.org/2011/06/the-three-essential-ingredient, accessed 29 May 2021.

Trompenaars, Fons and Hampden-Turner, Charles, *Riding the Waves of Culture: Understanding Cultural Diversity in Business* (London: Nicholas Brealey, 1997).

Van der Post, Lauren, *The Lost World of Kalahari, 1958* (London: Vintage, 2002).

Vann Gennep, Arnold, *The Rites of Passage, 1909* (Chicago, IL: University of Chicago Press, 1960).

Weick, Karl, 'Emergent Change as a Universal in Organizations', in *Breaking the Code of Change*, eds., Michael Beer and Nitin Nohria (Boston, MA: Harvard Business School Press, 2000) 223–241, 237.

Weick, Karl E. and Sutcliffe, Kathleen M., 'Organizing and the Process of Sensemaking', *Organization Science*, 2005, 16 (4):409–421.

Westerman, George, Calméjane, Claire, Bonnet, Didier, Ferraris, Patrick, and McAfee, Andrew, 'Digital Transformation: A Roadmap for Billion-Dollar Organizations', *MIT Center for Digital Business and Capgemini Consulting*, 17 November 2011, www.capgemini.com/resources/digital-transformation-a-roadmap-for-billiondollar-organizations/, accessed 29 May 2021.

Westerman, George, *Leading Digital: Turning Technology into Business Transformation* (Boston, MA: Harvard Business Review Press, 2014).

Wilson, David C., *A Strategy of Change: Concepts and Controversies in the Management of Change* (London: Routledge, 1992).

Xiao, Yan and Fan, Ziyang, '10 Technology Trends to Watch in the Covid-19 Pandemic', *World Economic Forum*, 27 April 2020, www.weforum.org/agenda/2020/04/10-technology-trends-coronavirus-covid19-pandemic-robotics-telehealth/, accessed 16 June 2020.

Zucconi, Eleonara, 'Toby Oliver (CTO @ Typeform) on Hiring, Managing, and Scaling Engineering Teams', *Medium*, 15 January 2018, https://medium.com/@eleonorazucconi/toby-oliver-cto-typeform-on-hiring-managing-and-scaling-engineering-teams-86bef9e5a708, accessed 29 May 2021.

5

SWARM 1.0

DEVELOPING A LOCAL HUMAN SWARM STRATEGY

As Kris Kendrick, Divisional Head of Business Strategy, resumed her seat, several colleagues nodded approval at her. She had just presented to the Executive Leadership Team and they were clearly impressed by her novel approach to preparing the divisional business strategy. It all started over six months ago when Kris discovered the fascinating way honeybees organised themselves and how this could support the strategic planning process.

In the past, she had followed a very traditional process-led approach to the strategic planning sessions. She convened a small planning committee who assessed the previous year's priorities and strategic plan and looked at the strengths, weaknesses, opportunities, and threats (SWOT analysis) for each priority. A revised set of priorities was then presented to stakeholders for input and feedback. The problem with this approach was that Kris always felt it was a tick-in-the-box exercise where none of the stakeholders related to the priorities drafted by the central team. This resulted in motivation and performance issues across the division because performance targets were set against the business plan. A swarm-based approach seemed to have some of the answers for her because it promised to optimise business intelligence and lead to collaboration and engagement across the division on a scale that hadn't been achieved before with

DOI: 10.4324/9781003215561-8

the conventional strategic planning process. Kris could see that this could potentially drive up business motivation and performance.

Kris set about building a swarm community. She identified a small coalition of trusted advisors to help her develop a swarm approach. She appointed swarm reps and formed a business intelligence network that worked with the swarm reps to identify critical business challenges. She established a swarm cluster, which was a dedicated group of self-organising sensemakers who processed the business intelligence. The swarm cluster worked remotely and face-to-face through swarm teams to come up with best-fit solutions to address the core business challenge. These solutions were played back to the business community for feedback and then presented for approval.

Kris found that there was a lot more energy and collective involvement in the strategic planning and that people seemed to own these priorities rather than merely read them on posters stuck up on the coffee machine. Kris received a WhatsApp later from the VP. 'Great presentation today, Kris. Your new swarm approach has certainly caused a buzz'. Kris groaned and replied 'zzzz'.

This fictional case study is based on true events. It is the story of the Divisional Head of Strategic Planning and business process owner, Kris, who approached the department's annual strategic planning session in a novel way. It represents a grassroots initiative for developing organisational muscle in collective decision-making in non-digital environments using human swarms. It encourages the formation of experimental pockets of self-organising swarm communities where ideation and decision-making is a collective and not central process. It adopts a nature-inspired swarm intelligence approach that encourages a more business intelligence-led, self-organising, and collective decision-making experience with wider inclusivity and a true stake in the process. Kris had created a small microbusiness transformation within her own division where new networks and sensemaking communities were formed and the business operating system was reinvented. New processes were established that in the future could be easily digitalised. New collective behaviours cultivated a localised hive mind.

This chapter explores how to set about establishing this independent structure, colonised by a swarm community of trusted advisors, reps, a business intelligence network (BIN), and swarm clusters. It goes on to detail some practical human-generated mechanisms – the human waggle dance – where information is distilled and consensus is reached without the need for designers, human facilitators, supervisors, or alpha leaders. It achieves this through the three business transformation levers outlined in Chapter 4; namely, system transformation, organisational change and development, and swarm facilitation. Let's look at each of these levers in turn.

Swarm 1.0: Lever 1: system transformation

In Chapter 4, a system transformation was characterised as a shift from current reality to future state. Lever 1 for Swarm 1.0 relates to system transformation. The following is a deep dive into organisational (structures and networks), digital (future-proofing the organisation for swarm tech solutions), and behavioural (developing willingness and ability) transformations.

Organisational transformation 1.0

Organisational transformation in relation to Swarm 1.0 addresses a key question: how can a one-off business meeting, event, or programme be more self-organising, collective, emergent, collaborative, and steered by business intelligence rather than governed by conditioning hierarchies? In natural honeybee systems, decisions are part of the collective group. This section reflects on how we can ditch the traditional organisational structure and run simple meetings in a more collective way through self-organising swarm communities and networks. Inspired by house-hunting honeybees, Swarm 1.0 is a self-organising grassroots initiative where ideation and decision-making is not pyramidal with ideas and decisions coming from the apex down, but is collective and deformalised and works through human swarms.

In simple terms, Swarm 1.0 is a self-organising complex adaptive cell (known as a swarm community) which nests within the broader traditional business community or enterprise. In this swarm community, you have influencers (business process owners and beekeepers), enablers (BIN, swarm clusters, and, swarm teams), and connectors (swarm reps and

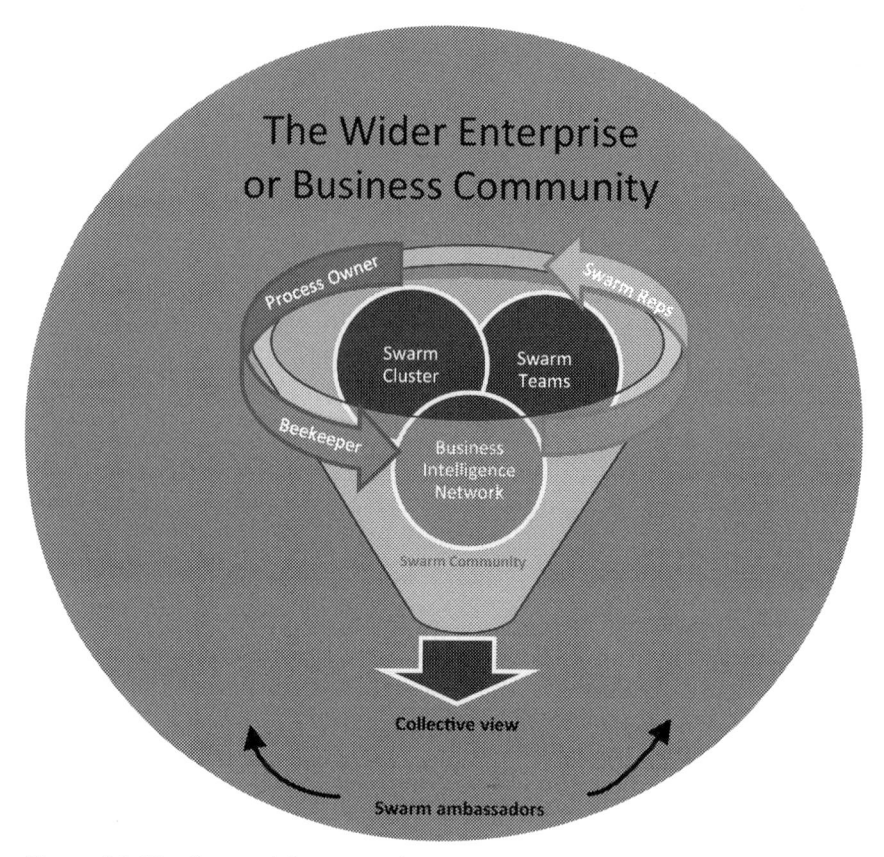

Figure 5.1 The Swarm 1.0 community.

swarm ambassadors) who evolve ideas and decisions and come up with a collective view. Figure 5.1 captures this.

Chapter 4 introduced an organic, honeycomb organisational structure. As swarm intensifies, this organic structure is going to prove to be critical for scaling up swarm across the organisation. Here we have the genesis of the organisational honeycomb structure: a single self-organising complex adaptive cell that has emerged from a local initiative that has the potential to replicate like DNA throughout the organisation. This is not planned and there is no organisational restructure required. At this stage, the single honeycomb cell that houses the swarm community is a seed. Let's explore in detail three key groups of agents (influencers, enablers, and connectors) that drive the organisational transformation at this level.

Influencers

These are the people that get things off the ground and running. Two key influencers here are business process owners and beekeepers. Let's look at each in turn.

Influencer: the business process owner

The business process owner is traditionally the key decision maker and sponsor of the meeting, event, project, or workshop who is in a position to adopt a local swarm approach. The business process owner could be anyone from a team leader who organises team events and meetings, to a project manager or head of department. Typically, business process owners, such as Kris, make independent decisions about the scope and design of the event without deferral, input, or approval from other sources or stakeholders.

The question is, why would a business process owner want to adopt a swarm approach for their local meeting or event? What's in it for them? It is a more intelligence-based approach that creates more engagement. The new generation of local frontline leaders are increasingly coming from the millennial generation who already makes up over half of the workforce. Over 50% of them manage people.[1] This generation has strong values around adaptiveness, flexibility, collaboration, inclusiveness, and people engagement/personal development. They are looking for more participatory, flexible, and collaborative ways of working and leading. They are digital natives who look to technological solutions to drive efficiencies. Many of them simply don't want to be hierarchical frontline leaders and managers. There are the young alpha millennial types, especially, from the entrepreneurial and start-up sector, but, on the whole, millennials are rejecting the traditional command and control Taylorist culture. Young managers and leaders are looking to engage with their teams, drive up collaboration, and create a more collective decision-making culture that promotes inclusiveness, adaptiveness, and trust. Swarm 1.0 achieves these objectives. Moreover, it is a steppingstone to digitalism and digital transformation (something that enthuses digital natives). Swarm 1.0 is a simple business process to adopt which does not require enterprise-wide input or planning. It requires a dedicated business intelligence input, greater collective involvement, and cross-collaboration which should lead to more engagement and a greater synthesis between working and learning. Each of these values should appeal to young managers and leaders and to the organisational goals around being more adaptive, collaborative, inclusive, and engaged. Another important reason to adopt swarm is that it facilitates a wider business transformation. It creates a networked and collaborative culture, futureproofs the division for digital transformation, and nurtures a global hivemind business environment.

What will the business process owner practically need to do?

- Familarise themselves with theories of collective decision-making, self-organising and emergent systems, swarm intelligence, and the swarm facilitation business process.
- Appoint trusted advisors; in particular, a beekeeper and swarm reps.
- Identify a meeting, event, workshop, or project that can adopt swarm.
- Establish a resourcing and financing model.
- Engage with all stakeholders in the business community.
- Create the BIN and nurture and moderate it for several months to get it established.
- Work with swarm reps to prioritise and shape the business intelligence that comes out of the BIN into a core business challenge.
- Form the swarm cluster.
- Become a swarm facilitation ambassador and exploit all opportunities to champion swarm in the business.

Influencer: the beekeeper

The beekeeper is appointed by the business process owner and is a thought leader, trusted advisor, and mentor to the swarm cluster and business process owner. The beekeeper can be someone from the department or project group who is a champion and promoter of swarm, or someone external such as a consultant. Just like an apiarist who nurtures and serves the hive, the organisational beekeeper provides the right environment for the organisational colony to swarm. The beekeeper is akin to Agile Scrum's scrum master. They serve the process and are experts in swarm intelligence as it relates to the local business community.

What will the beekeeper practically need to do?

- Mentor, coach, and advise the swarm community on the principles and properties of swarm and swarm facilitation.
- Support business process owners in key preparations, including setting up the BIN, creating the swarm cluster, and developing its function and capabilities.
- Participate in swarm meets and keep an eye on the process and be prepared to step in and counsel the swarm cluster and teams when required.

Enablers

Influencers can make things happen; but without dedicated enablers, the initiative would have little chance of success. Key enablers include the BIN, swarm clusters, and swarm teams.

Enabler: the business intelligence network (BIN)

The BIN is a collaborative network of influential stakeholders from the business community who have a deep alignment of core interest[2] who are willing and able to provide ongoing local emergent intelligence to the business process owner relating to issues affecting their area of business. They are a vital organisational sensemaking resource that drive the 'intelligence' component of swarm intelligence and provide crucial insights about what's going on at the ground level of the organisation. In traditional meetings or events, influencers undertake a business needs analysis or assessment to verify the need, seek more data, and engage key stakeholders. This needs analysis feeds into the competencies and objectives that shape the business design or agenda. Business needs assessments tend to be more political than instructional and can be influenced by groupthink. Swarm 1.0 differs from this traditional approach. It establishes an ongoing proactive feedback loop directly with the business through the diverse BIN whose experience and ideas can be drawn on to help departments shape new ideas, processes, and priorities. The business process owner, together with the swarm reps, process these priorities and establish a critical business challenge for the swarm cluster to make sense of. This is in the tradition of emergence and organisational sensemaking rather than evaluation or assessment. In Swarm 2.0, these BINs will be replaced by artificial intelligence (AI) technology; but here, process owners will need to manually build and maintain these collaborative intelligence networks that come out of such things as surveys, polling, interviews, and questionnaires.

Some basic principles to establish and maintain the BIN leading up to Swarm 1.0 includes:

1. *Identify and establish a diverse network*

   Influencers should draw a business stakeholder map that includes business contacts who have a stake in the department's decisions and ideas. Use the entire department to identify this business stakeholder network. Classic stakeholder mapping that plots degree of stakeholder commitment versus influence can be used to do a network analysis of the business community in order to identify their degree of influence and commitment. It is important to focus on building a diverse network of relevant agents with core interests that extend across a broad intelligence. It is also useful to have internal and external representation. External stakeholders include customers, clients, vendors/suppliers, employees, analysts, and even competitors. The aim here is to maximise intersectional thinking and experience – something Frans Johansson calls the '*Medici Effect*' – whilst at the same time maintaining a manageable and practical network.

2. *Make the case for the intelligence network – what's in it for the network?*

   It is obvious what's in it for the department – they get a live business network that provides them with ongoing organisational context and intelligence to make more effective and collective decisions within the department. When forming this intelligence network, it is important for influencers to be clear on the network's function, the commitment, and why, in the long term, it will be beneficial to participate. Clearly, the case for taking part is that participants get a chance to shape decision-making within a key department that impacts them.

3. *Keep it active by keeping it simple and focused*
   The success factor of an effective intelligence network is that it is up to date and actively participates. The network needs to be constantly reviewed to include new stakeholders and shifting influences and alliances. Actively shape the environment by constantly communicating the aims and objectives of the intelligence network and find diverse ways to elicit their views.

4. *Communicate quick wins and the strength of the network*
   If strategy, policy, ideas, and decisions have been shaped by the network, it is important to communicate this back to the BIN by demonstrating how their input and perspective influenced direction. It is vital for the business intelligence network to understand and appreciate the strategic importance of their contribution.

5. *Treat the network as an organic cybernetic system rather than as an oracle*
   The network needs to be maintained and nurtured and should be allowed to evolve organically and have some self-sufficiency.

6. *Build trust*
   Ensure that the network feels valued and that it is a respectful and confidential space.

What will the BIN practically need to do?

- Agree to be part of a BIN and to commit to the terms and conditions of that network.
- Communicate business challenges, issues, and incidents that impact the local business environment using an agreed format.
- Be prepared to engage with other BIN members to share learnings.
- Review the business process owner's assessment of key challenges coming out of the business intelligence.
- Review and comprehensively feedback on the swarm cluster's deliberations on the key challenges.
- Agree to be proactive members of the network, promoting it, and maintaining its integrity, efficiency, and confidentiality.

Enabler: swarm cluster

This is a problem-solving, idea-generating, and decision-making community that focuses on issues and business challenges that emerge from the BIN. We have seen how in the natural world, honeybees form beard-like clusters separate from the main colony in order to make important decisions. As we shall see shortly, this swarm is broken down into smaller groups. Ideally swarm clusters should be even numbered to conveniently divide into swarm teams and have no more than 30 participants because swarm clusters gather for swarm meets and, as a rule, larger groups present more practical challenges in terms of venues, logistics, and overall group self-management. The business process owner work with the swarm reps to identify business challenges that arise from the BIN. The swarm clusters will then be formed. In Swarm 1.0, which concerns local events, the swarm cluster will likely be resourced locally with participants who would have typically attended the conventional meeting, event, or workshop. The business process owner has overall say concerning swarm participation, but anyone may lobby the business process owner to be part of the swarm cluster. Once the group is formed, it will be self-organising and will be able to make group decisions, to retire members, or add new members based on the emerging business challenge. The swarm cluster's function is to work with the business challenge that emerges from the BIN and to build ideas and decisions around it. It will always remain a self-organising and self-resourceful network.

What will the swarm cluster practical need to do?

- Agree to take part in the swarm activities and work on the intelligence and business challenges that emerge from the BIN through the swarm reps.
- Partner with the business process owner on practical housekeeping issues around project scope, terms of reference, and resourcing.
- Design and agree a timetable and a collaborative process for working together during remote engagements and swarm meets.
- Split into swarm teams to work on the business challenge.
- Reach a group consensus in the swarm cluster.
- Convey the ideas and recommendations back to the business process owner via the swarm rep for further input with the BIN.
- Be prepared to engage in further swarms, if necessary, based on the feedback from the BIN and business community.

Enabler: swarm teams

We have seen that honeybees operate in small diverse groups and come together to make a collective decision. This is replicated in swarm facilitation with the creation of swarm teams. Chapter 3 raised the issue of the pitfalls of working in large groups. There have been many studies over the decades concerning the effectiveness of working in smaller groups.[3] Many successful modern group theories use smaller groups – such as action learning 'sets' and Agile's 'scrums'. In the early phase of formation, the swarm cluster needs to create working swarm teams and collectively agree on a process. The core philosophy of swarm facilitation is that it is not centrally managed or led; it is self-organising, deformalised, and emergent. It promotes diverse intersectional thinking. It is widely considered that diverse groups produce better outcomes.[4] This format allows for more engagement and focused group work as well as space for individual reflection. Each individual team works in parallel on the same business challenge or idea (just as honeybees work on the same challenge when identifying food patches or potential new nests). This means that the multiple views that emerge from the small groups feed into the larger group.

What will swarm teams practically need to do?

- Work collaboratively together on developing processes, ideas, and thoughts relating to the business challenge.
- Come up with elegant and best-fit solutions to present back to the swarm cluster.
- Work in the cluster distilling the diverse ideas into a collective cluster perspective for swarm reps to present to the business process owner.
- Refine ideas and decisions based on further intelligence and feedback from the business process owner and the BIN.

Connectors

Gladwell coined the term connector in *The Tipping Point* to mean people who spread ideas – 'The point about Connectors is that by having a foot in so many different worlds, they have the effect of bringing them all together'.[5] In Swarm 1.0, there are two key connectors who work across boundaries: the Swarm reps and the swarm ambassadors.

Connector: the swarm rep

Swarm reps are appointed directly by the business process owner. Swarm reps should be well connected with a networking perspective. They will work with the business process owner to review and prioritise the business challenge that emerges from the BIN. The swarm reps will go on to be part of the swarm teams in the cluster and will connect the cluster to the business process owner. They will also connect with the beekeeper to highlight any challenges or issues surfacing in the swarm team. This is a quick and practical way for the beekeeper and business process owner to remain connected to the swarm clusters. Finally, the swarm rep will be retained to represent the swarm community down the line in the implementation phase.

What will swarm reps practically need to do?

- Work with the business process owner to prioritise the business challenges that emerge from the BIN.
- Participate in the swarm team to represent its ideas, output, and perspective to the swarm cluster and the business process owner.
- Connect, where appropriate, with the beekeeper, swarm cluster and business process owner when clarity is required or an intervention is necessary.
- Liaise with the business process owner and BIN about the emergent ideas and go back to the cluster, if necessary, to rework ideas.
- Represent the swarm community in later implementation phases.

Connector: swarm ambassadors

These are business process owners who become swarm ambassadors and share their experience with the broader organisation. The role of the swarm ambassador is to share experiences, knowledge, and learning with the business community and executive decision makers and to champion swarm both inside and outside the organisation. Knowledge sharing channels should include mid- and after-action reviews, documenting the output, and using a wide and imaginative communication strategy to share the experience of working in local swarm communities.

Digital transformation 1.0

Swarm 1.0 is a human swarm that doesn't directly use technology to organise itself during swarm facilitation. So, what, it might be asked, is the relevance of digital transformation in a non-digital human-based system? In Chapter 4, it was opined that digital transformation is not just about promoting tech solutions and digital platforms, but preparing the ground for digitalisation. Digital transformation, therefore, is also as much about future-proofing and seeding the enterprise in terms of its structures, processes, and people as it is procuring tech solutions. Creating these networked complex adaptive systems at Swarm 1.0 prepares the ground for future digitalisation. Setting up BINs, cultivating hive mindsets, and putting in place swarm facilitation (which is algorithm based) creates a bridge mindsets, and putting in place for the future adoption of digitalism, digitalisation, and decision augmentation. This is building a grassroot culture and set of procedures that will be a good foundation and stepping stone towards digitalisation and embarking on a digital transformation journey.

Behavioural transformation 1.0

Chapter 4 introduced the willingness versus ability equation, the three behavioural quotients, and the nine swarm themes. It also introduced two types of learning interventions – developing ability and willingness as a preparation or transition to work in a swarm environment (pre-swarm development) versus developing abilities and attitudes in role to enhance performance in a swarm environment (in-swarm development). These are important considerations for developing behavioural transformation. Let's see how this plays out for Swarm 1.0.

Swarm community pre-swarm development

The principal players of the swarm community – influencers, enablers, and connectors – were carefully profiled earlier. Prior to the formation of clusters, these swarm community participants will need to prepare for swarm facilitation. Here is a summary of the specific learning initiatives that the swarm community needs to do at the pre-swarm stage.

Influencer: pre-swarm development for business process owner

Business process owners should not contemplate applying or practising swarm theory until they fully understand and appreciate the principles of swarm intelligence, the conditions in which swarm thrives in business, and how to put it into practice. One assumes that business process owners are already willing to adopt swarm, but they need to constantly develop their knowledge and abilities in this area. Specifically, they need to:

- Understand the history and impact of hierarchy on organisations and how it has negatively affected collaboration, agility, and collective decision-making.
- Research and reflect on the swarm approach and how it cultivates collective decision-making. They need to have an appreciation of the shortcomings of alpha leadership.
- Study the swarm facilitation approach and determine how it can benefit and be applied to a local meeting or event.
- Work with trusted advisors and thought leaders such as the beekeeper to develop pre-swarm and in-swarm learning interventions.

The learning methods that business process owners should follow to raise their knowledge and ability in this area are self-directed learning and learning from others.

Enabler: pre-swarm development for the business intelligence network

This network will require some background and context relating to the principles of swarm to help them understand their purpose and raison d'être. They do not require extensive educational programmes on the theory of swarm. They simply need to understand the context concerning why they are being asked to do something in a certain way. The primary communication and learning method will include a detailed introductory pack, one-to-one conversations by the business process owner, and a welcome induction when the network goes live. The business process owner will need to moderate, coach, and guide this network with support from the beekeeper.

Connector: pre-swarm development for swarm reps

Swarm reps are selected by business process owners prior to swarm facilitation. As discussed earlier, they are chosen for their business connections and network perspective and not for experience or knowledge relating to swarm. An important pre-swarm development initiative for this small group (there will typically be four to five swarm reps in a swarm community) is to build their knowledge and awareness of swarm. They could possibly join a small knowledge building network with the beekeeper and business process owner to cultivate their understanding. Most of the education effort can be done through self-directed learning.

Swarm community in-swarm development

This relates to the in-swarm community development that needs to be carried out during the swarm activity itself. As a quick refresher, it has been established that Swarm 1.0 is a wholly emergent approach. There is no top-down planning, directed, or centralised cultural and behavioural effort. It comes about through small-scale, local grassroots initiatives via informal networks and connectors. These local connectors and networks form a swarm community (which include influencers, the BIN, and the swarm clusters). They need to understand – to differing degrees – elements of swarm theory to achieve buy-in (willingness) and to support its goal and approach (ability). This will require some understanding about swarm intelligence and its application to business and an awareness and appreciation of swarm facilitation. Swarm learning and development initiatives at this level will not be as organised and formal as they are in Swarm 2.0. It will be informal and based on individual need.

Enabler: in-swarm development for swarm cluster

Most of the Swarm 1.0 in-swarm education effort should be targeted at this group. They will need to understand why they are using a swarm methodology rather than a more traditional approach (willingness) and gain practical guidance and approaches to thrive in a swarm environment (ability). The two quotients that are relevant for preparing Swarm 1.0 swarm clusters are developing agility and collaboration. The swarm cluster needs to be completely behind the idea of swarm facilitation (willingness) and have a high level of understanding and expertise in the theory and practice of swarm facilitation (ability). This group needs to understand the background, purpose, and mechanics of swarm facilitation to an advanced level and engage in swarm learning interventions that cover adaptive and collaborative quotients.

Adaptive quotient (AQ)

1. *Embracing complexity*
   Swarm cluster participants need to undertake a mindset shift away from being an individual contributor led by hierarchical leadership to being part of a self-organising complex adaptive system that exercise collective decision-making.
2. *Sensemaking*
   The swarm cluster needs to self-organise and make sense of the business intelligence within diverse teams using open technologies. They need to be able to distil this intelligence into a collective point of view.
3. *Perspectivism and letting go*
   The swarm cluster needs to suspend fixed assumptions and approach challenges through open thinking.

Collaborative quotient (CQ)

4. *Developing a hive mind*
   The swarm cluster needs to focus on 'we' rather than 'me' and build shared meaning and trust in others.
5. *Group creativity*
   The group needs to collaborate creatively and brainswarm ideas. They may need to collaborate remotely and come to a group agreement concerning working together.
6. *Negotiation and consensus building*
   The cluster and teams need to negotiate and build consensus. It will need mastery in interpersonal abilities to reach such group consensus.

In this in-swarm development, there are two types of learning methods that can develop the AQ and CQ of cluster participants: pre-swarm formal learning methods and in-swarm informal learning methods. Pre-swarm will include such methodologies as self-directed learning, general induction programmes, and bite-sized learning events. In-swarm will include such methodologies as one-to-one coaching, mentoring, and peer development such as swarm buddying.

Lever 2: organisational change and development approach

Swarm 1.0 is a wholly emergent, grassroots phenomenon rather than a planned organisational change. Inspired by relocating honeybees, pockets of the organisation create swarm communities to problem-solving, generate ideas, and make decisions. These complex adaptive cells have a honeycomb structure and nest in the more traditional hierarchy. As we have seen in Chapter 4, the honeycomb model becomes important as swarm organically grows and replicates. Swarm 1.0 will not change the organisation overnight but will create a seed. In 1993, Edward Lorenz mathematically explored how seemingly small incidents are all part of complex adaptive systems and can result in highly impactful occurrences and changes in other parts of the system, something known as the 'butterfly effect'.[6] Swarm 1.0 builds a momentum around approaching problem-solving, ideation, and decision-making in a more collective way. Practically speaking, this will mean a complex adaptive cell with no hierarchy or operant conditioning such as job titles, presenteeism, or formal ways of working. Swarm participants serve the challenge and not personalities and status. We have seen that there are roles in swarm communities just as there are roles in honeybee colonies (queen, workers, drones). But like honeybee colonies, the roles are all about serving the colony. There are also rules, but they are simple rules which are algorithmic and not prescriptive. Swarm clusters are groups of diverse people who are united by a common challenge, have roles to play within the community, and are guided by simple rules and business intelligence. This is about building a momentum through local emergence. Like the butterfly effect, this small change could well become the catalyst for significant organisation change down the line.

Lever 3: swarm facilitation

You recall that swarm facilitation is an algorithm that is modelled on the house-hunting habits of honeybees. This was illustrated in the swarm flow model (Figure 2.4). Let's look now in a detailed and practical way at how this plays out for Swarm 1.0.

Prepare

Prepare is a launch or start-up tier where influencers gain understanding of swarm, have conversations with stakeholders, ring-fence a budget, appoint a beekeeper, identify local programmes or events that could adopt a swarm facilitation approach, create the BIN, and appoint swarm reps.

Practical preparations that the process owner will need to carry out include the following.

Prepare stage: selection

Process owners need to identity likely meetings, events, or programmes that could benefit from a swarm approach. It is recommended that business process owners start modestly with a single event and use it as a learning experience to take forward into more ambitious swarm programmes. Selection criteria would include:

- Choose a single one-off event and not a multiple event.
- Choose an event organised by a single business process owner or decision maker with no other business process owners, executive stakeholders, or decision makers involved (business process owners do not want to be bogged down with endless stakeholder buy-in conversations).
- Choose an event with a clear objective or outcome. At this experimental stage, avoid such things as learning and training events/ programmes where there is no specific business outcome. Swarm might be used to develop a leadership strategy but not necessarily to develop individual leadership programmes.
- Choose an event that impacts the business and has various business stakeholder interests.

- Choose an event that will not create reputational issues. There are always hitches when new approaches are adopted. It is important to select a meeting or event where the stakes are low.

Prepare stage: budgeting

Swarm facilitation is not a structureless process. Honeybees have clear roles, deliverables, and priorities in the natural world. Managing a meeting or project using swarm theory necessitates clearly defined and costed terms of reference/deliverables.

Cluster

In Chapter 2, we saw that in the natural world, honeybees break away from the main colony to propagate the species. A swarm cluster forms with an objective to make sense of the business intelligence. This cluster should receive pre-swarm and in-swarm development. It needs to create smaller working groups called swarm teams.

Sensemake

The swarm cluster's raison d'être is to make sense of the business challenges that emerge from the BIN. There is a clear process/set of practical steps to sensemaking:

- Swarm reps from each swarm team need to work with the business process owner and the BIN to identify a key business challenge from the broad intelligence gathered over a period of months.
- The business challenge is communicated to the swarm cluster who then proceed to devise a group-considered set of Terms of Reference and a clear game plan and schedule for pre-swarm meet activities, swarm meet activities, and post-swarm meet activities.
- The swarm cluster works remotely on the business challenge and also on the design for the swarm meet (the main face-to-face event that will take place during the swarm cluster). The swarm reps will need to scope out venues for the swarm meet. They will require a large space suitable for swarm facilitation and its use of open space. Swarm

participants work in adaptive and collaborative ways. It is important to have a large room with natural lighting, break-out rooms, and pro-active conference personnel to support the swarm meet.

- The entire swarm cluster assemble off-site for the swarm meet. This is the major face-to-face swarm creativity session. The beekeeper is present but should not intervene unless the group gets tied up in mill knots.
- Swarm teams work in parallel on identical business challenges to create independent thinking and avoid groupthink. The swarm teams come together in the main swarm cluster and, like the honeybees, signal their ideas and then work in a group to distil and prioritise the good ideas.
- The swarm reps represent the ideas that emerge from their teams back to the main swarm cluster. The output of the swarm meet should be a collective group decision on the way forward that swam reps take back to the business process owner for further input.

Participatory methods in Swarm 1.0 sensemaking

The share and negotiation sessions in the main swarm cluster will not be formally facilitated. It is important, therefore, that there exists a mechanism to share and distil ideas. With collaborative technology, there is going to be more options and possibilities to optimise intelligence and distil ideas autonomously. At Swarm 1.0, however, the mechanism is manual and has certain limitations. Participatory, self-organising, and emergent group methods that do not use facilitators already exist and can be used for Swarm 1.0. It is the role of the swarm cluster and swarms to select processes, methodologies, and mechanisms to filter and synthesise ideas and data, but there are plenty of off-the-shelf participatory technologies that do not have complex structures or require external facilitators. These include such well-known and researched methodologies as open space technology (OST), brainstorming, brainswarming, dotmocracy, world café, agile teams, scrums, squads, group review, SWOT, crowdsourcing, gallery walks, dynamic facilitation, and fishbowl. All of these approaches share a common objective to create a more participatory, emergent, self-organising experience that maximises group participation and learning styles. Let's briefly profile some of the more well-known participatory technologies.

Speed dating

Speed dating is where you gather the entire swarm cluster into a single space and just let the network loose. Let people find connections and talk about their major discoveries with one big rule that they need to talk to at least ten other participants from outside their swarm team. A more structured way would be to have each swarm rep host a table and people join the table – this is more aligned with traditional speed dating. The entire group should then get together in a circle and talk about some of the emerging ideas with an attempt to influence the group like a waggle dance.

Dotmocracy

Dotmocracy is way of prioritising group ideas without the use of facilitators. The tool is of unknown origin but has been used in workshops since the 1980s. Here swarm reps can present to the group the teams' findings in a format such as a 'gallery walk' (where participants review ideas posted up on the wall) and participants physically vote with dots. Sometimes colour-coded dots are used where participants can make more than once choice.

SWOT analysis

This is a great tool for diagnosing ideas without the use of a facilitator. SWOT stands for strengths, weaknesses, opportunities, and threats and is often plotted in a four-box matrix where participants can review the idea (again as presentations or a gallery walk prepared by swarm reps) and add their observations in the appropriate boxes.

World Café/knowledge café

This is a useful participatory technology that is now widely used in workshops. The benefit of this mechanism is that it allows for a cross-pollination of ideas, a chance to build on ideas, and a simple process where participants from the group facilitate the discussions. Created by Juanita Brown and David Isaacs in 1995 and outlined in a 2002 book written by Juanita Brown entitled *The World Café: A Resource Guide for Hosting Conversations That Matter*, the World Café or knowledge café is where groups of tables are set up into themes selected by all participants. One host (the swarm rep) remains at each table to brief new arrivals on main insights from the ongoing conversations. A harvest occurs at the end where a group dialogue takes place picking out highlights. Knowledge/world café obviously fits in well with the idea of swarm facilitation at this level and is a good way to cross-fertilise ideas that have surfaced in individual swarm teams.

Six Thinking Hats

This is a self-organising group tool devised by Edward De Bono in his 1985 book, *Six Thinking Hats*, where participants use colour symbols (usually coloured hats) to collectively facilitate and manage group conversations. It is a way of disciplining and organising a conversation where the group follows a sequenced process. It is part of a group theory of how you can self-manage group conversations through signalling.

Act

Honeybees are driven by survivalism and unify and act around common purpose. Swarm communities are all about identifying common purpose and going with the wisdom of crowds. The beekeeper, again, serves the swarm community and helps it harvest its output.

Regenerate

We saw in Chapter 2 that the annual relocation of honeybees is about preserving, replenishing, and regenerating the colony. Regeneration and generativity are very important concepts for swarm. We saw that the in-swarm development at Swarm 1.0 is carried out via peer coaching and development. As more meetings and workshops adopt swarm, there is likely to be some people who served in other swarm clusters who can act as swarm mentors to help build swarm quotient. This brings fresh perspectives to the swarm environment. Pairing new resources with experienced resources who can peer coach and develop emerging talent will be a major strategic part of building swarm quotient at this level. Another crucial aspect of regeneration is the cycle of ideas and the looped feedback that occurs. After action reviews (AAR) are an essential part of the regenerative process at this level. Collective intelligence from the swarm meets and sessions is shared back to the BIN via the swarm reps for further input and the swarm rep goes on to represent the cluster during the implementation phase. The swarm community is recycled into other clusters. It is a way of making each swarm experience more successful than the last. The business intelligence community remains a constant legacy.

A comparison of swarm facilitation with other mainstream participatory approaches

Participatory meetings and workshops have been around for decades. A comparative study would be useful because it could help clarify and draw out distinctions between swarm facilitation and other participatory methods. I am focusing on technologies that are used in everyday meetings and events rather than general concepts such as Henry Chesbrough's *Open Innovation*. Here are a few participatory approaches:

Future Workshops (FW) and Future Search

Future Workshops are participatory events that adopt a visualisation tool. Participants are invited to brainstorm on a preselected topic by filtering key issues, visualising solutions, and creating action plans. The history of Future Workshops can be traced to the 1930s and 1940s, but Robert Jungk and Norbert Müllert published an influential book on Future Workshops in 1987 entitled *Future Workshops: How to Create Desirable Futures.* The principle of current state versus future state and the steps to get there was an important idea in Robert Fritz's 1984 *Path of Least Resistance.* Future Workshops are also the inspiration for the Future Search Conference which is a participatory method developed by Marvin Weisbord and Sandra Janoff that seeks to get the whole system in the room in order to create 'shared intentions' and a 'shared vision' through visualisation. It encourages participant self-management and responsibility.[7] There are clear commonalities between Future Workshops/Search and swarm facilitation. They are both participative technologies that concern problem-solving and decision-making opportunities in general meetings and workshops. There are, however, some key differences. Future Workshops/Search arrives at problems and decisions through the lens of visualisation;

swarm facilitation arrives at decisions through swarm intelligence. With Future Workshops (and to a lesser degree Future Search), the focus is contained to an event, whereas with swarm facilitation, the event consists of the entire end-to-end process that starts with harvesting business intelligence through collaborative networks and includes live swarm meets and post-engagement work with the broader business community. Finally (and crucially), Future Workshops and Future Search are designed and facilitated, they are not self-organising.

Open space technology (OST)

OST is a participant-led framework that was conceptualised in the 1980s by Harrison Owen and described in his book, *Open Space Technology: A User's Guide* (1992). Owen noticed how participants seemed to be more engaged during coffee breaks compared to the formal meeting and he sought to replicate the nature of these informal gatherings in the body of the meeting. OST is a one-off participatory and self-discovery event where participants create the agenda in real-time and work in groups. Topics are identified, prioritised, and facilitated by the group itself. Participants are free to move around the groups (known as the 'Law of Two Feet'). The process follows four principles:

1. Whoever comes is the right people
2. Whatever happens is the only thing that could have
3. Whenever it starts is the right time
4. When it's over, it's over

After the open space event, there is a group debrief and action planning. Similar approaches to OST include the Unconference Movement, Foo Camps and Birds of a Feather.[8]

There are some commonalities with swarm facilitation that includes the principle of diverse participation and a shift away from a centrally designed and facilitated event towards a more self-organising, emergent, and adaptive system. There are, however, major differences. OST is generally a one-off single process rather than a whole-system activity, will tend to surface issues in the room, relies on group discovery, and is very process driven and personality-led. OST is about contained groups constructing ideas and is in the tradition of constructivism; swarm facilitation is about strategically connecting ideas from across the enterprise in swarms and is more in the tradition of connectivism.

Agile Software Development/Scrum

Based on a rugby metaphor first conceived by Hirotaka Takeuchi and Ikujiro Nonaka in 1986, Scrum is a key collaborative and self-organising process for product development which came out of the software development industry.[9] Ken Schwaber and Mike Beedle wrote one of the earliest books on Scrum, *Agile Software Development with Scrum*. The book was based on the proceedings from a 2001 conference in Utah attended by software collaborators who discussed the problem of late and over-budget projects in the software industry. In the *2020 Scrum Guide*, Jeff Sutherland and Ken Schwaber describe Scrum as 'a lightweight framework that helps people, teams and organizations generate value through adaptive solutions for complex problems'.[10] It is a self-organising cross-functional process framework where small development teams collaborate together on product development. There are four 'events' in Scrum which include Scrum Sprint (a duration of product development time where the team does a lengthy session); a daily Scrum (a 15-minute connection and planning event during Sprint); the Sprint Review which is a product review at the end of the Sprint; and a Sprint Retrospective which is essentially an after-action review at the end of the project. There are three roles in the Scrum Team: the product owner (who is accountable for the product and maximises its value); the development team (an autonomous cross-functional skilled group who work on the product); and a Scrum Master (who is a 'servant-leader for the Scrum Team') who coaches and facilitates and is an ambassador in the organisation for Scrum. The Swedish music streaming platform Spotify has an agile culture that uses scrums and squads.[11] There are many striking similarities to swarm facilitation. Like swarm facilitation, Scrum comprises of self-organising, cross-functional, autonomous satellite working groups. It is in the tradition of complex adaptive systems, collective working, and decentralised structures where participants are involved in the planning and design. The role of the Scrum Master is the part-inspiration for the role of the beekeeper. There are major differences with Scrum Teams.

Swarm facilitation is not product-led; it is process-led. Second, swarm facilitation is intelligence-led and not specialist-led. Lastly, swarm facilitation aspires towards being a networked superorganism rather than an isolated Agile Scrum.[12]

Hackathon

A Hackathon is a contained innovation session that brings together specialists to work intensely on a critical problem. Its origins can be traced to June 1999 where software developers from around the world gathered together in a house in Calgary for a week and worked continuously to develop a software program.[13] Hackathons are very tech related and are focused on innovating new software programs. In recent times, the concept of the Hackathon has been incorporated into conferences and workshops where small sub-teams work on intense innovation sessions. Swarm facilitation shares the spirit of Hackathons where clusters of people work together intensely on common problems. Hackathon is the inspiration for the 'swarm meet' which is a swarm gathering where the swarm community collaborate face-to-face on a critical business issue over a short period of time. There are, however, differences. Swarm facilitation is a business process improvement that is intelligence-led and brings the whole system together, whereas Hackathons are one-off meetings attended by experts that focus on product innovation.

Charette

Charette is a collaborative public planning process that involves all key stakeholders intensely working together. Charette is the French word for 'cart' and has nineteenth-century origins where the architectural faculty of the *Ecole des Beaux-Arts* in Paris set strict deadlines for its students to submit final drawings to the proctors that were loaded onto a small cart (Charette). Most of the major research and articles about the Charette approach were published between 2005 and 2010. The three basic rules of collaborating with Charette include design with everyone, start with a blank sheet, and provide just enough information.[14] There are similarities to swarm facilitation. It is intelligence-led and involves the entire system in the design and decision-making process. There are, however, some important differences. Although Charette does have a pre- and post-event component, it is essentially a one-off, face-to-face, time-bound, designed event with a hard deadline, focusing on a single issue that (although shaped by participants) is extensively facilitated by designers based on early input from a steering committee in the context of public planning. Swarm facilitation is more self-organising and less time-bound.

Holacracy

Holacracy is a practice coined and developed by Brian Robertson. It is an organisational governance system that also accommodates small-scale meetings. It involves working and organising in a less hierarchical way where power is transferred from hierarchical decision makers to 'peer-to-peer' self-managing circle networks, governed by a written constitution. Holacracy is essentially a circle of networks nested in other circles of networks, including a 'super circle' (the GCC or General Company Circle) which sets enterprise-wide priorities and guidance, and the 'anchor circle' which includes board members. Robertson describes Holacracy as resembling a 'series of nested circles, like cells within organs within organisms'.[15] Each circle and sub-circle has a particular function with distinct roles (such as 'lead links') and autonomous governance. Zappos is one of the major companies that has adopted Holacracy. Similarities to swarm facilitation include that it is a decentralised and distributed authority where autonomous groups work on specific challenges. But comparisons stop there. Strictly speaking Holacracy is not a self-organising practice because it is governed by 'complex and detailed rules' and a written constitution.[16] Indeed, it is so complex that in March 2016, Medium abandoned Holacracy because they found it too hard to implement.[17] Moreover recently, Zappos has begun to scale back on Holacracy.[18] Swarm facilitation is a self-organising operating system that aspires to being a business superorganism rather than a governance system. Moreover, unlike Holacracy, swarm facilitation follows simple rules. Crucially, Robertson asserts that Holacracy only works 'when adopted as a complete system'.[19] Swarm facilitation works both as a complete system (Swarm 3.0) and a local system (Swarm 1.0). It is more adaptive and flexible than Holacracy.

This chapter has set out in a highly practical way how swarm can work for an everyday meeting or event without involving the broader organisation or state-of-the-art intelligent systems to augment the human swarm. Swarm 1.0 can be implemented immediately to become a complex adaptive cell within the broader organisation. It generates a more collective intelligence and collaborative decision-making at the local level. It requires an enthused business process owner and some enablers and connectors to help make it work. The swarm flow model (Figure 2.4) provides a good process to follow and there are already some off-the-peg methodologies that can support swarm facilitation. This is an emergent, grassroots form of swarm, a small seed that could start the organisation on its swarm journey. Swarm 2.0 replicates this emergent swarm community and accelerates it to a global and organisational planned effort. That's where we are going next.

Notes

1 Source: Jason Albanese, 'Four Ways Millennials Are Transforming Leadership', *Inc.*, 14 November 2018, www.inc.com/jason-albanese/four-ways-millennials-are-transforming-leadership.html, accessed 29 May 2021.

2 Inspired by Getraud Leimüller et al., which discusses networks as 'deeply aligned with the individual member's core interests'. Getraud Leimüller, et al., 'Next Generation Research & Innovation Networks to Inspire a Network on Learning through Play', *The Lego Foundation*, October 2014, www.playfutures.net/modules/core/client/documents/legofoundation_study-finalcor.pdf, accessed 29 May 2021.

3 Great source with good research in Besnik Avdiaj, 'Small Team Effectiveness on Decision-Making', *Thesis*, July 2017, www.researchgate.net/publication/318640183_Small_Team_Effectiveness_on_Decision-making, accessed 29 May 2021.

4 Good sources: Sian Beilock, 'How Diverse Teams Produce Better Outcomes', *Forbes*, 4 April 2019, www.forbes.com/sites/sianbeilock/2019/04/04/how-diversity-leads-to-better-outcomes/?sh=47f4efef65ce, accessed 29 May 2021; Scott E. Page, *The Diversity Bonus: How Great Teams Pay Off in the Knowledge Economy* (Princeton, NJ: Princeton University Press, 2017).

5 Malcolm Gladwell, *The Tipping Point: How Little Things Can Make a Big Difference* (New York, NY: Little, Brown and Company, 2000), 51.

6 Edward Lorenz, *The Essence of Chaos* (Seattle, WA: University of Washington Press, 1993).

7 Martin R. Weisbord and Sandra Janoff, *Future Search: An Action Guide to Finding Common Ground in Organizations and Communities* (San Francisco, CA: Berrett-Koehler, 1995), 3–4.

8 The four principles are discussed in Harrison Owen, *Open Space Technology: A User's Guide* (1992, San Francisco: Berrett Koehler, 1997), 95. Good resources: Michelle Boule, *Mob Rule Learning: Camps, Unconferences, and Trashing the Talking Head* (Medford, NJ: CyberAge Books, 2011); Kevin Ashley, 'IDCC16 Birds of a Feather Sessions – What, Why, How', *DCC*, 11 February 2016, www.dcc.ac.uk/news/idcc16-birds-feather-sessions-what-why-how, accessed 29 May 2021.

9 Source: Hirotaka Takeuchi and Ikujiro Nonaka, 'The New Product Development Game', *Harvard Business Review*, January 1988, https://hbr.org/1986/01/the-new-new-product-development-game, accessed 29 May 2021.

10 Jeff Sutherland and Ken Schwaber, 'The 2020 Scrum Guide', *Scrum Guides*, online, 2020, www.scrumguides.org/scrum-guide.html, accessed 29 November 2021.

11 Source: Henrik Kniberg, 'Spotify Engineering Culture Part 1', *YouTube*, 4:13, January 2014, www.youtube.com/watch?v=3YrRW4u9Rlo, accessed 29 May 2021.

12 This would appear to be currently worked on by Agile who are reportedly looking to incorporate swarm into their approach. See Brezočnik, Lucija, Fister, Iztok, and Podgorelec, Vili. 'Solving Agile Software Development Problems with Swarm Intelligence Algorithms', in Ibrahim Shadi, et al. (eds.), *Algorithms and Architectures for Parallel Processing* (Cham: Springer, 2017), 298–309.

13 Source: Colin Wood, 'Who Invented the Hackathon?', *Government Technology*, 15 November 2013, www.govtech.com/data/Who-Invented-the-Hackathon.html, accessed 29 May 2021.

14 Source: Patrick M. Condon, *Design Charrettes for Sustainable Communities* (Washington, DC/Covelo, CA/London: Island Press, 2008); and Rob Roggema (ed), *The Design Charrette: Ways to Envision Sustainable Futures* (Dordrecht/New York, NY: Springer, 2014).

15 Brian Robertson, *"Holacracy". The New Management System for a Rapidly Changing World* (New York, NY: Henry Holt and Company, 2015), 46.

16 Brian Robertson, *Holacracy*, 64.

17 Source: Andy Doyle, 'Management and Organization at Medium', *Medium*, 4 March 2016, https://blog.medium.com/management-and-organization-at-medium-2228cc9d93e9, accessed 29 May 2021.

18 Source: Aimee Groth, 'Zappos Has Quietly Backed Away from Holacracy', *Quartz at Work*, 29 January 2020, https://qz.com/work/1776841/zappos-has-quietly-backed-away-from-holacracy/, accessed 29 May 2021.

19 Brian Robertson, *Holacracy*, 175. He also argued, 'Holacracy is not simply a bolt-on technique that you can add on top of your existing structure, but a fundamental shift in the way power works and the way a company is organised'. Brian Robertson, *Holacracy*, 59.

Bibliography

Albanese, Jason, 'Four Ways Millennials Are Transforming Leadership', *Inc.*, 14 November 2018, www.inc.com/jason-albanese/four-ways-millennials-are-transforming-leadership.html, accessed 29 May 2021.

Ashley, Kevin, 'Birds of a Feather Sessions – What, Why, How', *DCC*, 11 February 2016, www.dcc.ac.uk/news/idcc16-birds-feather-sessions-what-why-how, accessed 29 May 2021.

Avdiaj, Besnik, 'Small Team Effectiveness on Decision-Making', *Thesis*, July 2017, www.researchgate.net/publication/318640183_Small_Team_Effectiveness_on_Decision-making, accessed 29 May 2021.

Beilock, Sian, 'How Diverse Teams Produce Better Outcomes', *Forbes*, 4 April 2019, www.forbes.com/sites/sianbeilock/2019/04/04/how-diversity-leads-to-better-outcomes/?sh=47f4efef65ce, accessed 29 May 2021.

Bohm, David and Nichol, Lee, *On Dialogue* (London/New York, NY: Routledge, 1996).

Boule, Michelle, *Mob Rule Learning: Camps, Unconferences, and Trashing the Talking Head* (Medford, NJ: CyberAge Books, 2011).

Brown, Juanita, *The World Café: A Resource Guide for Hosting Conversations that Matter* (Mill Valley, CA: Whole Systems Associates, 2002).

Chesbrough, Henry, *Open Innovation: The New Imperative for Creating and Profiting from Technology* (Boston, MA: Harvard Business School Press, 2003).

Condon, Patrick, *Design Charrettes for Sustainable Communities* (Washington, DC/Covelo, CA/London: Island Press, 2008).

de Bono, Edward, *Six Thinking Hats: An Essential Approach to Business Management* (New York, NY: Little, Brown, & Company, 1985).

Doyle, Andy, 'Management and Organization at Medium', *Medium*, 4 March 2016, https://blog.medium.com/management-and-organization-at-med ium-2228cc9d93e9, accessed 29 May 2021.

Fritz, Robert, *The Path of Least Resistance* (Salem, MA: DMA, 1984).

Gladwell, Malcolm, *The Tipping Point: How Little Things Can Make a Big Difference* (New York, NY: Little, Brown and Company, 2000).

Gloor, Peter A., *Swarm Creativity: Competitive Advantage through Collaborative Innovation Networks* (Oxford: Oxford University Press, 2006).

Groth, Aimee, 'Zappos Has Quietly Backed Away from Holacracy', *Quartz at Work*, 29 January 2020, https://qz.com/work/1776841/zappos-has-quie tly-backed-away-from-holacracy/, accessed 29 May 2021.

Isaacs, William, *Dialogue and the Art of Thinking Together: A Pioneering Approach to Communicating in Business and in Life* (New York, NY: Currency, 1999).

Johansson, Frans, *The Medici Effect: Breakthrough Insights at the Intersection of Ideas, Concepts, and Cultures* (Boston, MA: Harvard Business School Press, 2004).

Jungk, Robert and Müllert, Norbert, *Future Workshops: How to Create Desirable Futures* (London: Institute for Social Inventions, 1987).

Kniberg, Henrik, 'Spotify Engineering Culture Part 1', *YouTube*, 4:13, January 2014, www.youtube.com/watch?v=3YrRW4u9Rlo, accessed 29 May 2021.

Leimuller, Getraud, et al., 'Next Generation Research & Innovation Networks to Inspire a Network on Learning through Play', *The Lego Foundation*, October 2014, www.playfutures.net/modules/core/client/documents/ legofoundation_study-finalcor.pdf, accessed 29 May 2021.

Lorenz, Edward N., *The Essence of Chaos* (Seattle, WA: University of Washington Press, 1993).

Owen, Harrison, *Open Space Technology: A User's Guide* (1992, San Francisco: Berrett Koehler, 1997).

Page, Scott E., *The Diversity Bonus: How Great Teams Pay Off in the Knowledge Economy* (Princeton, NJ: Princeton University Press, 2017).

Robertson, Brian J. *"Holacracy". The New Management System for a Rapidly Changing World* (New York, NY: Henry Holt and Company, 2015).

Roggema, Rob (ed), *The Design Charrette: Ways to Envision Sustainable Futures* (Dordrecht/New York, NY: Springer, 2014).

Schwaber, Ken and Beedle, Michael, *Agile Software Development with Scrum* (Upper Saddle River, NJ: Pearson Prentice Hall, 2002).

Stephenson, Karen, *The Quantum Theory of Trust: The Secret of Mapping and Managing Human Relationships* (Upper Saddle River, New Jersey: Financial Times Prentice Hall, 2004).

Sutherland, Jeff and Schwaber, Ken, 'The 2020 Scrum Guide', *Scrum Guides*, online, November 2020, www.scrumguides.org/scrum-guide.html, accessed 29 November 2021.

Takeuchi, Hirotaka and Nonaka, Ikujiro, 'The New Product Development Game', *Harvard Business Review*, January 1988, https://hbr.org/1986/01/the-new-new-product-development-game, accessed 29 May 2021.

Weisbord, Martin R. and Janoff, Sandra, *Future Search: An Action Guide to Finding Common Ground in Organizations and Communities* (San Francisco, CA: Berrett-Koehler, 1995).

Wood, Colin, 'Who Invented the Hackathon?', *Government Technology*, 15 November 2013, www.govtech.com/data/Who-Invented-the-Hackathon.html, accessed 29 May 2021.

Woolley-Barker, Tamsin, *Teeming: How Superorganisms Work to Build Infinite Wealth in a Finite World* (Ashland, OR: White Cloud Press, 2017).

6

SWARM 2.0

DEVELOPING AN AUGMENTED WORKPLACE SWARM STRATEGY

Dieter Zetsche was Chairman of the Board of Management at Daimler AG and Head of Mercedes-Benz cars from January 2006 until May 2019. On his succession as Chairman, Dieter Zetsche anticipated that he would be leading the company during a period of unrivalled change and innovation. In an era of electric and self-driving cars and an increased competition from other luxury vehicle brands, he knew he had to transform the group and create a more collaborative and agile culture. In Dieter Zetsche's own words, 'We live in a disruptive world. We would rather be the disruptor than the disrupted'.[1]

The culture of decision-making and innovation in the group was traditionally top-down and hierarchical. As Roland Deiser points out, 'Industry leaders often have the hardest time to re-invent themselves, as a culture of success and top reputation can be major change inhibitors'.[2] Dieter Zetsche was keen to inspire a grassroots transformation. His personal epiphany was to realise that 'if you give people instructions, then ideally you will get the results you had expected. However, if you give them greater freedom you can get ideas far beyond expectations'.[3] He looked to create a more open and deformalised working environment and started to bring people together in informal networks (or swarms) to discuss openly the Daimler AG culture. The capstone of this was in 2016 when 1200

DOI: 10.4324/9781003215561-9

participants 'from all hierarchy levels and 50 different nations'[4] came together in a summit exploring how the Daimler AG culture might look in 2020. It was called the Leadership 2020 Summit. Dieter Zetsche describes it in his own words:

> It is a cultural revolution. We initiated a process six months ago involving around 1,000 employees. It went around the globe, across all age and hierarchy levels. What came out of it are prototypes for our corporate culture in the year 2020. A lot of revolutionary ideas were developed. We've just presented the results to our top 100 senior executives – and they were thrilled, which is something you can't normally expect from this group. I am convinced that we will soon be a fundamentally different company. Daimler will be much more faster and flexible in how it acts than before.[5]

The objective of Leadership 2020 was to slash hierarchy and bureaucracy and give people more freedom and decision-making capabilities though working in swarm networks.[6] 'Today we still have up to six levels of hierarchy that are involved in a decision', Dieter Zetsche reported to *Handelsblatt Today*. 'Now we're saying... we don't want more than two stages'.[7] What came out of this was the vision of the swarm organisation (Daimler AG's term). Drawing on self-organising principles from Agile Scrum,[8] Daimler AG started to work in self-organising swarm groups which had unprecedented freedoms and decision-making abilities to collaborate and innovate across hierarchies and function levels. Dieter Zetsche personally promoted this – 'I am supervising this field as mentor', he said. 'Many startups and tech companies work that way. This method supplements the hierarchical-management pyramid with cross-functional and interdisciplinary groups and eventually replaces them'.[9] In an interview with the Frankfurter Allgemeine in 2016, Dieter Zetsche said 'Wir stellen uns vor, dass wir kurzfristig, innerhalb von einem halben Jahr oder Jahr, rund 20 Prozent der Mitarbeiter auf eine Schwarm-Organisation umstellen' ['We imagine that in the short term, within six months or a year, we will switch around 20 per cent of our employees to a swarm organisation'].[10] The spirit of this strategic vision was reflected in the 2016 annual report.[11]

I had a conversation recently with Dr. Michael Poerner, who has worked in global organisational development and corporate leadership development for the group and was closely involved in building and practising the swarm approach. We discussed candidly ten key learnings and lessons that had come out of the experience of Daimler AG/Mercedes Benz journey to build a swarm organisation.

1. *Don't do swarm for swarm's sake.* There are some parts of the business that operate perfectly well in a traditional structure. Be realistic when you are selecting parts of the business to swarm.
2. *Don't expect quick results.* On paper, collaborative and collective innovation through swarm seems straightforward. This can be misleading; organising the enterprise into swarm communities is complex and you cannot expect a mature organisation with years of hierarchy and a strong culture of individual excellence to summarily self-organise into swarm communities. Hierarchical business operating systems are pervasive in traditional organisations, and it takes time for the traditional part of the organisation to embrace swarm. You can't 'switch' to being a swarm organisation, you have to transition to it.
3. *Having a strategy is imperative to success.* In the early days of adoption, Daimler AG built on their use of Agile Scrum and collaborated with external agile coaches as a preferred process to develop swarm.
4. *Targets are good but don't be governed by them.* Creating a swarm business target helps energise and motivate the organisation but treat it as an enabler and not a stipulation. In fact, Daimler AG/Mercedes Benz did not reach its 20% target, but the journey towards collective and collaborative ways of working became more important than the target figure.
5. *Expect curiosity and resistance.* Accept that any new initiative, particularly one as quirky and unconventional as swarm, will create curiosity and cultural tension. Swarm is about creating independent and self-organising complex adaptive cells and systems within the traditional hierarchy. This will generate curiosity and possibly even scepticism, mistrust, and fear. It is vital to invest effort into integrating and connecting swarm to the traditional side of the business in order to anticipate and mitigate these creative tensions. Communication is key.

6. *Keep it close to the business.* Daimler AG/Mercedes Benz initially developed an off-site campus for Leadership 2020 that was a modern purpose-built facility intended for swarm activity. They decided to close this facility because it symbolised exclusiveness and detachment from the business, and they reintegrated the swarm activity back to the business community.

7. *Strike a balance.* Swarm does require leadership endorsement, particularly in traditional organisations such as Daimler AG/Mercedes Benz, where there are multiple decision-making shareholders and partners to consider. The Chairman was personally involved in developing the swarm organisation and was the field mentor for the idea, convincing 100 senior leaders to endorse it. But this comes with a significant health warning. Natural swarms are not top-down occurrences; they are self-organising and emergent complex adaptive systems. A paradoxical tension exists when the top of the organisation decrees a cultural transformation to make the organisation more self-organising. A key learning is for leadership to reinvent itself as swarm leaders and find the right balance between guiding the organisation and creating organic structures for swarm to thrive (a planned approach to change) versus allowing the organisation to self-organise and cultivate swarm at the grassroots level, to build natural links with business, and to naturally develop swarm behaviours and a 'hive mind' (an emergent approach to change). Leadership needs to reinvent itself in Swarm 2.0 as consultative rather than prescriptive.

8. *Focus on integration as much as innovation.* Another takeaway is to connect the traditional part of the organisation with the self-organising swarm groups. The energy must not solely go on creating swarm communities; greater effort must go on wiring these communities up with the rest of the organisation. Daimler AG/Mercedes-Benz discovered that this required highly visible forms of communication. As Roland Deiser says, 'Realising the benefits resulting from a flat hierarchy, self-organization, and the abolishing of traditional leadership required clearly communicated top management commitment'.[12] The shift to swarm requires more than simply stating the vision in town hall gatherings, shareholder meetings, and in the company's annual reports. Another way of putting it is: don't just focus on the target or the technical accomplishment of setting up

swarm groups, focus on the culture; having the right culture make or break a swarm-based approach to business.

9. *Work out in advance the recruitment, remuneration, and perform-ance measures.* Swarm is a complex adaptive system that cannot be serviced by the traditional organisation in terms of recruitment, remuneration, and performance measures. A key learning is to have independent strategies in place for swarm communities; otherwise, they will be unduly influenced and conditioned by the traditional organisation.

10. *Continuously adapt and innovate.* Daimler AG/Mercedes Benz is constantly looking to improve the swarm process. For example, they are actively looking at intelligence augmentation to support decision-making in swarm environments. I will share some fur-ther conversations I had in this area later in the section on digital transformation.

Daimler AG's transition to swarm has transformed its culture and makes a great case study for Swarm 2.0. The key aspect of Swarm 2.0 is that it is an organisational-led rather than a local-led initiative. This chapter explores how swarm can be optimised more strategically across the enter-prise. This involves a planned and target-led business transformation drive that develops and populates the organic 'honeycomb' organisation struc-ture. It also prepares the ground for a digital transformation where smart technology and artificial intelligence (AI) systems are supporting human resources in unrivalled ways (helping to optimise business intelligence, ideation, and decision-making). Finally, it builds collaborative, agile, and digital mindsets fit-for-purpose for an augmented workplace. It is part of an overall phased change model that aspires to having significant parts of the enterprise adopt a swarm approach.

Let's follow Chapter 5's blueprint and look at each of the three business transformation levers in turn: system transformation, organisational change and development, and swarm facilitation.

Swarm 2.0: Lever 1: system transformation

System transformation represents a shift from current reality to future state. This trajectory drives swarm intelligence in the workplace and promotes organisational-led organic structures, decision augmentation, and hive minds. Swarm 2.0 is a phase that will kick in during the 2020s at a time of unprecedented levels of human and machine collaboration within augmented workplaces. One of the learnings from the Daimler AG case study is that there isn't a magic switch that flips the enterprise from a traditional to a swarm-based organisation. Swarm transformation is an evolution not a revolution – Daimler AG achieved swarm through the creation of targets. There will be a transition period from Swarm 1.0 to Swarm 2.0 where the organisation accelerates (to use John Kotter's term from Chapter 4). Let's see how this plays out at the organisational, digital, and behavioural levels.

Organisational transformation 2.0

If Swarm 1.0 was about local complex adaptive cells, functioning and emerging within the broader enterprise, Swarm 2.0 is a global swarm strategy. It is an organisational initiative, rather than a local one. We have established that swarm thrives in decentralised, deformalised, self-organising complex adaptive systems. Even a percentage of the organisation as swarm-based will have a significant impact on the global culture. That's why the organic honeycomb structure presented in Chapter 4 is a good organisational model for building a swarm-based enterprise; it is podular, organic, and accelerates at the pace of change. More will be said about the intricacies of developing the honeycomb organisation structure at Swarm 2.0 later in the organisational change theory section.

Swarm clusters processing business intelligence and coming up with best-fit solutions and decisions, is still a central activity in Swarm 2.0, but the swarm community and the business intelligence network will be more global and (increasingly) augmented by intelligent systems and decision augmentation. The Swarm 1.0 community model that was illustrated in Figure 5.1 together with the key agents (influencers, enablers, and connectors) will be different in Swarm 2.0. The revised model (Figure 6.1) is simplified with some different roles and functions to anticipate the rise of digital facilitation.

Let's look at some of the headline changes.

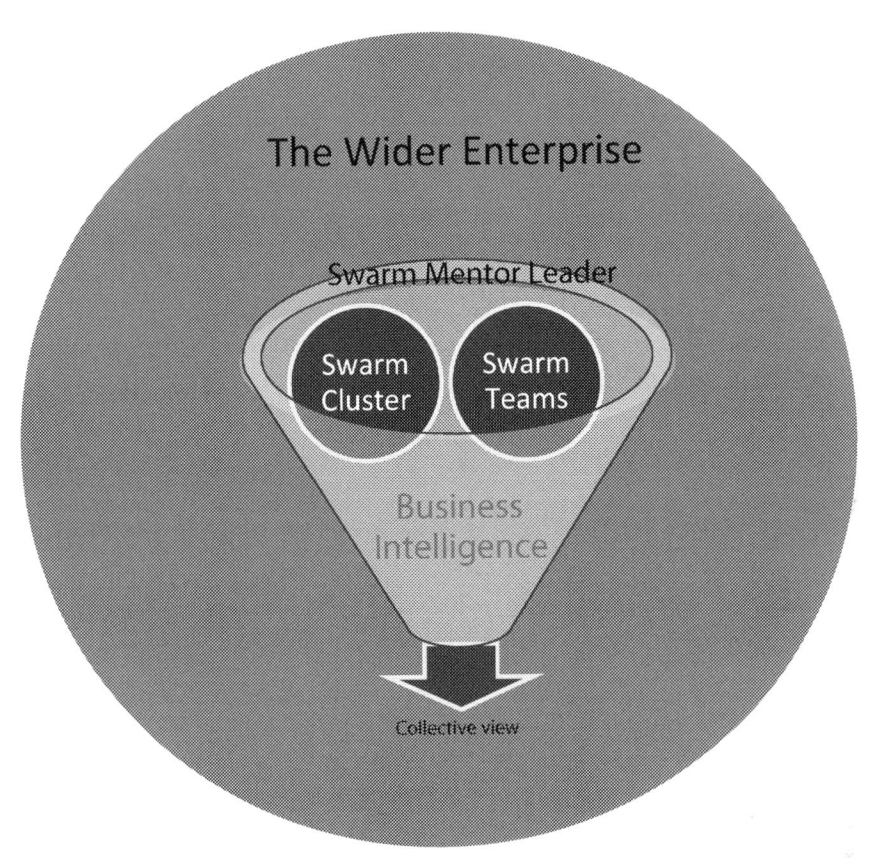

Figure 6.1 The Swarm 2.0 community.

Influencers: the swarm mentor leader (SML)

In Swarm 1.0, the key influencers were the business process owner and the beekeeper. This is because Swarm 1.0 is a local model that processes local business intelligence. The business process owner, with support from trusted advisors such as the beekeeper, drives the decision to adopt swarm. In Swarm 2.0, the business process owner is no longer an influencer, but a stakeholder and a local enabler. The decision for business locations to adopt swarm is centrally planned in Swarm 2.0. The role of the beekeeper as a local coach and mentor disappears and is part-replaced by swarm mentor leaders (SMLs).[13] The SMLs are executive-level leaders linked to the swarm community. SMLs form a conceptual bridge to my

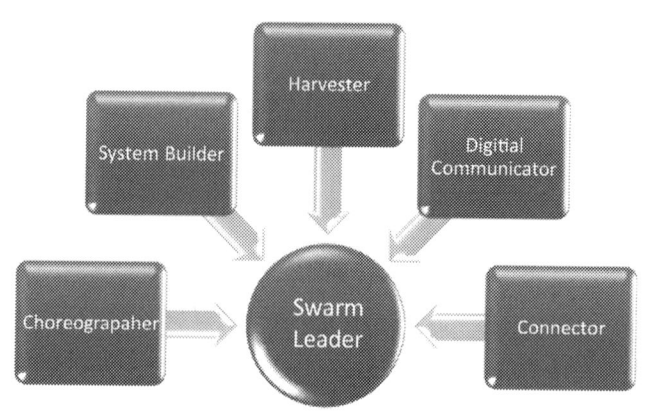

Figure 6.2 Five key roles of a swarm (mentor) leader.

previous publication, *Constructing Leadership 4.0*, which defines 'swarm leaders' as an 'adaptive, emergent, connected, responsive, and collaborative model that belongs broadly in the category of collective leadership'.[14] SMLs are enablers who lead through collaborative networks rather than formal structures; they navigate through complex adaptive systems where decisions, direction, and innovation emerge from within the system itself rather than from ego selves. It is an enabling rather than a governing leadership. Inspired by my study of swarm leaders, Figure 6.2 shows some key roles of swarm (mentor) leader.

Swarm mentor leadership is in the connectivist tradition where a connectivist leader focuses on how information flows through the enterprise rather than being preoccupied on the content of the information or the different personalities.[15] SMLs are responsive connectors who help shape the complex adaptive system and encourage collective intelligence and decision-making.[16] Practically speaker, SMLs will need to do the following:

1. Survey/scan the enterprise and identify sections of the business that can adopt swarm and become swarm communities. The criteria here would include sectors of the business that:
    - have already been exposed to swarm theory during the Swarm 1.0 phase;
    - have the potential to self-organise and function as a complex adaptive system;

- are digitally advanced;
- have an established business intelligence network;
- have business process owners who are sympathetic to the idea of being early swarm adopters and are prepared to invest personal time and effort into making it work;
- have a compelling strategic reason to become a swarm community and will contribute and promote swarm quotient across the enterprise.

2. Be a key link to the executive function.
3. Initiate conversations with business process owners, department heads, local decision makers, major stakeholders, partners, and investors about transforming the local environment into a swarm community.
4. Provide practical support, encouragement, and resources for local communities to reconfigure their business culture (structure, systems, and behaviours) to embrace a swarm approach.

Enabler: business intelligence

Swarm is an intelligence-led system. The second principle of swarm facilitation (see Figure 4.9 in Chapter 4) says swarm facilitation is an 'emerging intelligence-led complex adaptive system and not an assimilative knowledge-led sequential process'. In Swarm 1.0, this business intelligence is a physical (human) network. The business intelligence of Swarm 2.0 is a global business network (increasingly) supported by AI systems. Global business intelligence won't happen overnight. We have seen how swarm is a transition, not a sudden switch. The processes and technologies that amplify global business intelligence need time to evolve. Embryonic Swarm 2.0 will need to continue to lean on local business intelligence gathered through traditional business networks. The evolution of global business intelligence through advanced data analytics is part of the digital transformation story and will develop as Swarm 2.0 accelerates. The timeline for this will be spelled out in the conclusion of the book. The end game for Swarm 2.0 in relation to business intelligence is an augmented intelligence strategy where global business intelligence comes from big and wide data through such digital sources as organisational intelligence, innovation platforms, and social media (rather than physical networks).

Enabler: business process owner

Business process owners are no longer the local influencers and initiators that they once were in Swarm 1.0. In Swarm 2.0, the decision for swarm activity takes place at an organisational – and not local – level. That said, the success of Swarm 2.0 is very much dependent on buy-in from the local business process owners. It is important, therefore, for SMLs to continue to engage with business process owners.

Enabler: shareholders

Transforming the business by up to 20% is a significant organisational and governance change and may require shareholder approval depending on the type of relationship the organisation has with its investors. Daimler AG engaged with its shareholders about its aspirations to become a swarm organisation and published its ideas, vision, timeline, and goals relating to swarm in its annual shareholder report. This group of enablers cannot be sidelined.

Enabler: swarm cluster

In Swarm 2.0, human swarm clusters still exist, but their initiation and configuration will be a global strategic decision. In the early (transitional) phase of Swarm 2.0, there is likely to be limited cross-functional and department activity and swarm cluster participants will most likely continue to be locally resourced. The game changer will be when such technology as advanced people analytics is used to recruit swarm clusters and intelligent systems augment swarm facilitation. We have seen from Chapter 4 that Swarm 2.0 is part of a phased and accelerate change model that will transition into a swarm-based organisation over time. Daimler AG aimed to create a 20% swarm organisation target but still maintained 80% of its traditional structure.

Enabler: swarm teams

Swarm teams will remain a major component of swarm activity in Swarm 2.0. In Swarm 2.0, human creativity is still prized and humans will continue to collaborate in small teams linked to a cluster. The value of this theory of swarm intelligence in the workplace is not for human ideation and creation to be displaced by intelligent systems, but for intelligent systems to augment human creativity. Once intelligent systems are in place, they will augment business intelligence, ideation, and decision-making and support human swarm teams to self-organise, generate ideas, and make effective decisions. In the mature phase of Swarm 2.0, there will be no need for swarm team reps because (as we shall see later) this part of the swarm facilitation cycle will be automated.

Digital transformation 2.0

Back to my conversations with Daimler AG. I said they were actively looking to adopt intelligence augmentation. I was put in touch with senior experts working on business and digital transformation for the company. Based on my informal conversations, I began to understand from these senior practitioners, some of the philosophy and preparation needed for the digital transformation of a major organisation such as Daimler AG. Some key digital transformation learnings from these discussions included:

1. *Technology is an enabler, not a fix.* Augmented swarm and intelligent systems should be considered in the context of adding value by creating agile and connected organisations.
2. *Focus on data.* Automating business processes is not just about procuring or developing the latest AI system; it is about ensuring you have quality data. It is important to review the latest knowledge management and digitisation processes. This is a human behaviour and leadership issue.
3. *Use what's out there and start small.* There are plenty of off-the-shelf solutions in advanced data analytics and decision augmentation currently available on the market that can be immediately adopted to support swarm.
4. *Recruit the right talent.* Invest time in recruiting the right people in the digital business development field. Use traditional recruitment methods as well as people analytics to secure the best talent.
5. *Digital transformation is also about organisational and leadership transformation.* A digital business thrives in networks and complex

adaptive systems, not in hierarchies led by alpha leaders. A whole-system transformation is required.

6. *The future is augmented workplaces.* Machines will never replace human creativity and ingenuity, but from 2025 onwards, they will take care of routine business processes and augment human intelligence and performance.

Chapter 3 explored the current state of play regarding intelligent systems. John Launchbury of DARPA reviewed the third wave of AI and the shift away from scripted responses in artificial systems to a more human-simulated experience that understands context and meaning. The third wave will be a game changer in the next five years. It will require a digital and technology investment, but also a structure and mindset transformation. Without a comprehensive digital transformation strategy, there could potentially be significant digital disruption in the workplace.

The digital transformation pathway for Swarm 2.0 will need to attend to the following five areas:

1. Recruit data scientists and create digital leadership roles

Increasing the digital footprint of the enterprise is going to require some expertise and the most cost-effective and efficient way to achieve this would be through recruitment rather than internal retraining. Swarm 2.0 requires both a strategic digital leadership team and specialist data scientists and network analysts. Two important hires during the swarm business transformation that could make or break the digital transformation of the organisation would be a Chief Information Officer and a Chief Data Officer. Boris Groysberg et al. consider Chief Information Officers as critical appointments:

> Companies will seek 'hybrid' CIOs who have not only business savvy but also experience with analytics, organizational design, and infrastructure—and who know how to wire together a holistic system that can support global growth.[17]

Recent Gartner research indicates that companies are still reluctant to appoint a full-time CDO resource but that CDOs continue to grow in influence and impact.[18] The core activities of a Chief Data Officer will include:

- Overseeing recruitment of data scientists, network analysts, data analytics specialists across the enterprise to facilitate and bolster the organisation's digital transformation.
- Overseeing the rise of networks within the enterprise to replace formal governance and decision-making pyramids.
- Working with learning and development (L&D) to build digital quotient across the organisation, especially at midlevel.[19]
- Ensuring new recruits have required levels of digital quotient.
- Making the right procurement and development choices with others about the collaborative tech, data analytics, and decision augmentation tools required for swarm communities to be effective and thrive.
- Partnering with educationalists and policy decision makers to advise on the levels of digital quotient required by Industry 4.0.

Other important hires are data scientists, network analysts, and business intelligence analysts. In an HBR webinar, Michael Schrage argues that organisations need to have network and data science at the heart of their organisation.[20] Technical hires should be a mix of permanent employees and contingency workers because organisations need to be flexible. One strategy that companies are increasingly employing to build their talent and technical capability is acquiring where the organisation acquires a technical company and retains entire intact teams for a 'fast injection of talent'.[21] The organisational talent strategy needs to be led by what Zappos and others term hiring for cultural fit.[22]

2. Create a digital transformation strategy

As has been said elsewhere, technology is not always the fix or a shortcut. A digital transformation strategy should also focus on organisational structures and mindsets to create the right setting for digitalisation and there will need to be strategic partnerships formed with Organisational Development and Leadership Development. There should also be a mission plan concerning the strategic adoption of swarm and where/how to target resources. This will need to be planned and costed and shared with key stakeholders. Such a digital transformation strategy should include such things as timelines, budget, and talent retention strategies.

3. Procurement

At the technical level, digital transformation in the workplace is about using AI solutions to augment and improve business processes. It concerns preparing and future-proofing the enterprise to take full advantage of this technology. An important organisational decision would be the procurement of emerging technologies of the type discussed in Chapter 3 to help optimise business intelligence and digitally facilitate ideas and decisions. The lesson learned from Daimler AG is to start small and use technologies that are already developed.

4. Digitisation

Any Swarm 2.0 digital transformation strategy will need a digitisation plan with an aspiration to digitise all forms of human activity and experience, including vocalised expressions (conversations and collaborations) and non-vocalised expressions (human emotion, reactions, and feeling) into a digital format. By Swarm 3.0, we may even have the capacity to digitise human deliberation and thoughts in the form of thought recognition. The breakthrough of Swarm 2.0 will be when both online and offline conversations and collaborations are digitised and AI systems crunch this data to aid collective decision-making. This will be the game changer that narrows the digital divide and enables the entire system to be instantaneously involved in organisational sensemaking. This is just as much a behavioural as it is a technical challenge. People need to understand that every conversation and idea that is not digitally captured, documented, and recorded will not be part of the collective organisational data store and memory. Today's digitised human experience is tomorrow's data for the digital organisation to act upon and collectively transform the enterprise. Carlos Velasco and Marianna Obrist correlate the coronavirus pandemic with the 'rapid digitisation of human experiences'.[23]

5. Integration

In the Daimler case study, Dr. Michael Poerner identified connectivity and communication as a major organisational learning when adopting swarm. It is important to connect the enterprise both internally and externally. It needs to be a collaborative learning organisation that optimises collective impact. For this to happen, the traditional side of the organisation needs to be integrated with the swarm side. You also need to do some very practical things relating to transparency and data access. Swarms and collective decision-making do not thrive in closed systems that are firewalled.

Behavioural transformation 2.0

It was posited in the last chapter that Swarm 1.0 will be an emergent (local) initiative and that building ability and mindsets will be the responsibility of the local business process owner. Learning interventions were largely contained to in-swarm development. Swarm 2.0 is an organisational-led effort. Building ability and mindsets are part of a group-level strategically planned initiative with pre-swarm and in-swarm organisational learning interventions that develop willingness and ability built around the swarm quotients and themes presented in Chapter 4. Let's see how this plays out in Swarm 2.0.

Adaptive quotient in Swarm 2.0

In Swarm 2.0, people will be working in more complex adaptive environments and collaborating more globally via augmented intelligence. They will need to make sense of the increased data coming from inside and outside the organisation and make fast connections and decisions through others. Working in a swarm environment, or a function that supports a swarm environment, requires collective thinking and the ability, supported by intelligent systems, to put things in perspective and learn to suspend individual preferences outside of the collective view. The three adaptive quotient themes (embracing complexity, sensemaking, and perspectivism) will directly contribute to meeting these Swarm 2.0 challenges.

Collaborative quotient in Swarm 2.0

In Swarm 2.0, people will find themselves collaborating more with others through smart technology. The days of the lone cognitive genius are truly numbered in Swarm 2.0. People who will succeed in the organisation of the future will have a collective hive mindset. With augmented intelligence and data analytics, this should free up people to be more co-creative with each other. Decision augmentation means people won't need to constantly crunch data. They just need to go with the collective flow. They should be accomplished in the various collaborative tools and will naturally be able to build consensus. The three collaborative quotient themes relevant here are building a collective mindset/hive mind, engaging in group creativity, and building consensus through negotiation.

Digital quotient in Swarm 2.0

In Swarm 2.0, people will need to increasingly collaborate through technology and that means understanding it, adopting digitalisation, and embracing digitalism. Getting into a healthy mindset of promoting personal digitisation and being fluent in navigating around technology and managing its risks/dangers as well as its benefits is all part of the digital transformation journey. The digital worker of the future will need to pay attention to digital etiquette and raising e-charisma. The three anchors connected with digital quotient are embracing emerging technology, cultivating a digital mindset, and working in a digital culture.

Pre-Swarm 2.0 learning interventions

Building willingness and ability in the transition period leading up to swarm is going to require a dedicated L&D input. The core content of such programmes will come from the three swarm quotients. Here are some pre-swarm learning delivery models to consider for Swarm 2.0, partitioned into directed and self-directed interventions.

Directed intervention: formal global swarm learning programmes

Organisational sponsored learning swarm events need to be developed to on-board participants in swarm clusters. The objective of the pre-swarm global programmes will be to prepare participants' abilities and willingness to work in a swarm environment. Such programmes are likely to be online offerings and be blended with self-directed learning and cultural boot camps.

Directed intervention: intact team development

In early manifestations of Swarm 2.0, entire departments or divisions will be exposed to swarm environments and it makes sense that the entire division or department attend learning interventions as an intact team. At this level, any learning intervention will be aimed at building willingness and ability and should cover all three quotients and all nine swarm themes.

Directed intervention: culture camp events and cultural boot camps

These proved to be very effective in Zappos' transition to Holacracy.[24] They are one-off events where participants are immersed in the new culture and can be a highly effective way of raising willingness and ability. A programme can be designed around the history, background, and purpose of swarm intelligence.

Directed intervention: bite-sized learning

The nine swarm themes that make up the three mindset quotients may conveniently be designed into a bite-sized learning experience that can be delivered online or face-to-face as lunch and learns.

Directed intervention: immersive training

Immersive technology such as virtual reality is already widely used in corporate education settings such as Walmart.[25] A recent Price Waterhouse Coopers (PWC) report determined that virtual reality (VR) learners learnt more quickly than classroom learners, were more confident applying their learning, were more engaged with the content, and were more focused than their e-learning peers.[26] One of the fastest growth areas for VR and augmented reality (AR) applications is in the field of education. The next five years should see this technology add real value to the corporate education sector.

Self-directed interventions

Self-directed intervention: swarm learning and resource portal

One of the things that needs to be developed to create a standardised – yet flexible – L&D offering to support swarm would be a swarm learning and resource portal. This is an enterprise-wide learning management system where users can manage their own development. It can house all the self-directed material, online courses, articles, and user experiences associated with building swarm capacity. Moreover, it could function as a real-time appraisal system which manages performance-related feedback. It could also be a resourcing and professional network resource for shared learning, swarm community resourcing, and endorsing others. LinkedIn comes to mind as a good model for such a portal. This portal would need to be developed by specialists in learning and networking but should ultimately be self-organising. It would need to be funded centrally and be a major strategic tool in the organisation's bid to increase swarm quotient across the enterprise. The additional merit of a central portal is that the enterprise, through AI, can monitor and identify the swarm capability and easily match resources through people analytics. Organisations can collect employee data such as current skill sets, qualifications, and experience for developing personalised learning solutions. This system should also link to remuneration where a participant's experience and input into the swarm process should automatically determine their compensation.

Self-directed intervention: self-directed learning

This could be an online self-paced programme that provides essential background and reading around the theory and purpose of swarm and information on the three quotients. This could be reinforced by pre-swarm learning support networks.

Self-directed intervention: observation

Swarm cluster on-boarding could include observing a live or recorded swarm cluster and then having a group discussion about it.

In-Swarm 2.0 learning development

In-swarm development takes place once the swarm cluster is formed and is focused more on raising skills and abilities during the swarm activity. It is principally a peer coaching model. The swarm cluster community will be an eclectic group. Some may have worked in swarm communities before (maybe on other projects or in Swarm 1.0); others may be working in this environment for the first time. Much of the pre-swarm intervention is around raising willingness and ability. In-swarm is about raising ability and performance. Some significant in-swarm interventions will include the following.

Induction programmes

As new resources join swarm clusters, they will need some form of project induction and a refresher of best practice related to working in a swarm environment. The induction programme will build on pre-swarm development and, for the sake of consistency, will need to be designed around the three swarm quotients and nine swarm themes.

Swarm coach

A core strategic approach for building swarm competence in Swarm 2.0 is for experienced practitioners of swarm to coach and mentor less experienced cluster participants. Some criteria to be a swarm coach would include:

- Experience working in a swarm community environment for at least two assignments and to have gained above average feedback and endorsements.
- Good understanding of swarm intelligence and swarm facilitation.
- Agreeing to attend peer coaching sessions organised by the local L&D consultants to build skill in this area.

Swarm buddy

Swarm buddies are colleagues who are paired to support each other. It would be preferable to match experienced swarm practitioners with less experienced ones to help build swarm quotient and contribute to the overall organisational swarm capacity. This would include reverse mentoring where digital natives and technically advanced participants are paired with less technically minded participants to help build their confidence and understanding of the new technology.

e-Coaching and cobot feedback

One of the benefits of being in a digital environment is the potential for e-feedback and e-endorsements. This feedback can be machine assisted with e-coaching and feedback bots that assess your ability to navigate the system. There are already some established e-coaching bots such as Coach Otto.[27] Cobots can also help raise user ability and help users navigate around new systems. This feedback could appear on the learning portal dashboard and automatically feed into an ongoing peer performance assessment.

Collaborative learning networks and forums

The swarm learning and resource portal should have built-in forums and learning networks for swarm participants to connect and engage with other swarm participants. Here they can post challenges and share experiences.

Implications for L&D

It has been said often that Swarm 1.0 is a local initiative and Swarm 2.0 is a more organisation-led and global effort. A major part of this will involve transforming mindsets. L&D will need to be on-board. This will have a major impact on L&D and additional L&D resources may have to be recruited. L&D hires will need to have experience in self-organising systems, sensemaking, self-directed learning within a blended context, remote and virtual learning (through networks), augmented intelligence, and peer coaching. Specific core activities and tasks of L&D specialists for Swarm 2.0 are as follows:

- Work with the Chief Data Officer and their team to build and recruit digital quotient across the enterprise.
- Partner with technical specialists to develop the learning and resource portal which will be a one-stop-shop for development, personal feedback, resourcing and networking.

- Support the organisation to develop pre-swarm and in-swarm interventions.
- Develop guidelines, competence, and skills in peer coaching, including practical peer coaching sessions.
- Manage the on-boarding and induction of new resources joining swarm communities.
- Build and maintain a cache of self-resourceful and self-directed resources and materials.
- Have some experience as a change agent to advise on the journey of change where appropriate.

Lever 2: organisational change and development

It has been established that Swarm 2.0 accelerates local swarm initiatives to a group-wide level and that swarm activity will be amplified and enhanced by having access to global resources, functions, systems, and talent. Traditional parts of the organisation coexist with group functions and swarm communities in the honeycomb structure, and are all interconnected. It will become clearer in the concluding chapter that Swarm 2.0 is a phased transitional process rather than something that is switched on. A key learning from the Daimler AG case study is that the transition to swarm includes being highly realistic and strategic about which parts of the organisation need to convert to swarm.

If one were to create an action list for transitioning/migrating to Swarm 2.0. it should include the following:

- Do a feasibility study for the organisation to become swarm-based. Include practical experiences from business process owners. Incorporate these findings into a strategy paper and use this as a communication document for senior leadership, business leaders, partners, and investors.
- Identify areas of the organisation that could convert to swarm and work with the local business process owners as part of the feasibility study.
- Work with a legal team to reach agreement at board and investor levels to adopt a swarm approach.

- Work closely with OD and L&D resources to help build the swarm communities and raise their willingness and ability.
- Consult with identified parts of the organisation and provide resources to adopt swarm.
- Recruit senior executives as SMLs to support the different swarm communities.
- Task the chief data officer and data scientists to work on a digital transformation to support augmented swarm.

We discovered in Chapter 4 that the accelerate change model is designed to be low impact, organic, and phased over time. Change recipients won't feel much impact from this transition. Much of the organisation (up to 80%) will remain the same. Slowly over time, the organisation will evolve and emerge. The system transformation will be slow-burning and will accelerate at its own pace of change. A notable difference will be in the emergence of new roles. But (as we saw in the Kotter 'accelerate' model) it will remain business as usual for the rest of the organisation. The traditional organisation will slowly connect with these new swarm communities and coexist alongside them in the honeycomb model. In terms of digital transformation, this is not going to be a technological disrupter – digital business teams will work in the background on developing intelligent systems to augment business intelligence and decision-making. This will be integrated with the traditional business. Swarm communities will collaborate and work in a more agile and collective way. They will have access to transitional learning programmes and in-work learning activities to cultivate a hive mind. When we look at Swarm 3.0 in Chapter 7, it will feel much more disruptive than Swarm 2.0 which is all about mitigating disruption, delivering business as usual (to use John Kotter's term from his Accelerate theory), and having a quiet systems transformation on the back burner.

Lever 3: swarm facilitation

Inspired by house-hunting honeybees, swarm facilitation, you recall, is a business process model that applies to all levels of swarm within organisations. It was inspired by the swarm flow model in Chapter 2 (Figure 2.4). Let's run through the cycle and relate it to Swarm 2.0.

Prepare

In Swarm 1.0, collective ideation and decision-making is made possible through humans manually gathering local business intelligence and processing ideas through local human swarms. This human-centric system requires a lot of local preparation, planning, and effort in preparing the business community and swarm cluster. As we progress to the more global centric Swarm 2.0, swarm facilitation will still be conducted through human swarms. The preparation will not be done locally, but globally. SMLs, OD, and LD resources will all be involved. Swarm 2.0 will have access to global intelligence networks and systems. As Swarm 2.0 further accelerates and becomes established, intelligent systems will go live and support the swarm process. This will include data-driven methods that will be used to identify and prioritise critical business issues and needs from a wide dataset that spans inside and outside the enterprise. Swarm communities across the enterprise will be able to access business intelligence through a dashboard to help them identify their individual critical challenges. In the future, swarm facilitation preparation will be an ongoing, emergent, evolving automated business intelligence that is driven by advanced analytics accessed through business intelligence dashboards.

Two practical considerations in Swarm 2.0 preparation

Swarm meets

In Swarm 2.0, swarm activity will largely be carried out online. The notion of human versus digital presence was discussed in Chapter 1 where it was considered that even with spatial web and immersive technology, 2025 may still need to rely on human presence. If a face-to-face is required, the swarm cluster will need to arrange and prepare this just as they did in Swam 1.0. The swarm cluster will need to identify a process and timeframe and flag the costs to the SML. By 2025, there is sure to be many more smart meeting rooms available with Internet of Things (IoT) and digital boards. A recent Jones Lang LaSalle (JLL) report noted that offices may scale down by 2025 with less need for physical office space because of Covid-related hybrid working. They think that the culture of the densified office will change with larger spaces becoming available as collaboration areas, innovation zones, teamwork, and learning hubs.[28]

Budget and resourcing

Just as in regular projects, an important element of swarm preparation involves determining budgets and resources. In terms of budget, there will need to be a centrally approved budget to fund the swarm clusters' time and costs. As was discussed in Chapter 4, swarm and complex adaptive systems are not a license to spend. There will be a need for a far more flexible approach than traditional models and this may require a flexible or variable budget. In terms of securing resources, swarm clusters will no longer be restricted to departments; swarms can be drawn from across the enterprise, but they must be able to contribute something to the business challenge. The size of the group can be more flexible than swarm facilitation 1.0, but online work groups can get unwieldy and suffer from the kind of group processing disadvantages outlined in Chapter 3. Online work groups can be more difficult than face-to-face groups to build cohesion.[29] Resourcing is most likely to be a combination of open resourcing where perspective candidates self-nominate and a nominated model. There will be an increasing reliance on people analytics as and when this becomes available through online systems and AI recruitment tools. Swarm clusters need to be diverse with a broad degree of experience, cultural background, educational background, as well as having a good mix of gender, race, and preferences. We have discussed how a learning and resource portal could support resourcing and recruitment. This will need to be developed but could prove to be another game changer.

Cluster

The principle of working in swarm clusters (vital for the success of honeybees) continues under Swarm 2.0 but these clusters are global and will be increasingly supported by intelligent systems as and when they are phased in. The cluster group will need pre-swarm learning that includes an induction along the lines outlined in the previous section. It was noted in Chapter 5 that breaking the large swarm cluster down into small self-organising teams who work in parallel on ideas is hugely beneficial in terms of mitigating groupthink.

Sensemake

The newly formed swarm cluster needs to work on business challenges just as they did in Swarm 1.0, but the difference here is (as we have discussed throughout the book) technology will increasingly augment these swarm sessions particularly in business intelligence, ideation, and decision-making. In Swarm 1.0, such things were manually processed using non-digital participatory technologies to distil ideas. In Swarm 2.0, intelligent systems will augment the human creative decision-making process. Conversations, collaborations and even brainswarming will be digitised so that intelligent systems can crunch, filter, and process the data. In Swarm 1.0, we looked at some off-the-shelf participatory tools that can support self-organising meetings and events. There is an increasing use of intelligent systems being used in workshops and conferences that are helping to organise and distil data and intelligence. Entrepreneurs such as Ginny Santos, founder of NeOlé Inc, lead the field in this area, creating interactive workshops using collaborative technology for some prestigious clients.[30] Below are some extant technologies that will most likely feature in Swarm 2.0 sensemaking from the mid-twenties onward.

Online collaboration tools

The coronavirus pandemic has raised the bar regarding how people collaborate remotely. Also, we have more millennials and digital natives in the workplace who are skilled and comfortable with online collaboration. We detailed in Chapter 3 the expanding commercial market of these tools, especially collaboration platforms. The shift to online collaboration will mean more global team diversity.

Transcription software

There is a new generation of transcription software using advanced voice recognition that transcribes person-to-person conversations in live and virtual meetings.[31] In a few years, this technology will most likely be a standard (wearable) tool in virtual and face-to-face meetings. The real benefit of transcription devices is that everyday conversations are digitalised and can be used in data science contexts. Microsoft is also active in this field and has recently produced an AI-powered meeting transcription device that uses facial recognition as well as voice recognition.[32]

IoT/Smart meeting rooms

Smart meeting rooms and conference facilities that monitor environments and equipment and adjust to the environment are coming into their own and will be crucial in non-human-facilitated environments.[33] There may be future possibilities for the IoT smart rooms to connect with wearables that track mood and productivity levels.

Interactive touch screens, digitables, and digital whiteboards

Touch screen and digitables are growing in popularity in workspaces because they cater for visual and co-creative learners. Many start-up companies are venturing into this market, including Digitable, Mural, and Eyefactive. Digitables could revolutionise the World Café experience. Stormboard (previously called Edistorm) is a touch screen technology that embraces the concept of swarming ideas and digital dotmocracy. This technology allows for the collaborative building of ideas in both virtual and face-to-face environments. It improves the flow of ideas (allowing for instant changes and efficient collaboration) and allows for the easy digitalisation of ideas which can be instantly shared with stakeholders and networks and be incorporated into data analysis.

Wearable technologies

Wearable technologies such as smart glasses, smart watches, smart bracelets, necklaces, rings, and hearables are beginning to 'augment employees abilities'.[34] There is growing market for them to be used as emotional sensors.[35] Wearables are becoming even more important as they link to IoT and provide real-time data of human experience. This data can increasingly be used for decision-making purposes. There is future scope for GPS technology in wearables to physically track people in large conferences when using such thing as Open Space Technology's 'Law of Two Feet'. This could easily be paired with data visualisation or data viz graphs.[36] Increasingly, wearable technology is likely to be superseded by microchip implants.[37]

Act

In the Daimler AG case study, we discussed the importance of having swarm communities being close to the business. Intelligent systems will be able to supply real-time data. As swarm clusters work on challenges, the business community, the business process owners, executive sponsors and other major stakeholders will be able to monitor the flow of ideas and input and steer the process in real time. This is going to allow for quick action and greater transparency.

Regeneration

Swarm 2.0 is a global initiative which reaches across the enterprise and beyond. It transcends organisational boundaries and has collective impact. Intelligent systems will help improve this connectivity. More of the system is involved and benefits from the swarm process. In Swarm 2.0, participants become more experienced at swarm and build its capacity by cross-resourcing with other swarm clusters. This builds swarm quotient. It is also the seed for a global learning system. The swarm's digitalised appraisal and analysis feeds into an ongoing business improvement (*Kaizen*). In Swarm 2.0 (a global initiative), every engagement and collaboration builds ideas and swarm capacity and, therefore, builds the enterprise.

In this chapter, we have positioned Swarm 2.0 as an organisational-led initiative. The complex adaptive cells described in Chapter 1 replicate into a complex adaptive system that extends strategically across the organisation, coexisting with the more traditional parts of the organisation. In

Swarm 2.0, SMLs partner with local business process owners to build organisational swarm capacity and capability. SMLs form strategic partnerships to devise central strategies around procuring technology, recruiting, and developing willingness and ability. A key lesson learnt from Daimler AG, who adopted swarm and calls itself a swarm organisation, is that swarm doesn't happen overnight and is not something you switch on.

This chapter has explored how you can build swarm with limited disruption to the organisation using Kotter's Accelerate model where business can continue as normal whilst swarm is scaled up. Apart from involving the organisation in the planning, preparation, and execution of swarm, a key differentiator between Swarm 1.0 and 2.0 is that Swarm 2.0 uses intelligent systems to support the decision-making process. This is phased in over time and supports both business intelligence and the swarm cluster activity which allows for organisations to be more intelligence-led and achieve greater collaborative efficiency. It also helps connect and integrate swarm creativity to the traditional side of the business. This use of technology and intelligent systems intensifies in Swarm 3.0 creating the opportunity to build a business superorganism. Let's turn our attention to Swarm 3.0, the final phase of the swarm transformation journey.

Notes

1 Greg Ring, 'Daimler Chief Plots Cultural Revolution', *Handelsblatt Today*, 25 July 2016, www.handelsblatt.com/english/companies/future-drive-daimler-chief-plots-cultural-revolution/23539560.html?ticket=ST-18438435-yYvenMdlKh51Qqyim2XP-ap5, accessed 29 May 2021.

2 Roland Deiser, 'Part 5: Agility in Practice: The Swarm Organization at Daimler', *The Digital Transformation People*, 7 May 2019, www.thedigitaltransformationpeople.com/channels/people-and-change/agility-in-practice-the-swarm-organization-at-daimler/, accessed 29 May 2021.

3 Dieter Zetsche, 'Going Viral with Cultural Change', *LinkedIn*, 30 May 2017, www.linkedin.com/pulse/going-viral-cultural-change-dieter-zetsche/, accessed 29 May 2021.

4 Diester Zetsche, 'Going Viral with Cultural Change'.

5 Greg Ring, 'Daimler Chief Plots Cultural Revolution'.

6 Dieter Zetsche discussed the swarm organisation approach where, 'It isn't the decision-making pyramid that is of primary importance, but rather the network'. Source: Dieter Zetsche interviewed by WirtschaftsWoche staff 'Daimler Chief Plots Cultural Revolution', *Handelsblatt Global*, 25 July 2016, https://global.handelsblatt.com/companies/daimlerchief-plots-cultural-revolution-574783, accessed 29 May 2021.

7 Sven Afhüppe, Markus Fasse, Martin Murphy, 'Daimler's Cultural Revolution', *Handelsblatt Today*, 31 October 2016, www.handelsblatt.com/english/companies/handelsblatt-exclusive-daimlers-cultural-revolution/23542004.html, accessed 29 May 2021.

8 The link to Agile Scrum is made by Roland Deiser, 'Part 5: Agility in Practice: The Swarm Organization at Daimler'.

9 Greg Ring, 'Daimler Chief Plots Cultural Revolution'.

10 'Daimler baut Konzern für die Digitalisierung um', *Frankfurter Allgemeine*, 7 September 2016, www.faz.net/aktuell/wirtschaft/daimler-baut-konzern-fuer-die-digitalisierung-um-14424858.html, accessed 29 May 2021.

11

> Leadership 2020: The transformation now has a name and a mission. We have been engaged in constant activity and dialogue since January 2016—across all hierarchies and national borders, in a digital, transparent and networked manner. Above all, we've focused on authenticity and tried to make sure that every employee can see and understand our efforts. Leadership 2020 means change. Initial results have already been achieved. Daimler is undergoing a transformation that's being supported by all employees for all employees.
>
> > 'Daimler Annual Report 2016', www.daimler.com/documents/investors/reports/annual-report/daimler/daimler-ir-annualreport-2016.pdf, accessed 29 May 2021, 56

12 Roland Deiser, 'Part 5: Agility in Practice: The Swarm Organization at Daimler', *The Digital Transformation People*, 7 May 2019, www.thedigitaltransformationpeople.com/channels/people-and-change/agility-in-practice-the-swarm-organization-at-daimler/, accessed 20 March 2021.

13 Mentor leaders are an established part of leadership. See, for example, Tony Dungy, *The Mentor Leader* (Carol Stream, IL: Tyndale House, 2011).

14 Richard Kelly, *Constructing Leadership 4.0: Swarm Leadership and the Fourth Industrial Revolution* (Basingstoke: Palgrave Macmillan, 2018), 184.

15 Richard Kelly, *Constructing Leadership 4.0*, 12.

16 Richard Kelly, *Constructing Leadership 4.0*, 116.

17 Boris Groysberg, Kevin Kelly, and Bryan Macdonald, 'The New Path to the C-Suite', *Harvard Business Review*, March 2011, https://hbr.org/2011/03/the-new-path-to-the-c-suite, accessed 29 May 2021.

18 Source: Jackie Wiles, 'Do You Need a Chief Data Officer?' Gartner, 18 May 2021, https://www.gartner.com/smarterwithgartner/do-you-need-a-chief-data-officer, accessed 30 November 2021.

19 'The most critical thing is midlevel talent: the "boots on the ground" who can make or break digital initiatives and are ultimately responsible for bringing products, services, and offers to market'. Tanguy Catlin, Jay Scanlan, and Paul Willmott, 'Raising Your Digital Quotient' in McKinsey Digital, 'Raising Your Digital Quotient', *McKinsey & Company*, December 2015, www.eurasiancommission.org/ru/act/dmi/workgroup/materials/Pages/Бизнес-среда%20в%20цифровом%20мире/Доклады%20консалтинговых%20агентств/Mckinsey_Raising%20your%20Digital%20Quotient_2016.pdf, accessed 29 May 2021, 16.

20 Michael Schrage, 'Leadership and Big Innovation', *HBR Webinar*, 13 December 2013. https://hbr.org/webinar/2016/12/leadership-and-big-data-innovation, accessed 29 May 2021.

21 Kate Smaje, 'What's Your Digital Quotient?', *Harvard Business Review*, Ideacast, Episode 483, 3 September 2015, https://hbr.org/podcast/2015/09/whats-your-digital-quotient.html, accessed 20 May 2021.

22 Good analysis Rob Gray, 'Can Recruiting for Values Go Too Far?', *HR Magazine*, 27 January 2015, www.hrmagazine.co.uk/content/features/can-recruiting-for-values-go-too-far, accessed 29 May 2021.

23 Carlos Velasco and Marianna Obrist, 'Life After Corona and the Rapid Digitisation of Human Experiences', *BI Norwegian Business School*, 2 April 2020, www.bi.edu/research/business-review/articles/2020/04/life-after-corona-and-the-rapid-digitisation-of-human-experiences/, accessed 29 May 2021.

24 Source: 'Culture Drives Success', *Zappos Insights*, 2021, www.zapposinsights.com/, accessed 29 May 2021.

25 Source: Sarah Fister Gale, 'Case Study: Walmart Embraces Immersive Learning', *Chief Learning Officer*, 23 March 2021, www.chieflearningofficer. com/2021/03/23/case-study-walmart-embraces-immersive-learning/, accessed 29 May 2021.

26 Scott Likens and Daniel L. Eckert, 'How Virtual Reality is Redefining Soft Skills Training', PWC, 2021, https://www.pwc.com/us/en/tech-effect/ emerging-tech/virtual-reality-study.html, accessed 30 November 2021.

27 Source: Amy MacMillan Bankson, 'Could an Artificial Intelligence-Based Coach Help Managers Master Difficult Conversations?', *MIT Management*, 23 February 2017, https://mitsloan.mit.edu/ideas-made-to-matter/could-artificial-intelligence-based-coach-help-managers-master-difficult-conver sations.

28 Source: Aayat Ali, 'Why Hybrid Working and the Employee Experience Are Needed', *All Work/The Future of Work*, 25 January 2021, https://allwork. space/2021/01/why-hybrid-working-and-the-employee-experience-are-nee ded/, accessed 29 May 2021.

29 Good resource: Sherry Piezon and Robin Donaldson, 'Online Groups and Social Loafing: Understanding Student-Group Interactions', *Online Journal of Distance Learning Administration*, 8, 2005.

30 For good a example of digital facilitation, see, for example, Laura Bowley, '5 Benefits of Hybrid Events', Neole, 19 July 2021, https://www.neole.ca/5-benefits-of-hybrid-events/, accessed 30 November 2021.

31 Good source: Jason Hiner, 'AI Breakthrough: Otter.ai App Can Transcribe Your Meetings in Real Time, For Free', *ZD Net*, 2 March 2018, www.zdnet. com/article/ai-breakthrough-otter-ai-app-can-transcribe-your-meetings-in-real-time-for-free/, accessed 29 May 2021.

32 Chris Burt, 'Microsoft Unveils AI-Powered Meeting Transcription Device with Facial and Voice Recognition', *Biometric Update*, 8 May 2018, www. biometricupdate.com/201805/microsoft-unveils-ai-powered-meeting-transcription-device-with-facial-and-voice-recognition, 29 May 2021.

33 Giorgos Sfikas, Charilaos Akasiadis, and E. Spyrou, 'Creating a Smart Room Using an IoT Approach', *Semantic Scholar*, 2016, www.semanticscholar. org/paper/Creating-a-Smart-Room-using-an-IoT-approach-Sfikas-Akasiadis/bb0e5be1105b80e3c8d9fc7061566389cb659aa2?p2df, accessed 29 May 2021.

34 Source: David Schatsky and Navya Kumar, 'Workforce Superpowers: Wearables are Augmenting Employees' Abilities'. *Deloitte Insights*, 25

July 2018, https://www2.deloitte.com/us/en/insights/focus/signals-for-strategists/wearable-devices-in-the-workplace.html, accessed 29 May 2021.

35 Good resource: Michael Sawh, 'Getting All Emotional: Wearables that Are Trying to Monitor How We Feel', 27 May 2019, www.wareable.com/wearable-tech/wearables-that-track-emotion-7278, accessed 29 May 2021.

36 There is a commercial version of dot voting available now. See 'What is Dot Voting?', *Pollunit*, https://pollunit.com/en/tutorials/dot_voting, accessed 29 May 2021. Johnathan Stray provides a superb application of data visualisation on his website. See Johnathan Stray, 'Using Clustering to Analyze the Voting Blocs in the UK House of Lords', *Computational Journalism*, 18 September 2018, www.compjournalism.com/?p=13, accessed 29 May 2021.

37 Good sources: Agence France-Presse, 'Thousands of People in Sweden Get Microchip Implants for a New Way of Life', 13 May 2018, www.scmp.com/news/world/europe/article/2145896/thousands-people-sweden-get-microchip-implants-new-way-life, accessed 29 May 2021; Haley Weiss, 'Why You're Probably Getting a Microchip Implant Someday', *The Atlantic*, 21 September 2018, www.theatlantic.com/technology/archive/2018/09/how-i-learned-to-stop-worrying-and-love-the-microchip/570946/, accessed 29 May 2021.

Bibliography

Afhüppe, Sven, Fasse, Markus, and Murphy, Martin, 'Daimler's Cultural Revolution', *Handelsblatt Today*, 31 October 2016, www.handelsblatt.com/english/companies/handelsblatt-exclusive-daimlers-cultural-revolution/23542004.html, accessed 29 May 2021.

Ali, Aayat, 'Why Hybrid Working and the Employee Experience Are Needed', *All Work/The Future of Work*, 25 January 2021, https://allwork.space/2021/01/why-hybrid-working-and-the-employee-experience-are-needed/, accessed 29 May 2021.

Burt, Chris, 'Microsoft Unveils AI-Powered Meeting Transcription Device with Facial and Voice Recognition', *Biometric Update*, 8 May 2018, www.biometricupdate.com/201805/microsoft-unveils-ai-powered-meeting-transcription-device-with-facial-and-voice-recognition, 29 May 2021.

Deiser, Roland, 'Part 5: Agility in Practice: The Swarm Organization at Daimler', *The Digital Transformation People*, 7 May 2019, www.thedigitaltransformationpeople.com/channels/people-and-change/agility-in-practice-the-swarm-organization-at-daimler/, accessed 29 May 2021.

Dungy, Tony, *The Mentor Leader* (Carol Stream, IL: Tyndale House, 2011).

Fister Gale, Sarah, 'Case Study: Walmart Embraces Immersive Learning', *Chief Learning Officer*, 23 March 2021, www.chieflearningofficer.com/2021/03/23/case-study-walmart-embraces-immersive-learning/, accessed 29 May 2021.

France-Presse, Agence, 'Thousands of People in Sweden Get Microchip Implants for a New Way of Life', 13 May 2018, www.scmp.com/news/world/europe/article/2145896/thousands-people-sweden-get-microchip-implants-new-way-life, accessed 29 May 2021

Gray, Rob, 'Can Recruiting for Values Go Too Far?', *HR Magazine*, 27 January 2015, www.hrmagazine.co.uk/content/features/can-recruiting-for-values-go-too-far, accessed 29 May 2021.

Groysberg, Boris, Kelly, Kevin, and Macdonald, Bryan, 'The New Path to the C-Suite', *Harvard Business Review*, March 2011, https://hbr.org/2011/03/the-new-path-to-the-c-suite, accessed 29 May 2021.

Kelly, Richard, *Constructing Leadership 4.0: Swarm Leadership and the Fourth Industrial Revolution* (Basingstoke: Palgrave Macmillan, 2018).

Kotter, John, 'Accelerate!', *Harvard Business Review*, November 2012, https://hbr.org/2012/11/accelerate, accessed 29 May 2021.

Kotter, John P., *Accelerate: Building Strategic Agility for a Faster-Moving World* (Boston, MA: Harvard Business Press Books, 2014).

MacMillan Bankson, Amy, 'Could an Artificial Intelligence-Based Coach Help Managers Master Difficult Conversations?', *MIT Management*, 23 February 2017, https://mitsloan.mit.edu/ideas-made-to-matter/could-artificial-intelligence-based-coach-help-managers-master-difficult-conversations, accessed 29 May 2021.

Piezon, Sherry and Donaldson, Robin. 'Online Groups and Social Loafing: Understanding Student-Group Interactions', *Online Journal of Distance Learning Administration*, 2005, Volume 8, Number 4.

Ring, Greg, 'Daimler Chief Plots Cultural Revolution', *Handelsblatt Today*, 25 July 2016, www.handelsblatt.com/english/companies/future-drive-daimler-chief-plots-cultural-revolution/23539560.html?ticket=ST-18438435-yYvenMdlKh51Qqyim2XP-ap5, accessed 29 May 2021.

Sawh, Michael, 'Getting All Emotional: Wearables That Are Trying to Monitor How We Feel', 27 May 2019, www.wareable.com/wearable-tech/wearables-that-track-emotion-7278, accessed 29 May 2021.

Schatsky, David and Kumar, Navya, 'Workforce Superpowers: Wearables are Augmenting Employees' Abilities'. *Deloitte Insights*, 25 July 2018, https://www2.deloitte.com/us/en/insights/focus/signals-for-strategists/wearable-devices-in-the-workplace.html, accessed 29 May 2021.

Schrage, Michael, 'Leadership and Big Innovation', *HBR Webinar*, 16 December 2013, https://hbr.org/webinar/2016/12/leadership-and-big-data-innovation, accessed 29 May 2021.

Sfikas, Giorgos, Akasiadis, Charilaos, and Spyrou, Evaggelos, 'Creating a Smart Room Using an IoT Approach', *Semantic Scholar*, 2016, www.semanticscholar.org/paper/Creating-a-Smart-Room-using-an-IoT-approach-Sfikas-Akasiadis/bb0e5be1105b80e3c8d9fc7061566389cb659aa2?p2df, accessed 29 May 2021.

Smaje, Kate, 'What's Your Digital Quotient?', *Harvard Business Review, Ideacast, Episode*, September 2015, 483 (3), https://hbr.org/podcast/2015/09/whats-your-digital-quotient.htm, accessed 20 May 2021.

Stray, Johnathan, 'Using Clustering to Analyze the Voting Blocs in the UK House of Lords', *Computational Journalism*, 18 September 2018, www.compjournalism.com/?p=13, accessed 29 May 2021.

Velasco, Carlos and Obrist, Marianna, 'Life After Corona and the Rapid Digitisation of Human Experiences', *BI Norwegian Business School*, 2 April 2020, www.bi.edu/research/business-review/articles/2020/04/life-after-corona-and-the-rapid-digitisation-of-human-experiences/, accessed 29 May 2021.

Weiss, Haley, 'Why You're Probably Getting a Microchip Implant Someday', *The Atlantic*, 21 September 2018, www.theatlantic.com/technology/archive/2018/09/how-i-learned-to-stop-worrying-and-love-the-microchip/570946/, accessed 29 May 2021.

Zetsche, Dieter, 'Going Viral with Cultural Change', *LinkedIn*, 30 May 2017, www.linkedin.com/pulse/going-viral-cultural-change-dieter-zetsche/, accessed 29 May 2021.

7

SWARM 3.0

TOWARDS A BUSINESS SUPERORGANISM

Su-Jin checked the time on her wearable and carried her steaming flask of memil-cha to her pod chair and slipped on her augmented reality glasses. It was time to join Summit 2035. Su-Jin was a contingent worker from Seoul with a strong marketing and sales background who divided her time among several companies providing sales and marketing expertise. One of her clients, a global smart e-bike company, had been a swarm-based organisation since 2024. It was 2032 and the enterprise was now at a defining moment. It had organised a virtual summit to review where it would like to be in 2035 and to start a dialogue and decide collectively whether to remain with swarm as a strategic lever and sidebar of the business or to accelerate swarm and transform the entire enterprise into a business superorganism. This virtual summit had been organised for every stakeholder in the organisation, including salaried employees, contingent workers, shareholders, and partners. Su-Jin was excited to attend. With her latest augmented reality glasses, it really felt like she was a participant in the room. She was experiencing a high-quality augmented reality experience. Su-Jin was 'met' by a personal holobot, who briefed her on the background and itinerary. The figure of the Collective Enterprise Optimiser (CEO), Ashley Harris, appeared ghost-like via holoportation and she carefully set out the three-month road map. She spoke about

DOI: 10.4324/9781003215561-10

the challenges and crossroads they faced. As she spoke, her words were converted from speech to text and appeared as subtitles which instantaneously translated into preferred languages. A data viz with scattergraphs was displaying the collective reaction (including emotional responses) gathered from the wearables and implants of the virtual participants. Participants could give real-time feedback to the CEO during her keynote delivery. Concepts mentioned by the CEO were visualised as hologram models which participants could interact with. After the CEO's opening remarks, Su-Jin linked up with her remote swarm cluster. They were tasked to brainswarm the CEO's keynote in their swarm teams Su-Jin took her flask and walked over to her digitable table. The real work was about to begin.

This fictional vignette set in 2032 depicts a contingent worker in the knowledge sector participating in a virtual business summit of an established swarm organisation that was collectively deciding whether it should transform into a business superorganism.

The Nature of Business Transformation is a phased approach to building a swarm-based organisation. It started with a local emergent initiative of complex adaptive cells (Swarm 1.0) and accelerated into an organisational-led planned strategy (Swarm 2.0), a process known as swarm transformation. This final stage of the transformation is one that will require the most effort and is potentially the most disruptive because it involves a critical decision concerning the future governance of the enterprise.

Swarm 3.0 is effectively a decision to take established swarm communities within the organic honeycomb structure and accelerate them into a business superorganism. A business superorganism, you recall, is not defined by bricks and mortar, personalities, or rigid structures and governance; it is organic and networked – a complex adaptive system of self-organising, self-replicating, cross-functional swarm communities. These are augmented and shaped by intelligent systems. A business superorganism is defined by its brand, with no central headquarters or traditional CEO. It is a nexus for people and ideas that is shaped and organised by artificial intelligence (AI) and smart technology. The organisation knows at any given moment the full data snapshot of the enterprise. There is no need for management, supervisors, and analysts in this world.

Let's look now at the transition to Swarm 3.0 via the familiar template of the three business transformation levers. Although the structure of this chapter follows former chapters, the discerning reader will note a difference in approach. Whereas Chapters 5 and 6 (which explored Swarm 1.0 and 2.0, respectively) were very practical with clear steps, this chapter is less prescriptive. The reason for this is Swarm 3.0 is most likely to happen in the next decade in an unpredictable operating environment. This chapter, therefore, presents guiding principles and projected scenarios rather than future certainties.

Swarm 3.0: Lever 1: system transformation

We have seen how the organic honeycomb model, the digital strategy, the concept of the hivemind, the hybrid organisational change and development approach, and the swarm facilitation process have all been instrumental in supporting the growth and transition of organisational swarm. A key decision that the Swarm 2.0 organisation needs to take is whether it stays functioning as a part-swarm and benefits from the adaptiveness, collaboration, and engagement that this brings, or whether it accelerates towards a business superorganism. If it opts to accelerate, then this will require further system transformation which will be disruptive. Let's explore Swarm 3.0 now by starting with the organisational, digital, and behavioural system transformations.

Organisational transformation 3.0

Swarm 3.0 represents a tipping point for the organisation. The choice involves committing to a deeper swarm which will require a radical change of the governing structure and set the organisation on the path to becoming a business superorganism where the entire organisation functions as a self-organising, collective, swarm-based entity glued together by smart technology. The transition to this level of swarm is going to require a critical organisational commitment – to deformalise the entire enterprise so that it works entirely through connected networks/communities and functions as a complex adaptive system. In previous versions of swarm, only parts of the organisation were impacted; here the entire organisational set-up will be subject to the business transformation. Expressed succinctly, the choice here is whether the enterprise continues as an assemblage of organised complex adaptive cells which raise agility and engagement, but continues to operate within a tradition context, or does it exploit the full potential of becoming a complex adaptive system? This choice is all about abandoning hierarchies and traditional Business Operating System (BOS) 1.0 legacies. Superorganisms and hierarchies cannot coexist together; superorganisms work through collective networks and not rigid reporting lines and chains of command. The next three points on 'rethinking governance, leadership and management', 'rethinking resourcing', and 'deformalisation' are all practical steps to creating networked organisations.

Rethinking governance, leadership, and management

One of the most comprehensive descriptions of these complex terms and their interrelatedness was expressed by Michael Gallagher in the context of whether universities should be run as academies or enterprises. Gallagher said,

> Governance is the structure of relationships that bring about organisational coherence, authorise policies, plans and decisions, and account for their probity, responsiveness and cost-effectiveness. Leadership is seeing opportunities and setting strategic directions, and investing in and drawing on people's capabilities to develop organisational purposes and values. Management is achieving intended outcomes through the allocation of responsibilities and resources, and monitoring their efficiency and effectiveness.[1]

This traditional composition has been in place for centuries and contributes to the classic BOS explored in Chapter 1. It is fit-for-purpose for a hierarchical organisational structure; it is not fit-for-purpose for a swarm-based organisation that is aspiring towards becoming a business superorganism. Superorganisms have zero central governance, leadership, and management. In the natural world, swarm colonies are organic, generative, self-governing, self-organising, complex adaptive systems.

Governance

To become a business superorganism, the rigid governance structure that has concentrated power in investors, directors, and senior executives will need to be redistributed. Power in business superorganisms lies in the complex adaptive system and not in power hierarchies. That said, and speaking practically, investors and equity shareholders do have considerable power in large established organisations, so there will need to be some legal consultation to try to establish a model where decisions made in the swarm clusters and endorsed by the business community are not blocked by equity shareholders. An important conversation needs to take place with investors and a legal framework should be agreed and produced before the organisation sets out on a path to becoming a business superorganism. There are historic examples of investors seeking to change the culture of organisations they acquire. Amazon's acquisition of Whole Foods, for example, is an interesting case study. Amazon insisted it would not change Whole Food's business model of team-led decision-making, but there has been a centralisation of operations and some purchasing and sales decisions are now driven directly by Amazon.[2] It does seem that even solid commitments in acquisitions by buyers to protect the core culture of an acquisition are not sufficient. The governance issue, for sure, needs to be carefully considered with legal teams and meticulously documented before contemplating any bold moves.

Leadership

In swarm models, leadership is collective. The role of swarm mentor leader was pivotal in Swarm 2.0. This role will cease to exist in Swarm 3.0. In superorganisms, no single agent is more important than another. In a business superorganism (Swarm 3.0), there should be no power titles or job grades, but a collective group of self-organising agents who exercise collective leadership that is 'managed' by intelligent systems. In Swarm 3.0, leadership is not going to be a role; it will be a collective enabling behaviour, facilitated by intelligent systems. The CEO will be the Collective Enterprise Optimiser. S/he will no longer be an organisational figurehead who is the central and all-powerful decision maker or influencer, but, like the queen bee, will be a nurturer and an enabler and an enterprise ambassador for the organisation – someone who serves to optimise connectedness, collectivism, and generativity.

Management

Put simply, management has no place in an organisation that is aspiring to become a business superorganism. Management and supervisory structures do not exist in natural swarm environments. We saw in the *Preface* that DreamWorks Animation representation of directive and management-type characters (such as decorated general Lou Lo Duca) bears no reality to honeybee colonies. Superorganisms do not have such directive agents. A transition to Swarm 3.0 and business superorganism status would practically mean the total eradication of management. It would be a seismic cultural earthquake to remove all supervisory and management roles in preference for self-organising swarm communities.

Rethinking resourcing

Swarm 3.0 will require some major rethinking of the way organisations are resourced. There will need to be a radical programme of redirecting talent from management to swarm clusters. This may result in one of the largest redundancy programmes in corporate history and would certainly mean that the enterprise of the future won't have the amount of human resources that they currently have. A company is likely to have many workplace providers[3] (independent workers who digitally bid for involvement in assignments or 'gigs' or who are identified by people analytics as likely resource fits). Peter Schwartz refers to this in a *Salesforce* piece as the rise of the independent worker.[4] A Citrix 2035 study of 1500 surveyed business leaders believed that by 2035 (the timeline for Swarm 3.0), the fixed and permanent resourcing model is likely to be superseded in preference for on-demand talent.[5] Traditional companies tend to use dedicated resources that are tied to divisions and departments. Business superorganisms are decentralised and deformalised complex adaptive systems which require a more flexible and broader human (and machine) resourcing model that is not bound by precedence or conventions. By 2035, shared or pooled human resourcing such as freelancers, contingent workers, and cloud workers across varied organisations will be inevitable. Post-Covid companies will move towards more flexible and organic structures and will require a more flexible resource model. Mruthyanjaya Rao Mangipudi et al. argue human resource pooling improves efficiency.[6] It certainly will be an excellent resourcing model for business superorganisms and Swarm 3.0. Machines will play a significant part in the work communities of the future which will include service robots and smart technology to augment human intelligence. They will work alongside human resources as cobots.[7] The big unknown here, as we explored in Chapter 3, is to what degree machine/artificial intelligence will be in the third AI wave and have advanced automated business processes.[8] Organisational restructuring in Swarm 3.0, therefore, will be about limiting permanent resources and maximising shared and pooled resources. The organisation will need to engage with their legal teams to implement this model and consider staged redundancies. Classic organisational charts and organograms which symbolise status and a sense of 'belonging' to specific departments will be abandoned. The learning and resource portal developed in Swam 2.0 will prove to be a game changer and strategic lever here and AI people analytics will also be key to identify ongoing resources. A flexible billing model will need to be worked out. Most large organisations work on the principle of internal billable hours. This can be a conditioning factor and isn't workable in a swarm context.

In summary, the organisation will not be divided into departments or divisions but human and machine resources will be in a shared pool that is called upon to resource global swarm communities. The traditional 'boss' or supervisor who allocates tasks and oversees hiring, remuneration, performance appraisal, and termination will not be necessary and employment terms and data will be managed by AI systems. Performance feedback will come from colleagues and cobots and the algorithm will determine remuneration.

Deformalisation

Superorganisms thrive in deformalised settings. Likewise, swarm clusters and communities flourish in less formal environments. In Swarm 1.0, it was advised that business process owners abandon formalities and operant conditioning such as rank, job titles, pay grades, and the like and cultivate a culture of peer equality within complex adaptive cells. This deformalisation accelerated in Swarm 2.0 as swarm communities became a substantive part of the enterprise. The connections between the swarm-based parts of the organisation and the more traditional elements were also deformalised, passing through wirearchies rather than hierarchies. Swarm 3.0, will need to accelerate deformalisation to an enterprise-wide level. We have already discussed what this may look like for leadership, management, and governance where power transfers away from influential decision-making individuals. There will need to be initiatives like ongoing peer and cobot reviews rather than end of year appraisals, peer compensation rather than formal management grading, endorsements rather than promotions. Plenty talk about the merits of a boss-less organisation[9]; likewise, plenty consider it to be impractical and impossible.[10] The reason why it is possible with augmented swarm is because the end-game of augmented swarm – the business superorganism – is a complex adaptive system that is facilitated through intelligent systems and not alpha leaders. It is not just an internal phenomenon. Organisations need to cultivate collective impact and this means being more open and transparent with such things as reassessing firewalls and sharing resources and experiences with external partners. A business superorganism requires more open relationships with shareholders, partners, suppliers, and customers.

Digital transformation 3.0

By 2035, organisations are likely to be within John Launchbury's AI third wave where artificial systems will be able to understand context and meaning. We saw from Chapter 3 that a generation of smart technology and swarm augmentation is already underway. Major digital transformation milestones that need to occur at Swarm 3.0 that will propel the organisation towards being a business superorganism include human digitisation; universal wirearchy/digital facilitation; tech development, digitalisation, and human/machine collaboration. Let's review each in turn.

Human digitisation

We saw in Chapter 3 that there are many AI recognition systems that decipher and digitise human output and emotion. Emotional recognition is increasingly being developed especially through implants and wearables.

The next phase of AI human recognition that is under development and could be ready as early as the next decade is thought recognition. These technologies are supporting the concept of the digitised human where every human thought, conversation, emotion, and expression, are instantaneously captured digitally. This technology has the potential to be a powerful swarm tool where thoughts, emotions, physical reaction, and expressions are captured during ideation and fed into decision-making. The game changer will occur when this technology determines inner human landscapes rather than just external ones and produces digital human datasets that augment ideation and decision-making.

Wireacracy and digital facilitation

Jon Husband's theory of wirearchy has been widely presented in this study. Wirearchy raises understanding of the knowledge flow across boundaries and is key for a borderless self-governing entity, such as swarm, that connects and links to networks, communities, and enterprises. Jon Husband's theory analyses what happens to power and authority in an interconnected machine and human environment. This perspective belongs more to the connectivist tradition than the behavioural and cognitivist traditions that shaped hierarchical organisations. In Swarm 1.0, organisations were connected through human-managed networks and communities; in Swarm 2.0, data analytics became the connecting force; in Swarm 3.0, the entire enterprise will shift from hierarchy to wirearchy and become a super connectivist organisation. The honeycomb structure is optimised through linked cells. For networks, communities, stakeholders, and partners to be truly aligned in a non-hierarchical way, we will need to examine how these cells and clusters are linked and connected using intelligent systems. Human digitisation is key in this transformation together with the development of smart technology to progress the integration of people and machines. This should all be developed in parallel with organisational and behavioural transformations. As the enterprise becomes more digitally connected and interconnected, the concept of digital facilitation will grow in importance. Digital facilitation is where human thought and decision-making are facilitated by systems and technology.

Tech developments, digitalisation, and human/machine collaboration

Digitalisation, you recall, is different from digitisation. Digitalisation is the evolution of systems and technology; digitisation is converting non-digital systems to digital formats. We don't know for sure what technology will exist by the mid-2030s, but we can have a good guess based on current research and development. Most likely, the next 15 years will see a dramatic progression towards augmented decisions and autonomous intelligence. We saw in Chapter 3 that AI is currently on a par with the human intelligence of a young child. By the time we get to the mid-2030s, AI should come of age. Technology will be semi-supervised and able to crunch unlabelled and disorganised data. This will make it increasingly useful in the collaborative tech and augmented decision space where technology can assist human effort. Also, as we have already mentioned in this chapter, humans and human intelligence will become more augmented by machine intelligence with wearables and implants. Effectively, humans will become integrated cyborgs.[11] By the mid-2030s, humans and machines will have an unprecedented level of collaboration. Service robots, chatbots, wearables, Internet of Things will all contribute to our human connectivity and augment our intelligence. Swarm 3.0 is not singularity, but it is advanced augmented intelligence that promotes connectivity, digitisation, and deep learning. All of this has the potential to facilitate human thought, ideas, and decisions. Practically speaking, organisations will need to make global and joined-up decisions about this emerging technology and procure systems that can be applied universally across the enterprise. This ongoing strategic procurement of digitalised systems will be a major part of the digital transformation journey of the organisation, but it will be one that is coordinated with the structural and behavioural transformation of the organisation.

Behavioural transformation 3.0

By the time organisations are contemplating and discussing Swarm 3.0 and growing into a business superorganism, the enterprise – if it follows the swarm transformation formula – would already have spent over a decade future-proofing its structures, digital systems, and behaviours. In terms of the latter, the subject of this section, we have already seen that pre-swarm and in-swarm learning interventions can raise the willingness and ability of swarm whether is it locally organised (Swarm 1.0) or organisationally sponsored (Swarm 2.0). By the time organisations deliberate on Swarm 3.0, the enterprise should already be firmly transitioning into a hivemind enterprise. There are additional initiatives that the organisation would need to undertake to further progress and reinforce hivemind behaviours.

Embrace emerging technology to support learning and development

By 2035, the smart tech scenarios portrayed in the opening vignette to support learning such as virtual and augmented reality (VR and AR) smart glasses, holograms,[12] holoportation, VR, chatbots, wearables, advanced data visualisations, and digitables that feature now on our Twitter feeds are likely to be mainstream. The future could see other nascent technologies supporting corporate learning such as robot educators.[13]

Building a cross-boundary swarm learning enterprise

In 1973, Peter Senge's colleague, Donald Schön, wrote about learning systems:

> We must become able not only to transform our institutions, in response to changing situations and requirements; we must invent and develop institutions which are 'learning systems', that is to say, systems capable of bringing about their own continuing transformation.[14]

The idea of 'continuing transformation' is something very important for building swarm, but it is particularly relevant for Swarm 3.0. As we have asserted throughout, swarm is generative – the system supports progress and learning. There needs to be a culture of kaizen or continuous improvement and the collective nature of swarm should be about supporting each other through collaborative learning networks.

Influence the broader traditional education sector

By 2035 and the rise of Industry 4.0 and the connected economy, it simply will not be enough for organisations to develop their own talent. They will need to send their swarm ambassadors outside of the company walls and help shape and influence the broader traditional education sector. Carolina Milanesi says, 'the private sector must work with the public sector so that we can create a proper skillset supply to match the demand. The current education system is simply not doing enough to help mold an appropriately skilled talent pool'.[15] By the time we get to the end of this decade, the core business attributes of hiveminds, digital quotient, collaborate mindsets should be taught in schools and universities as a matter of course and swarm business ambassadors should be partners and advisors for the educational sector. Business superorganisms need to play a direct part in the educational system of the future. This is the true meaning of generative cross-boundary learning systems.

Lever 2: organisational change

What we have seen so far in Swarm 1.0 and Swarm 2.0 is a phased hybrid model of change that accelerates over time. Swarm 1.0 was a grassroots emergent initiative; Swarm 2.0 formalised swarm in the enterprise and scaled it up over time. Swarm 3.0 is a game changer; it shifts the enterprise towards becoming a business superorganism. This is when the honeycomb structure becomes an entire complex adaptive system. Swarm 3.0 is the most ambitious and disruptive phase of the swarm transformation and will require the most organisational change effort. Here are some important steps in the transition phase from Swarm 2.0 to 3.0.

Do an organisational pulse check

Taking the organisation beyond a percentage of the enterprise being swarm-based to a majority swarm-based organisation/business superorganism is a big step that will require a significant change in governance and structure. This is a key moment where the company needs to decide whether to take swarm to the ultimate step. This will require a considerable organisational commitment and investment which will impact such things as governance and resourcing. The pulse check senses the enterprise-wide mood to deepen swarm and should include a feasibility study that weighs up costs and benefits. Some specific conditions of this organisational pulse check should include:

- It needs to be boundary spanning. There needs to be full involvement of employees, contingent workers, shareholders, partners, customers, and suppliers. Listen to all views and seek to eliminate rank and status during this process. Also, conduct some benchmarking with similar organisations who are also aspiring towards being business superorganisms.
- For larger organisations, it will most likely be virtual and should use the swarm techniques and the smart tech augmentation that it is aspiring to adopt.
- It should be a transparent, open, and honest appraisal of the business. The pros and cons of accelerating the business into a greater swarm-based entity must be considered.
- In the drive to have a swarm organisation, remember to keep the customer in mind not just the organisational need. Don't redesign the soul of the company.
- Give it the time it needs. Honeybees leave the colony and reside in bivouacs to determine their future. They take the time they need for the important decisions connected to their survival.
- Embrace the Medici Effect.
- Keep the vision of the organisation in mind. Don't lose sight of the summit.

Develop an acceleration strategy

If the organisational pulse check recommends taking things to the next level, then the next task is to develop a Swarm 3.0 acceleration strategy. The strategy is about scaling up the enterprise from current reality (which may typically be up to 25% of the organisation as swarm-based) to a majority state where the enterprise is a majority swarm. A good way of conceptualising this is by likening it to climbing a mountain. Warren Bennis uses a mountaineering analogy in *On Becoming a Leader*. He says,

Mountain climbers don't start climbing from the bottom of the mountain. They look at where they want to go, and work backward to where they're starting from. Like a mountain climber, once you have the summit in view, you figure out all the ways you might get there.[16]

If the summit is a business superorganism, the climb to this summit will include a number of important camps:

Preparing for the journey

This relates to the organisational pulse check. It is desirous to consult with the organisation and get everyone committed to the journey.

Base camp

This relates to the governance restructure and refocusing of the organisational powerbase away from investors, directors, and senior executives towards a more collective governance. Getting to base camp and creating a new collective culture base will be a significant challenge.

Camp 1

This relates to rethinking the resourcing and budgeting model. As has been discussed, there is no place for fixed resourcing and fenced-off departments in a complex adaptive system such as Swarm 3.0. The organisation will need to migrate to a pooled/shared resourcing model, supported by open resourcing and people analytics. Freelancers, contingency workers, crowdsourcing participants, paid ideators, and pooled resources from across the enterprise, including partners, should all be involved.

Camp 2

This relates to the restructuring of management and deformalising the organisation. This will be a challenging part of the climb and is the single factor that could change the face of the organisational culture. Managers will need to be assessed, retrained as swarm participants, or phased out of the organisation. This step will need to eliminate conditioning factors such as job titles, rigid budgeting models, bonuses, recruitment policies, and the like. As discussed elsewhere, these are operant conditioners that have no place in complex adaptive systems such as Swarm 3.0.

Camp 3

This connects to the digital transformation discussed in Lever 1. Camp 3 is about exploiting the latest technology that supports self-organising complex adaptive systems. This concerns future technology that will come from the third wave of AI where machines provide efficient business intelligence analytics and decision augmentation.

Reaching the summit

The summit in this case is a full adoption of Swarm 3.0 and the succession of the organisation to a business superorganism. That said, the hybrid approach of planned and emergent change needs to continue to allow the business to evolve. That's why transitioning to Swarm 3.0 could take several years (and for large organisations up to a decade). This is in keeping with Kotter's theory of minimising disruption and evolving the business. In mountaineering, climbers need to acclimatise to the different camp levels. Climbing Mount Everest, for example, takes two months. Most mountaineering activity is about acclimatisation. It is also important that businesses acclimatise to the incremental changes. In mountaineering, climbers have the choice to abort the climb if the conditions are not right and in business it should be the same. Maybe the organisation reaches a higher percentage but is happy staying at that level. Maybe the organisation will want to abandon the climb or continue to the summit and be a business superorganism. Establishing camps and acclimatising to them is all part of the change journey and integral to Kotter's Accelerate approach. Having the summit in mind (becoming a business superorganism) and knowing the milestones and options to get there, it will allow the business to be adaptive and responsive while pursuing business as normal.

Lever 3: swarm facilitation

You recall, swarm facilitation is based on the swarm flow model (Figure 2.4) which is an algorithm for relocating honeybees. This model serves the organisation as a self-organising ideation and decision-making cycle without the need for alpha leaders, facilitators, or designers. This model becomes more automated in Swarm 3.0. Let's follow the template of the last two chapters and explore each process and how it plays out in Swarm 3.0.

Prepare

Preparation in Swarm 3.0 is a fully digital and autonomous process. Business intelligence comes out of boundary-spanning advanced analytics. Swarm communities will be resourced through open resourcing and people analytics and onboarded and remunerated through central management systems. Swarm 3.0 simply does not need the kind of preparation that other phases of swarm needed.

Cluster

There will still be human participation in 2035, but forming swarms into clusters and teams will be supported by intelligent systems that will create the swarm clusters/teams and set them the business challenge. The challenge is generated from data analytics.

Sensemake

Clusters of human creativity will still prevail in 2035, but it will be augmented. In Swarm 3.0, sensemaking will be a human/machine collaboration where human ideation and creative intuition will be machine processed. By 2035, there will be an unprecedented collaboration of humans and machines. Humans will create; machines will digitise these impressions, compute them, visually represent them, and implement them.

Act

This will be machine assisted at Swarm 3.0, but it needs to be supervised. Machines cannot just act on swarm creativity from the cluster; it needs to be overseen by humans. This is part of the ethical dimension of intelligent automation discussed in Chapter 3. Machines will not be capable at this stage in their evolution to make creative choices concerning human need. By 2050, Su-Jin (from our opening story) would probably be a machine supervisor or ethical controller.

Regenerate

Creating a real-time double-loop system between the cluster and community encourages generativity. Also, we have seen at this level, Swarm 3.0 will be a global 'learning system'.

This chapter is the final phase of swarm transformation where future organisations will need to decide how far they develop swarm in their organisations. A business superorganism (Swarm 3.0) means full organisational connectivity and integration where human creativity across the enterprise is augmented and supported by intelligent systems at each phase of swarm facilitation. The organisation would have had over a decade to prepare for this phase in terms of its structures, systems, and behaviours. That said, Swarm 3.0 is still an ambitious step that will create organisational disruption. Swarm 3.0 will generate job displacement and a reorganisation of governance. It also has the potential to become the kind of learning system that early transformationalists such as Donald Schön and Peter Senge theorised about. Ultimately, despite concerns about technological singularity, Swarm 3.0 is still all about human choice.

Notes

1 Michael Gallagher, 'Modern University Governance – A National Perspective', in *Conference Paper. Conference Organised by The Australia Institute and Manning Clark House, The Australian National University, Canberra*, 26 July 2001, http://ncgdvn.blogspot.com/2008/12/modern-university-governance-national.html, accessed 29 May 2021.

2 Good source: Steve Banker, 'How Amazon Changed Whole Foods', *Forbes*, 26 June 2019, www.forbes.com/sites/stevebanker/2019/06/25/how-amazon-changed-whole-foods/?sh=33af00e978dd, accessed 29 May 2021.

3 Source: 'The Future of Human Resources', *Monitor Deloitte*, www2.deloitte. com/content/dam/Deloitte/de/Documents/strategy/Future-of-Human-Resources-2030-Deloitte-Glimpse-Paper.PDF, accessed 29 May 2021.

4 Peter Schwartz, 'The Future of Work: Technology, Jobs and Augmented Intelligence', *Salesforce Blog*, 9 October 2017, www.salesforce.com/au/blog/ 2017/10/the-future-of-work--technology--jobs-and-augmented-intelligence. html?utm_content=buffer36b7e&utm_medium=social&utm_source= twitter.com&utm_campaign=buffer, accessed 29 May 2021.

5 Source: 'How People and Technology Will Pioneer New Ways of Working', *Citrix*, 2021, www.citrix.com/fieldwork/employee-experience/new-ways-of-working-2035.html, accessed 29 May 2021.

6 Mruthyanjaya Rao Mangipudi, et al., 'Optimization of Human Resources: Does Human Resource Pooling in an Organization Help in Improving Capacity Building and Efficiency? A Case Study', *JHRSS*, 7, 3, 2019, https:// m.scirp.org/papers/94789, accessed 29 May 2021.

7 Good source: Jeanne Meister, 'AI Plus Human Intelligence Is the Future of Work', *Forbes*, 11 January 2018, www.forbes.com/sites/jeannemeister/ 2018/01/11/ai-plus-human-intelligence-is-the-future-of-work/?sh= 7709d7c52bba#39f9278a2bba, accessed 29 May 2021.

8 The issue is neatly captured by Dalith Steiger, Co-founder of Swiss Cognitive when she says,

> Eventually, autonomous industry systems will not only be able to compile and analyze data from different sources, but reach independent conclusions based on that information. They will thus be in a position to make correct decisions, even in situations they have not been programmed to handle.
>
> Source: 'On Course for Sustainable Future with Artificial Intelligence', *ABB Interview*, ABB, 22 January 2020, https://new.abb.com/news/detail/55794/on-course-for-a-sustainable-future-with-artificial-intelligence, accessed 29 May 2021

9 Source: Gary Hamel, 'First, Let's Fire all the Managers', *Harvard Business Review*, December 2011, https://hbr.org/2011/12/first-lets-fire-all-the-manag ers, accessed 29 May 2021.

10 Source: André Spicer, 'No Bosses, No Managers: The Truth Behind the "Flat Hierarchy" Façade', *The Guardian*, 30 July 2018, www.theguardian.com/ commentisfree/2018/jul/30/no-bosses-managers-flat-hierachy-workplace-tech-hollywood, accessed 29 May 2021.

11 Elon Musk predicts this. Source: Thomas Ricker, 'Elon Musk: We're Already Cyborgs', *The Verge*, 2 June 2016, www.theverge.com/2016/6/2/11837854/ neural-lace-cyborgs-elon-musk, accessed 29 May 2021.

12 Good source: R. Dallon Adams, 'Hologram Virtual Meetings? Envisioning the Future of Remote Collaboration, Hiring, and More', 20 August 2020, www.techrepublic.com/article/hologram-virtual-meetings-envisioning-the-future-of-remote-collaboration-hiring-and-more/, accessed 29 May 2021.

13 Good source: Douglas P. Newton and Lynn D. Newton, 'Humanoid Robots as Teachers and a Proposed Code of Practice', *Frontiers in Education*, 5 November 2019, www.frontiersin.org/articles/10.3389/feduc.2019.00125/ full, accessed 29 May 2021. Also Stuart Nathan, 'A Real Step towards the Virtual Holodeck', 26 March 2019, www.theengineer.co.uk/real-step-towards-virtual-holodeck/, accessed 29 May 2021.

14 D.A. Schön, *Beyond the Stable State. Public and Private Learning in a Changing Society* (New York, NY: Random House, 1971), 30.

15 Carolina Milanesi, 'Digital Transformation and Digital Divide Post COVID-19', *Forbes*, 11 May 2020, www.forbes.com/sites/carolinamilanesi/2020/ 05/11/digital-transformation-and-digital-divide-post-covid-19/?sh= 3753fb616565, accessed 29 May 2021.

16 Warren Bennis, *On Becoming a Leader, 1989* (New York, NY: Basic Books, 2003), 126.

Bibliography

Banker, Steve, 'How Amazon Changed Whole Foods', *Forbes*, 26 June 2019, www.forbes.com/sites/stevebanker/2019/06/25/how-amazon-changed-whole-foods/?sh=33af00e978dd, accessed 29 May 2021.

Bennis, Warren, *On Becoming a Leader, 1989* (New York, NY: Basic Books, 2003).

Gallagher, Michael, 'Modern University Governance – A National Perspective', in *Conference Paper. Conference Organised by The Australia Institute and Manning Clark House, The Australian National University, Canberra*, 26 July

2001, http://ncgdvn.blogspot.com/2008/12/modern-university-governance-national.html, accessed 29 May 2021.

Hamel, Gary, 'First, Let's Fire All the Managers', *Harvard Business Review*, December 2011, https://hbr.org/2011/12/first-lets-fire-all-the-managers, accessed 29 May 2021.

Husband, Jon, 'What Is Wirearchy?', *Wirearchy* (blog), 16 February 2013, http://wirearchy.com/what-is-wirearchy/, accessed 29 May 2021.

Mangipudi, Mruthyanjaya R., Prasad, Kanaka D.V., and Vaidya, Rajesh, 'Optimization of Human Resources: Does Human Resource Pooling in an Organization Help in Improving Capacity Building and Efficiency? A Case Study', *JHRSS*, 2019, 7 (3), https://m.scirp.org/papers/94789, accessed 29 May 2021.

Meister, Jeanne, 'AI Plus Human Intelligence Is the Future Of Work', *Forbes*, 11 January 2018, www.forbes.com/sites/jeannemeister/2018/01/11/ai-plus-human-intelligence-is-the-future-of-work/?sh=7709d7c52bba#39f9278a2bba, accessed 29 May 2021.

Milanesi, Carolina, 'Digital Transformation and Digital Divide Post COVID-19', *Forbes*, 11 May 2020, www.forbes.com/sites/carolinamilanesi/2020/05/11/digital-transformation-and-digital-divide-post-covid-19/?sh=3753fb616565, accessed 29 May 2021.

Ricker, Thomas, 'Elon Musk: We're Already Cyborgs', *The Verge*, 2 June 2016, www.theverge.com/2016/6/2/11837854/neural-lace-cyborgs-elon-musk, accessed 29 May 2021.

Schön, Donald A., *Beyond the Stable State. Public and Private Learning in a Changing Society* (New York, NY: Random House, 1971).

Schwartz, Peter, 'The Future of Work: Technology, Jobs and Augmented Intelligence', *Salesforce Blog*, 9 October 2017, www.salesforce.com/au/blog/2017/10/the-future-of-work--technology--jobs-and-augmented-intelligence.html?utm_content=buffer36b7e&utm_medium=social&utm_source=twitter.com&utm_campaign=buffer, accessed 29 May 2021.

Spicer, André, 'No Bosses, No Managers: The Truth Behind the "Flat Hierarchy" Façade', *The Guardian*, 20 July 2018, www.theguardian.com/commentisfree/2018/jul/30/no-bosses-managers-flat-hierachy-workplace-tech-hollywood, accessed 29 May 2021.

CONCLUSION

SWARM TRANSFORMATION AT A GLANCE

Professional texts can come up empty if they fail to clearly demonstrate how to implement the ideas discussed in a book. This conclusory chapter presents a clear no-nonsense summation and road map for building a more swarm-based organisation and business superorganism. This will promote a more agile, collaborative, engaged, and connected enterprise. Processes and swarm transformation phases are disseminated throughout the book. I am conscious that structuring the book in this way can lessen its impact and diminish it as a step-by-step guide that adopters need to take to implement swarm. This final conclusory chapter, therefore, revists swarm transformation but organises it in a practical, sequential, and visual way: a clear and logical span from pre-swarm to business superorganisms. It highlights the transitions and key milestones that adopters should take. The objective of the chapter is to cover the distance travelled, but also to be a handy road map for adopting swarm in the organisation. Central to the chapter is a detailed timeline (Figure C.2) of the swarm transformation. This will appeal to visual learnings, but I will also go on to document the stages in some detail.

Overview

The core of the book concerns the need to have upgraded and fit-for-purpose business operating systems (BOSs) within organisations that are

DOI: 10.4324/9781003215561-11

compatible with Industry 4.0. The study takes inspiration from swarm intelligence and, in particular, the house-hunting habits of honeybees (*Apis mellifera*). The traditional BOS 1.0 is hierarchical, prescriptive, and centripetal. It is structured so that ideas and decisions are formed at the top and driven down the scalar chain of command. Business input and endorsement of executive ideas come about through predetermined needs assessment rather than through business intelligence. This approach fails modern business. In an era where machine intelligence is coming of age and augmenting (and even replacing) human resources and where the younger generation are rejecting traditional business structures and are feeling disengaged in the workplace, the system is out of date. The experience of the coronavirus pandemic has exposed the flaw but also revealed the fix. Knowledge workers have spent most of 2020 and 2021 working from home. They rose to the challenge to be agile and flexible to keep their organisations running. The culture of workplace presenteeism, supervision, and scalar chain decision-making was suspended and the business world didn't collapse; in fact, as we revealed earlier, initial indication points to a rise in productivity compared with pre-Covid findings.

Part 1 of the book focuses on the theoretical issues of the business transformation related to swarm and machine intelligence. Part 2 focuses on the swarm transformation itself. Evolving the enterprise into a swarm-based organisation necessitates a phased system and culture transformation at the structure, digital/technology, and mindset level. This requires a comprehensive phased approach to change that involves both planned and emergent change. It has three levels of adoption (see Figure C.1). A universal change and development strategy and swarm facilitation (modelled on relocating honeybees) are applied to each level.

Let's now do a deep dive into these three levels of adoption and view them in the full swarm transformation context. Figure C.2 represents a detailed timeline of swarm transformation.

This is an entire overview of the book and you see it has five distinct stages. Let's investigate them.

Stage 1: transition to Swarm 1.0 (six months)

Swarm 1.0 is where a business process owner with full budgetary and decision-making authority associated with a local meeting, event, or

Swarm 3.0. Optimising business improvement through business superorganisms
The enterprise is a complex adaptive system of fully wired and integrated swarm communities. Business intelligence is automated and human digitisation and decision augmentation supports human creativity.

Swarm 2.0. Optimising business improvement through human and machine systems and networks
Complex adaptive swarm communities are organisationally-led. The swarm communities are business intelligence led and are global decision-making networks. Business intelligence and group processing is augmented with intelligent systems.

Swarm 1.0. Optimising business improvement through human systems and networks
Swarm communities are formed to support local meetings and events. They are not centrally designed or planned, but are self-organising complex adaptive cells where intelligence, ideas, and decisions come about through human communities and networks using the principle of swarm intelligence.

Figure C.1 Three levels of swarm adoption.

programme decides voluntarily to adopt a swarm approach by setting up a swarm community (which includes a trusted advisor/beekeeper, business intelligence network, swarm cluster, and swarm reps). The purpose of this swarm community is to make sense, through swarm teams, of business challenges emerging from the business intelligence network and provide recommendations back to the business process owner via the swarm reps. This swarm process is organic and emergent, rather than prescriptive. Voluntary self-organising swarm communities adopt swarm facilitation to optimise collective intelligence and decision-making through human swarms that are not supported by technology. It operates as a complex adaptive cell bivouacked within the broader hierarchical structure. Four important tasks at this stage include the following:

1. Influencer to research into swarm theory and identify and recruit trusted advisors

Business process owners should not contemplate adopting a collective decision-making approach, such as swarm, without first understanding some basic principles of self-organising complex adaptive systems. We saw in Chapter 5 that this can be gained through self-directed learning

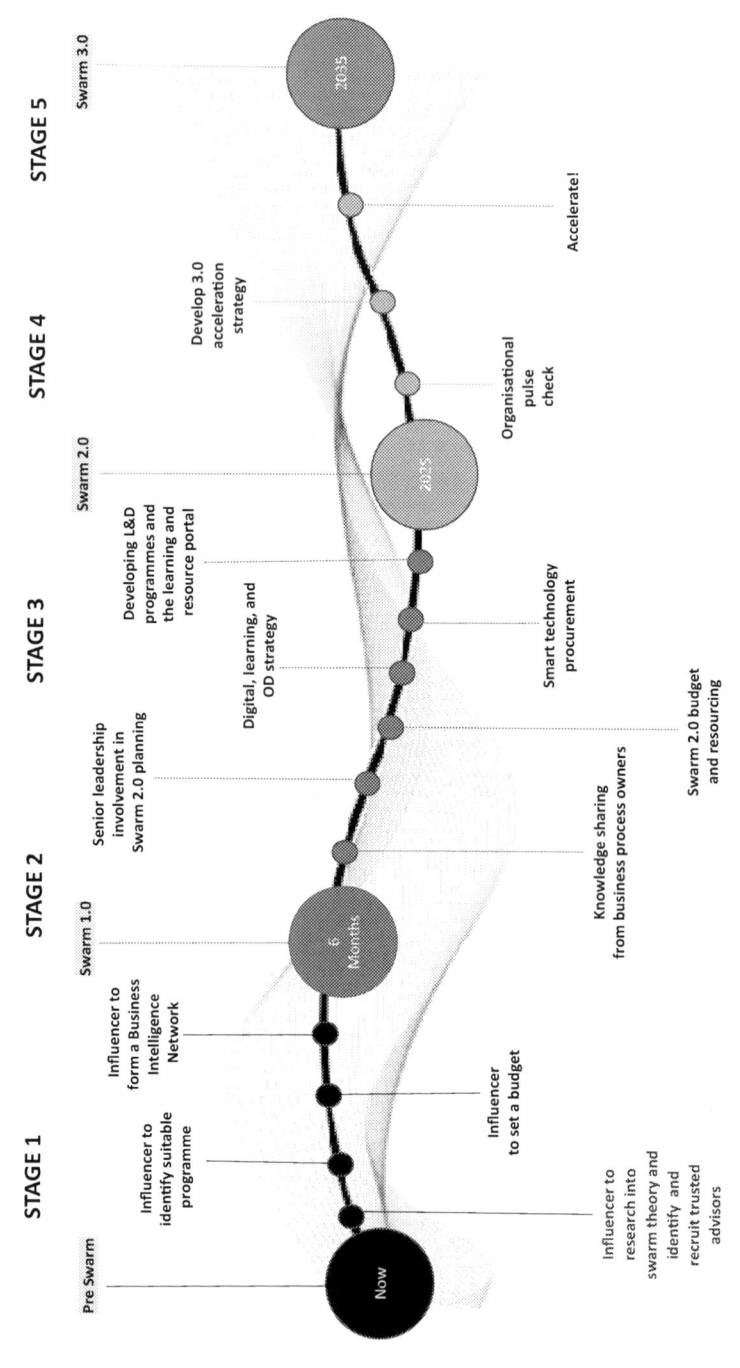

Figure C.2 Detailed timeline of the five stages of swarm transformation.

and through building a network of trusted advisors, including beekeepers, swarm reps, and thought leaders in the field.

2. Influencer to identify suitable programme

This is part of the swarm facilitation preparation. Business process owners need to identify a local meeting, event, or programme where swarm facilitation can be applied.

3. Influencer to set a budget

A local swarm process is no different from any other project and will need to be resourced and budgeted. This is a key part of the preparation for swarm facilitation. Identical with general project budgeting, business process owners will need to budget for resources, third-party support, venue, and material costs.

4. Influencer to form the Business Intelligence Network

Swarm is intelligence-led rather than knowledge-led. The Swarm 1.0 Business Intelligence Network is a physical network of local business stakeholders. They are part of the swarm community. This is a component of the swarm facilitation preparation and should be established several months ahead of forming the swarm cluster. Chapter 5 provided some basic principles to establish this network.

Stage 2: Swarm 1.0 timespan

This is the second stage of the five-stage swarm transformation and it covers the time span of Swarm 1.0. Here, business process owners who have prepared the ground are now ready to operationalise Swarm 1.0. They need to establish a swam cluster and develop the cluster's willingness and ability through pre-swarm and in-swarm interventions. These interventions are based on adaptive and collaborative quotients. The swarm cluster will work on the core business challenge identified through the swarm rep and create a working timetable. The swarm cluster will divide into teams who work on the business challenge both remotely and in swarm meets. Output from these sessions is shared with the business process owner via the swarm reps for approval and implementation. Swarm reps represent the swarm cluster at the implementation phase. The business process owner goes on to become a swarm ambassador to promote swarm across the organisation.

Stage 3: transition to Swarm 2.0

Swarm 1.0 has been characterised as a local meeting or event that follows the swarm facilitation process where ideas and decisions emerge from human swarms. Swarm 1.0 is a self-organising and emergent change model that works through complex adaptive cells. This local building of awareness and understanding should hopefully gain grassroots momentum and contribute to the overall swarm transformation of the enterprise. Swarm 2.0 accelerates this to a global level. It is a more strategic and planned effort where a select percentage of the organisation formally adopts swarm to optimise collective intelligence and decision-making at the global level. To achieve a successful strategic and global swarm-based organisation, there needs to be a micro systems transformation which will materialise through three levers. Lever 1 is a systems transformation. The organisational structure needs to be organic in order to encourage a strategic partnership between influencers and enablers. Intelligent systems need to be procured to augment the swarm process. Alpha attitudes and behaviours need to be replaced with more collaborative and collective decision-making (hive mind). Lever 2 is an organisational change and development model. Lever 3 is the swarm facilitation process. There are six important milestones in the (stage 3) transition to Swarm 2.0.

1. Knowledge sharing from business process owners

Progressing to an organisational-led swarm approach requires organisational input/knowledge sharing and a feasibility study leading to a key strategy paper. Business process owners who practised Swarm 1.0 will assume the role of swarm ambassador where they are expected to share Swarm 1.0 learnings with executive decision makers and Organisational Development practitioners. Beekeepers will also input into this process. This should all contribute to a strategy or white paper that provides essential background, organisational experience, and recommendations for the broader organisation. The strategy paper should address the pros and cons of a global-led approach to swarm. It should also consider ideas concerning the organisational change and development approach, the behavioural transformation needed, and ideas on introducing intelligent systems to augment business intelligence gathering, digitisation and decision, augmentation. It should also include an assessment of key stakeholders and an estimate of costs.

2. Senior leadership involvement for Swarm 2.0 planning

A key activity for organisational-led swarm (which is part of the preparation stage in the swarm facilitation model) is around planning. This is different from the earlier consideration to decide whether to adopt swarm. This involves working with investors to ensure buy-in, appointing swarm mentor leaders, and scanning the enterprise for suitable parts of the business to adopt swarm.

3. Swarm 2.0 budget and resourcing

Operational planning will also be needed around securing a budget and resourcing model to transition to Swarm 2.0. There are specialists that need to be resourced, including learning and development (L&D) and OD resources to help with the business transformation, and various data and network specialists at both the technical and executive levels to help with the digital transformation. This will need to be budgeted for.

4. Digital, learning, and OD strategy

This is the formal approval of the agreed strategy. It should involve digital, learning, and OD strategy. It makes sense to wait for the new resources to be onboarded before approving the strategy.

5. Smart technology procurement

This follows the digital strategy. As we saw in Chapter 3, intelligent systems, digitisation devices, and decision augmentation support swarm and are an important differentia from Swarm 1.0. They are also part of the digital transformation of the organisation (although as discussed in Chapter 4, procurement is not the whole picture as digital transformation is not just about procuring new systems, but undertaking an entire systems transformation). An important decision must be made by digital business development experts and the CDO (or their equivalent) about procuring or developing in-house intelligent systems to support future swarm. Priority should be given to improving existing data, digitisation, and processing intelligent systems such as decision augmentation. An important investment would be the development of a business intelligence dashboard. Swarm 2.0 is not a switch; it is a transition. Development and procurement decisions will not happen overnight and are a slow burn phase-in.

6. Developing L&D programmes and the learning and resource portal

In Swarm 1.0, pre- and in-swarm development were carried out locally; in Swarm 2.0, it is organisational-led. One of the key initiatives we looked at in Chapter 6 was for newly resourced L&D professionals to help develop an L&D central learning and resource portal. This portal is an urgent priority as it will help connect the organisation and manage resources in Swarm 2.0 and Swarm 3.0. This portal will contain such things as resourcing opportunities, self-directed learning material, personal development plans, and remuneration data. To repeat the earlier message, such a system must be developed and phased into Swarm 2.0 rather than introduced abruptly.

Stage 4: Swarm 2.0 time span

This is stage four of the five-stage process and it covers the period of building and maintaining a percentage of the organisation as swarm-based. This time span could stretch across a decade or more and slowly develop and introduce new digital support systems such as business intelligent systems, learning and resource portals, and swarm augmentation systems. It starts with the appointed swarm mentor leaders getting everything swarm-ready and future-proofing the organisation to be swarm-based. Global business intelligence needs to be tapped to identify critical business issues (something that will be automated over time). Swarm clusters will be globally resourced (manually at first but increasingly through global portals). Swarm clusters break into teams and work on business challenges. Increasingly, intelligent systems, collaborative tools, and augmented decision-making will all support and augment swarm clusters and assist sensemaking. As we have seen with the example of Daimler AG, it could take up to five years for a large organisation to be proficient at Swarm 2.0 where a significant percentage of the organisation functions as a swarm. Daimler AG was ambitious and sought to have 20% of its organisation functioning as a swarm in two to three years – a target that proved to be over-optimistic.

Stage 5: transition to Swarm 3.0

The transition to Swarm 3.0 accelerates the organisation from being an established swarm-based organisation (Swarm 2.0) to a business superorganism (Swarm 3.0). A business superorganism, you recall, is inspired by natural superorganisms and will be a global complex adaptive connected system. Swarm 3.0 comprehensively abandons the old BOS; it reconfigures governance and alpha leadership and veers away from permanent resourcing, fixed roles, supervisory management, and presenteeism. Business superorganisms are organic networked complex adaptive systems of diverse interconnected swarm communities, augmented by intelligent systems that facilitate business intelligence, creative thinking, and decision-making. Important transition steps include the following:

1. Organisational pulse check

This is an enterprise-wide assessment and feasibility study to see whether the swarm-based organisation (Swarm 2.0) is ready, willing, and able to deepen its swarm culture, undergo the necessary system transformation, and replicate its swarm base across the enterprise to become a business superorganism. This step will require a feasibility study, a strategy review, and an organisational assembly or summit to assess Swarm 3.0 viability.

2. Develop Swarm 3.0 acceleration strategy (from base camp to summit)

A comprehensive acceleration strategy must be drawn with clear steps to success. In Chapter 7, a mountaineering analogy was used where base camp is about addressing the leadership and governance issues; camp 1 explores resourcing and budgeting; camp 2 is about deformalising the organisation, including abandoning management structures; camp 3 looks at procurement/development of enabling technology and intelligent systems to support acceleration (part of digital transformation). Reaching the summit is about achieving objectives and becoming a business superorganism. These steps are all part of an ambitious climb and an acclimatisation to the new realities and conditions.

3. Accelerate!

John Kotter's accelerate model was introduced in Chapter 4. Kotter's model is about managing change using a two-tiered system which ensures regular business gets done whilst accelerating the transition to Swarm 3.0. Swarm transformation is a circa 15-year process of small steps. Once the organisation has decided to become a business superorganism, it needs to take the giant leap. This leap is a technological one where networked cells of humans and machines work together to optimise business intelligence. If that sounds implausible, just take a walk in your local wood. Look in the tree stumps at the honeybees, lift up stones, glance in streams, and look up to the branches. Nature has been organising itself as superorganisms since this world began. It is time for us to catch up.

Final thoughts

This book is about organisational reinvention and business transformation inspired by nature and swarm intelligence. Swarm complex adaptive cells, swarm-based organisations, and business superorganisms need adaptive, borderless, self-organising environments of the type found in the natural world. But it would be a mistake for readers to dismiss this as a quirky little book about turning our workplaces into honeybee colonies. If you feel that there has been too much emphasis on honeybees in this book, let's talk instead about elephants. There is a jumbo elephant sitting in meeting rooms across the world. It is called business as usual. It astounds me that some organisations are not facing up to the challenge that is staring them in the face. The BOS that has given so much stability, productivity, and profitability to organisations for decades is no longer fit for purpose. New intelligent technology is changing the game and the rules.[1] Young talent doesn't want to work in a pyramid where the privileged few in the apex get to make all the decisions and have all the fun. A five-minute coffee break on LinkedIn is all it takes for your best talent to find a new job. We are going through a paradigm shift that could wipe out organisations that don't upgrade their BOS and create fit-for-purpose work environments. For too long, we have been told that a self-organising working environment is years away and too complicated to set up – that people need structure and supervision and that productivity would suffer if we abandoned the old structures. The coronavirus pandemic has disproved this. It has shown how the workforce can be quickly mobilised and can continue to be productive – even more productive – through collaborative technology and without the culture of supervision and presenteeism.

My final thought, therefore, is not about swarms and honeybees, but a heads-up. Organisations need to sensemake their environment and see that augmented, brickless, and borderless workplaces are just around the corner. Emerging studies are urging organisations to future-proof and prepare themselves for Industry 4.0. Organisations need to appraise their business processes – I call it business genome sequencing – and revitalise their creaky BOSs.[2] It is essential for organisations to transform themselves and embrace the new post-Covid/artificial intelligence business realities that are on the horizon. After all, birds do it, bees do it, even educated fleas do it…

Notes

1   Andrew Ng, Chief Scientist at Baidu Research, opines, 'Just as electricity transformed almost everything 100 years ago, today I actually have a hard time thinking of an industry that I don't think AI will transform in the next several years'. Cited in Shana Lynch, 'Andrew Ng: Why AI Is the New Electricity', *Stanford Business*, 11 March 2017, www.gsb.stanford.edu/insights/andrew-ng-why-ai-new-electricity, accessed 29 May 2021.

2   This McKinsey discussion paper, for example, says,

> To harness the new technologies to their full effect, companies will need to retool their corporate structures and their approaches to work. That change will require redesigned business processes and a new focus on the talent they have—and the talent they need.
>
> Jacques Bughin, et al., 'Skill Shift: Automation and the Future of the Workforce', *McKinsey Global Institute*, www.mckinsey.com/featured-insights/future-of-work/skill-shift-automation-and-the-future-of-the-workforce, accessed 29 May 2021

Bibliography

Bughin, Jacques, Hazan, Eric, Lund, Susan, Dahlström, Peter, Wiesinger, Anna, and Subramaniam, Amresh, 'Skill Shift: Automation and the Future of the Workforce', *McKinsey Global Institute*, 23 May 2018, www.mckinsey.com/featured-insights/future-of-work/skill-shift-automation-and-the-future-of-the-workforce, accessed 29 May 2021.

Kotter, John, 'Accelerate!', *Harvard Business Review*, November 2012, https://hbr.org/2012/11/accelerate, accessed 29 May 2021.

Kotter, John P., *Accelerate: Building Strategic Agility for a Faster-Moving World* (Boston, MA: Harvard Business Press Books, 2014).

Lynch, Shana, 'Andrew Ng: Why AI Is the New Electricity', *Stanford Business*, 11 March 2017, www.gsb.stanford.edu/insights/andrew-ng-why-ai-new-electricity, accessed 29 May 2021.

INDEX